PRAISE FOR *FROM PATRIOT TO PIRATE: THE OUTLAW LIFE OF SAM MASON*

"*From Patriot to Pirate: The Outlaw Life of Sam Mason* by Carter F. Smith is a wildly entertaining romp through late eighteenth-century Western colonial and post-Revolutionary America. While the brilliant but roguish Samuel Mason was the epitome of 'the good, the bad, and the ugly,' he is quintessentially American. Revolutionary Patriot, horse thief, frontiersman, judge, tavern keeper, justice of the peace, criminal gang leader, and river pirate—Mason was a factotum before the word was invented. Smith knows his history and has written a great swashbuckling tale of the early American frontier and the blurry gray lines that separate the heroic and lawful from the criminal."

—**Samuel Marquis**, bestselling and award-winning author of *Captain Kidd: A True Story of Treasure and Betrayal*

"A truly riveting story about river piracy and land piracy along the Mississippi. Based on trial transcripts, criminal reports, and saucy stories from the 'hearsay' side of things, Smith and his research team successfully pieced together the life of Sam Mason as one of the lesser-known outlaws of the eighteenth century, doing full justice to his dazzling character as that of a 'noble bandit' (I'm sure his victims, in particular Colonel Joshua Baker, would disagree though). And on top of all that, there are copious travel and tasting notes waiting for all those who want to follow in the footsteps of Sam Mason (figuratively speaking, mind you!) to see what he saw and to eat what he ate (I might just try the bramble pie . . .)."

—**Peter Lehr**, author of *Pirates: A New History, from Vikings to Somali Raiders*; Senior Lecturer, University of St Andrews, Scotland

"Samuel Mason and his gang threatened US westward expansion at the turn of the nineteenth century. We are indebted to Smith for meticulously unearthing Mason's complex story, along with the stories of the people he robbed. Readers will come away from this book with a richer understanding of the limits of federal authority during the Early Republic. Smith nicely situates Mason and riverine piracy alongside Thomas Jefferson, the Louisiana Purchase, and other familiar figures and events."

—**Chris Magra**, author of *Poseidon's Curse: British Naval Impressment and Atlantic Origins of the American Revolution*; Professor of American History and Director of the Center for the Study of Tennesseans and War, The University of Tennessee, USA

FROM PATRIOT TO PIRATE

The Outlaw Life of Sam Mason

CARTER F. SMITH

BLOOMSBURY ACADEMIC
NEW YORK • LONDON • OXFORD • NEW DELHI • SYDNEY

BLOOMSBURY ACADEMIC
Bloomsbury Publishing Inc
Bloomsbury Publishing Inc, 1359 Broadway, New York, NY 10018, USA
Bloomsbury Publishing Plc, 50 Bedford Square, London, WC1B 3DP, UK
Bloomsbury Publishing Ireland, 29 Earlsfort Terrace, Dublin 2, D02 AY28, Ireland

BLOOMSBURY, BLOOMSBURY ACADEMIC and the Diana logo are trademarks of
Bloomsbury Publishing Plc

First published in the United States of America 2025

Copyright © Carter F. Smith, 2025

Cover design: Sally Rinehart
Cover image © Fiverr International Ltd.

All rights reserved. No part of this publication may be: i) reproduced or transmitted in any form, electronic or mechanical, including photocopying, recording or by means of any information storage or retrieval system without prior permission in writing from the publishers; or ii) used or reproduced in any way for the training, development or operation of artificial intelligence (AI) technologies, including generative AI technologies. The rights holders expressly reserve this publication from the text and data mining exception as per Article 4(3) of the Digital Single Market Directive (EU) 2019/790.

Bloomsbury Publishing Inc does not have any control over, or responsibility for, any third-party websites referred to or in this book. All internet addresses given in this book were correct at the time of going to press. The author and publisher regret any inconvenience caused if addresses have changed or sites have ceased to exist, but can accept no responsibility for any such changes.

A catalog record for this book is available from the Library of Congress.

ISBN: HB: 978-1-5381-3997-4
ePDF: 979-8-8818-5771-4
eBook: 978-1-5381-3998-1

Typeset by Deanta Global Publishing Services, Chennai, India
Printed and bound in the United States of America

For product safety related questions contact productsafety@bloomsbury.com.

To find out more about our authors and books visit www.bloomsbury.com and sign up for our newsletters.

Dedicated to the descendants of Sam Mason, the most complex character I have ever pursued.

CONTENTS

Preface: Prelude to a Pirate ix
Acknowledgments xix

PART I 1739–76 1

1 Origin Story (1739–57) 3
2 The Battle Tested Colonies (1754–76) 19

PART II 1777–83 37

3 Wild Western Virginia (1777–78) 39
4 Mason Bought the Farm (1779–80) 53
5 Life After the Military (1781–83) 63

PART III 1784–1801 73

6 Fraud on the Frontier (1784–97) 75
7 Escape to the Cave (1797–99) 87
8 Pirating the Mississippi (1799–1801) 101

PART IV 1802–04 113

9 Enough Is Enough (1802–03) 115
10 Good Days and Bad (1803–04) 147
11 Sam Mason 161

Appendix A: Investigative Team Traveling and Tasting Notes 173
Appendix B: Timeline of Samuel Mason's Life 206
Appendix C: Incidents of Historical Misinformation 211
Appendix D: Thomas Mason Timeline and Reference Documentation 219
Appendix E: Additional Reading, Watching, and Listening 226
Notes 228
Bibliography 243
Index 247
About the Author 257

PREFACE
PRELUDE TO A PIRATE

The Ohio and Mississippi Rivers were the lifeblood of the American frontier in the late eighteenth century, carrying settlers, traders, and soldiers to new opportunities. But while they provided vital transportation routes, the rivers were also fraught with danger. River piracy threatened the very trade that was so crucial to the region's development. With the newly formed government stretched thin, pirates operated with near impunity, turning the rivers into lawless highways. Flatboats and keelboats, packed with goods like furs, tobacco, and grain, made their way downriver—until the pirates showed up, attacking ships and stealing cargo. For merchants, the stakes were high: losing their goods often meant losing their investments, if not their lives. Still, despite the dangers, trade along the rivers flourished.

In the spring of 1801, Colonel Joshua Baker set out on a trip to New Orleans—something he'd done many times before. Baker was a merchant and planter from Hardin County, Kentucky, about 30 miles south of the Ohio River, in the area we now know as Elizabethtown and Fort Knox. He and his crew traveled over 600 miles, arriving in New Orleans by mid-summer, where they sold their livestock and produce. In early August, Baker and two companions began their long journey back to northern Kentucky on horseback, with five pack mules laden with provisions. As they passed through Natchez, Mississippi, they picked up a fourth traveler—a man who, like them, sought safety in numbers as they rode through the dangerous wilderness along the trail that would later be known as the Natchez Trace.

But danger found them anyway. On their second morning, about 90 miles north of Natchez, they stopped at a creek to bathe, likely thinking it was a moment of respite. No sooner had they dismounted and stepped into the water than four land pirates—bandits of the wilderness—appeared, demanding all their money and property. The thieves made off with their horses and $2,300 in cash earned from selling their goods in New Orleans.

Colonel Baker wasn't about to let a robbery stop him. The following spring, he headed back down the river from Kentucky with another load bound for the New Orleans market. But just as he neared his destination, river pirates attacked. That time, Baker and his crew fought back. Baker survived the encounter and quickly reported the incident to the territorial governor, who alerted military commanders throughout the region. The call went out: find and capture the pirates!

Pirates like Samuel Mason. While many traders feared the thieves drawn to both the rivers and the Natchez Trace, Mason stood out as one of the most dangerous, a leader among the lawless. Like Baker, Mason had served in the Revolutionary War, fighting for the United States' independence from England. But unlike Baker, Mason had taken a far darker path after the war. Rather than seek out an honest living, he turned to river piracy, preying on those trying to carve out a life in the West. And for those brave enough to follow the rivers and trails, Mason and his gang were a constant, looming threat—one they'd have to face if they wanted to make it home alive.

For the discerning student of history, this story serves as a portal into the realities and challenges faced by pioneers in the early nineteenth century. Colonel Baker's narrative, stripped of embellishments, invites readers to traverse the corridors of time and witness a chapter in American history where the promise of territorial expansion is entwined with the struggles of human survival. However, this book is not just the story of Colonel Baker's perilous journey; it is the "rest of the story" regarding the dangers along the western expansion following the Revolutionary War. It is a deeper exploration of the realities of the early years of the Natchez Trace. In delving into this meticulously researched account, true crime readers, historians, pirate fans, and general readers alike are offered a window into the complexities that shaped the course of a nation forging its path across an untamed frontier.

This book is a story of adventure, violence, and lawlessness, telling the story of river piracy on the Ohio and Mississippi Rivers. It is also a story of the resilience and determination of those who lived on the frontier in those times. I hope that this book will give you a better understanding of this fascinating and important period in American history!

The Mason Mystery

While researching for another book, I learned about Samuel Mason, the Revolutionary War Captain who retired to become an American River and Land Pirate. After spending much of the last decade of my military career and the first decade or so of my academic career investigating and researching military-trained

PREFACE

gang members (MTGMs), I wrote a book on the subject. During the initial research for that book, I was intrigued to learn that Mason was the first US MTGM and was also the most documented. Unfortunately, I found that much of the documentation had been inconsistent and inaccessible to most readers and researchers.

I realized that both Mason's military and criminal activities began near the area now known as Pittsburgh, Pennsylvania. He joined the Colonial Militia under General George Washington and served on the front lines of the frontier in what is now Wheeling, West Virginia. After he left the Militia, he spent some time in eastern Tennessee and western Kentucky. While he had stolen a few things here and there, he significantly escalated his criminal activity once he reached his fifties and moved to the Ohio River in northwestern Kentucky in the area known as Red Banks (now Henderson), Kentucky. Mason and his gang soon moved west along the Ohio River to southern Illinois, at Cave-In-Rock, then down the Mississippi River to New Madrid, Missouri, and later to Natchez, Mississippi.

There, Mason strategically ran his criminal operation on the east (United States) side of the Mississippi River while living in many places in the Louisiana Territory, both while under the control of Spain and France (more on that later). Mason was ultimately tried in 1803 in Spanish Louisiana and, through a bizarre twist of fate, was released and killed shortly after. There's more detail later in the book, but my interest was already piqued, so I started a more thorough investigation of Mason once the military gang book was finished.

I was pleasantly surprised when I learned of the existence of trial transcripts documenting the inquiry when Mason and his gang were arrested for river piracy. I confirmed that the Mississippi Department of Archives and History had the trial manuscript (Z/0273.000).[1] Unfortunately, upon contacting them, I found the original handwritten paper transcript was in French and was far too fragile to copy. The administrator advised that there was also a handwritten paper English translation, so I hoped for the best, although I suspected the two transcripts were on the same paper and stored in the same place. Sadly, it was also too fragile to be photocopied. The archivists later found microfiche copies of the two records among their unprocessed holdings, though. They told me that because the transcripts were so lengthy, the time it would take them to copy either document would exceed the time they could devote to a public request. The options presented to me were visiting the library and copying the material or contracting with a freelance researcher to do the work.

Locating the Trial Transcripts

Thankfully, the Genealogy Division of the Dallas Public Library (DPL) had obtained a paper first copy of the transcripts. I found that after a simple search on the

WorldCat database, a public-access resource for identifying and locating library books and publications, and was very relieved.[2] The DPL copy was made in 1978 from the original manuscript before it became too fragile to handle. The letter that the Mississippi Archives' head sent to accompany the transcript in 1978 said there was a French and English translation of the Samuel Mason trial in their private manuscript collection—manuscript number Z273v.

Most, if not all, libraries have a program called the Interlibrary Loan program, where participating library members can request specific documents and publications be sent to their local library to be examined, and often checked out. When asked, the head of the DPL Genealogy Division advised me that I could request Interlibrary Loan copies of the DPL material. However, their Interlibrary Loan Department could only provide up to 50 pages per request (the document was 111 pages).

Not one to let simple administrative policies or procedures keep me from accomplishing important things, I agreed and suggested that I would submit three requests: one for pages 1–50, one for pages 51–100, and the third for pages 101–111. Problem solved! I was quite happy that my plan was coming to fruition. Imagine my disappointment and surprise when this brilliant idea was met with a hard "no." And she wasn't joking, either!

The policy they followed, put in place by the ILL Program, was that multiple requests could not circumvent that policy. While I wondered how books over fifty-one pages were sent out under this policy, I shifted instead to solution mode. I summarized what I had learned: "So about the only way I can get a copy of the transcripts is if I or someone who knows me walk(s) into the library?" I was assured that this option would satisfy the need.

Ultimately, I obtained a digital copy of the translated transcript by coordinating with colleagues at the University of Texas–Dallas. One of the first tasks was to transcribe and digitize the handwritten document. Thankfully, I found two outstanding university students to help with that task, which we accomplished in a little over a year.

The Hunt Commenced

With my curiosity as a retired criminal investigator and researcher completely piqued, I decided to begin *From Patriot to Pirate*. I didn't know where it would lead me, how long it would take, or whether it would be successful. I have "hunted" (investigated, tracked, and located) many criminals before, but never one like this. This hunt was over quite a long distance and over quite a long time, and that time was in the past.

PREFACE

In my criminal justice courses, I am fond of noting that police officers often depend on others for assistance in conducting their investigations. I didn't realize it at the time, but there were quite a few people I would come to depend on during this hunt. It was as if a group of investigators were brought together supernaturally to form a task force that traversed time and space to assist me in my quest. I'll introduce many of them to you as we proceed.

You might find this odd, but I never cared about pirates or history until I met Sam Mason. Criminals interested me when I was investigating or teaching. Military issues were a passing interest when I (or one of my sons) was a service member. Pirates? I couldn't have cared less, and history? The extent of my thought on the subject was summed up in a quote I'd read years ago on a supervisor's wall and found insightful: "those who don't remember the past are doomed to repeat it" (Seneca). I was surely not a *student* of history, much less a history *nerd*.

And then Sam Mason came along.

Assembling the Team

In typical situations, the team for investigating, tracking, or hunting a suspect is assembled based on willingness, availability, skills, and expertise. The better investigative teams are made up of several competent, available folks with similar interests who work together as best they can to learn things, share information, and document their combined efforts. I have been privileged to be on many teams of that sort, early in life with the military police, later as a criminal investigator, and most recently in professional academic settings, finding ways to improve the learning process for students or to evaluate and explain why a process or system works the way it does.

The assembly process of this team was different, though, as it radically traversed time and space. When I've shared the idea with my students that the police need to find cooperative witnesses, I've explained that it is necessary because they cannot predict the future and cannot access a time machine or a crystal ball. While that is true for historical investigations, too, one thing can help investigators that doesn't entail time travel, and we all have it. It's called *imagination* and includes (depending on the application) creative vision, fantasy, mental pictures, fancy, daydreaming, inventiveness, and artistic insight.

Imagination is beautiful and allows us to exist firmly rooted in the present while traveling or projecting ourselves in thought to either the future or the past. Using the imagination enables us to put ourselves in situations others face, are facing, or will face to identify things they may have done or missed and to anticipate problems they may not have seen coming. The imagination helps many criminal investigators anticipate their adversaries' next move, not unlike a chess match.

The investigative team that I assembled ended up being, at the same time, a motley crew, a task force, a dream team, and a group of draftees. Here is what I know about each. Remember that our experiences and goals shape our perceptions, so you will likely see differences in what each reported. The brief list of attributes and experiences I provide should explain that, for the most part.

The primary team included (in alphabetical order):

- Herbert Asbury (1891–1963) was an American journalist, writer, and historian best known for his works on the history of crime and urban life in the United States.
- Leland D. Baldwin (1897–1981) was an American historian and author known for his expertise on the history of the American frontier and river piracy.
- Raymond Martin Bell (1907–96) was an American historian and genealogist known for his extensive research and publications on the history of southwestern Pennsylvania and neighboring regions.
- James Branch Cabell (1879–1958) was an American author and journalist best known for his works of fantasy fiction and satirical novels.
- Robert M. Coates (1897–1973) was an American writer, art critic, and editor known for his contributions to American literature and art criticism.
- Marc Coker is an independent historian/scholar of Texas history. His forte has been using family and local histories as a springboard to better understand state and US history. In the case of Sam Mason, it is family history.
- Samuel Draper (1815–91) was best known for the Draper Manuscripts, a significant body of work collected from the colonial period through the early nineteenth century. Draper's work has provided a foundational source for understanding the complexities of frontier life and the expansion of the United States during a formative period in its history.
- Edward L. Lach Jr. is an American historian and editor known for his scholarly contributions to American history and his editorial work on significant historical publications.
- Ronald R. Morazán is a scholar noted for his work on historical records related to Latin America. He particularly focuses on the Cabildo records and municipal council records from the colonial and early republican periods.
- Stanley Nelson is a journalist and editor of the Concordia Sentinel in Ferriday, Louisiana, dedicated to uncovering historical truths and

providing in-depth coverage of significant events and figures, particularly in Southern history.
- Earl Nicodemus is a West Liberty University Professor Emeritus and a charter member and founding president of the West Liberty Historical Society, who authored numerous articles on the history of West Liberty and the surrounding areas.
- Otto Arthur Rothert (1871–1956) was an American historian, author, and editor renowned for his contributions to documenting the history and folklore of the Ohio Valley.
- Joe Roxby is a historian and writer interested in the outlaws and lawmen of America's frontier days, providing detailed and well-researched narratives that highlight the complexities of the times.
- Mark Wagner is an archaeologist and academic known for his expertise in the American Midwest. He focuses on the interactions between Native Americans and Euro-Americans during the eighteenth and nineteenth centuries, characterized by his extensive field research and ability to uncover and interpret historical artifacts and sites.

While I was one of the few, if not the only, investigator who conducted on-site investigations, albeit in a different century, and was undoubtedly the one who visited most of Mason's haunts over his sixty or so years of life, this investigation would not have been possible without the drafted investigative team members.

About the Book

This book is historical fact, not fiction.

It is a chronological and geographic recollection of historical events based on the life and times of Sam Mason. I have devoted a good part of the last five years to the project. Indeed, multiples of that would have been needed to complete the project to cover the investigative team's time. In tracking down the truth, I found that some of the essential sources were various documents (letters, journals, notes, reports, court records, and more) written in and shortly after the time we are studying. As you will see, investigators and other historians do not agree in some areas. We are calling those areas *historical misinformation*, and have tried to identify, address, reconcile, and explain all of them. See the collection in Appendix C near the end of the book.

To provide continuity and interest for the reader, I have tried to adapt the writing style to one more conversational, without too many tangents or interruptions. It was, admittedly, a tricky balance to maintain. I tried to present the best analysis where there was conflict in investigative reporting. Where there was a consensus, I summarized and credited the investigators at the end of the chapter. Many of the facts are referenced with endnotes. However, the list of investigators and bibliography would be a more thorough source to consult, as the project required embedding in the historical period and location to pull it all together.

Additionally, for consistency, when a name or word is spelled differently in multiple sources *(also known as* or *AKA)*, I will identify how it is most likely or often spelled. Then, where it is spelled differently in a source document, I will identify that spelling in parentheses the first time, proceeding with the most common name from that point on. Finally, where a word that reflects a quote or segment in the original document appears misspelled, I will leave it as is for context. Leaving it as it was bothered me a lot, but I believe historical context is essential. There were consistency issues with names, and they were often spelled phonetically in early American English, without the concern for purist spelling and grammar found in so many professions today.

I extend a most special thanks to the following, as their contributions were pivotal to the success of this enthralling project:

Alexis Wynn, an alum of my academic department at Middle Tennessee State University, accomplished most of the transcript conversion to digital (typed and thus searchable) format. Alexis is an avid adventurer with a curious mind and a no-quit attitude.

Mary Cate Rose is a former student of my academic department and an alumna of the history department. She is a historian who helped document and investigate Mason's life by researching it, verifying his court records, identifying additional researchers, and initiating contact with them. She has a master's in history and enjoys exploring the Civil Rights Movement.

Bob Taylor, a professor of Criminology at the University of Texas at Dallas, is a friend in the academic business who helped me acquire a copy of the Mason Trial transcripts.

Chelsey Narvey, then a graduate student of Bob Taylor's and now an assistant professor at the Sam Houston State University College of Criminal Justice, without whom I would not have a copy of the trial transcripts (and you might not have a copy of this book).

Stephanie Bennett and Gayla Bush, in the Genealogy & History Division of the Dallas Public Library, kept the records safe while I tried to acquire them.

The book will document the first-person investigation of this historical figure. It aims to summarize the investigative research process in an exciting format that appeals to general readers, history nerds, pirate fanatics, and general researchers so they can reach their own conclusions.

PREFACE

The book has five parts, each starting with a map showing the areas covered. Part I (with Chapters 1 and 2) provides the foundation for the book, including Mason's early years and the time he served in the French and Indian and Revolutionary Wars and coverage of the historical misinformation regarding Mason's lineage. Part II (Chapters 3–5) covers his time at Fort Henry in Wheeling, West Virginia, through his retirement from the militia and his time directly after the war in eastern Tennessee. Part III (Chapters 6–8) includes most of his time in Kentucky and Illinois and his transition to river piracy as a primary career. Part IV (Chapters 9–11) reviews the activities in his last years in the Natchez and New Orleans areas.

The Appendices inform the first four parts of the book and provide a foundation for understanding the times in which Mason lived. They were designed to fill in the many blanks you will find in history, adding a readable and enjoyable accompaniment to the first part of the book. Appendix A provides comprehensive information to expand on the investigative team's travel and tasting notes and some delicious information to help you understand colonial food and drink. Appendix B provides a timeline of Samuel Mason's life, with dates and locations. Appendix C lists and explains several incidents of historical misinformation. Appendix D is a timeline of the life of Thomas Mason, Sam Mason's father. Finally, Appendix E includes a list for additional reading, watching, and listening in case you don't feel satisfied after our adventure.

As you transition from one part of the book to another, take the time to reflect on the transitions during Mason's life, so you can better imagine what he was experiencing. I included a map at the beginning of each part. I did that because I hadn't lived in or traveled to most of the places where Mason was, and I liked seeing them in relation to each other, so I could imagine how long the travel took, what might have been different, and things of that nature. Familiarize yourself with the locations to prime your imagination for the journey ahead.

Join the Team: Tips for Immersive Reading

As with the team assembly, I recommend approaching the book with a healthy dose of imagination. Take the time to join the team in your mind before embarking. We will wait for you! Many chapters include helpful distances, times, locations, and historical events. Familiarize yourself with distances between places of interest to you, identify a person you know who is similar in age to the one mentioned, and recall a time in your life that happened a certain number of years ago to help put the events in perspective. Additionally, access to the map at the beginning of each part and the entire map of the eastern United

States in Appendix B would be helpful so you can see how far folks traveled or moved before the invention of the automobile or the steamboat. You may find the timeline of Mason's life in Appendix B helpful, too, in addition to the maps.

Each of the chapters includes travel and tasting notes at the end. When the contemporary investigative team traveled to many locations, we planned historical visits, side adventures, and meals. Many of those, along with other notes for context, were offered for your optional enjoyment should you plan to be near any of these locations, find your calendar sufficiently empty, and desire to take a trip of your own. We listed them at the end of the chapter and described them in more detail in Appendix A. As with learning a language, immersion is the best way to fully experience history. While you cannot *go* back in time, you can learn about the historical events and visit several of the places listed.

If you cannot physically travel, use a mapping program and a travel application to see what the location looks like now and what others (including me) have said about it. It's truly the next best thing to being there. Look in the travel and tasting notes section and the extended notes in Appendix A, and try some period recipes for another sensory experience. And then share some with friends! I encourage you to plan a day trip, a long weekend, or more if you are close to any of these locations and can make the time to do so. Please make sure to reach out to me if you do. I would love to hear about your adventures, perceptions, and discoveries! Visit www.PirateSamMason.com to comment, learn more, amd join the community!

A Note to the Reader

This is not a typical biography. To write *Patriot to Pirate*, I had to pursue Sam Mason the way the frontier did, by following the rivers, the rumors, and the records scattered across time and place. You won't find Mason on every page because his life wasn't lived in isolation. He was a product of the geography, the wars, and the fractured loyalties that defined the American frontier after the Revolution.

The book moves intentionally through geography and chronology. Understanding the places Mason lived and the people he encountered, both notorious and forgotten, reveals how a respected militia captain became a pirate and land criminal feared across the Ohio and Mississippi Rivers.

For those looking for a tighter biographical account, that story comes next, in the forthcoming volume focused on Mason's arrest, trial, and violent end. But to fully understand the man, you must first understand the world that made him.

ACKNOWLEDGMENTS

I offer a most earnest tip of the tricorn hat to Sharmyn Smith, Mark Coker, Lucian Cayce, Shane Atkinson, Ben Stickle, Joshua Powell, and Jennell Brown for bravely navigating this manuscript before it ever found its way to you, dear reader. They combed through the pages like well-practiced river pirates looking for valuables hidden on a flatboat, listing all manner of necessary edits and excellent revision suggestions to keep this book afloat. Should there be any errors or historical detours that remain, know they are entirely of my own making—for these valiant reviewers gave their finest in editing this tale.

With great Respect
Your Hble Srvnt
Carter F. Smith

PART I
1739–76

Figure 1.1 Winchester, Virginia; Pittsburgh, Pennsylvania; Wheeling, West Virginia. Sketched by Rotna, with Fiverr.

It may be helpful to bookmark and reference Appendix A (additional travel and tasting notes), Appendix B (Timeline of Mason's life), Appendix C (Historical Misinformation), and Appendix D (Thomas Mason Timeline) as or after you read this chapter to help provide a foundation for the historical commentary.

1
ORIGIN STORY (1739–57)

Samuel Mason was born to English citizens living in an English colony on another continent—land England claimed to have a legitimate right to possess. His birthplace? Virginia—a colony that would later become a commonwealth, famous for its central role in history. But here's where things get interesting: there's been some debate over exactly which part of Virginia that was. As we'll soon see, Sam's birthplace is just one of many nuggets of historical information that has been argued over. So, let's dive in and untangle the facts from the *historical misinformation* as we go!

Sam was born in 1739, well before the United States even existed. Some historians suggest he might have been born in Norfolk, Virginia.[1] Now, Norfolk in southeastern Virginia sits near the North Carolina border, right along the Atlantic coast. In 1739, it was a small port town on the Elizabeth River, boasting about 500 residents. Established in 1682 as a shipping and trading hub, Norfolk was one of the earliest English settlements in the area, making it a magnet for piracy and privateering as ships from England and its colonies docked to trade tobacco, rice, indigo, and yes, slaves. The town had a courthouse, several churches, and even a school—but only for the children of the wealthy. To protect its people from attacks by Indians (or Native Americans, Savages, Indigenous Peoples—pick your term depending on the historical period) and European rivals, Norfolk also had a small military presence. Given all that, it would make sense to think Sam was born in Norfolk, right? But no, it seems that wasn't the case.

Mason was more likely born up north in Frederick County, Virginia, right at the tip where today's West Virginia, Virginia, and Maryland converge. Frederick County, named after Frederick Louis, Prince of Wales (the eldest son of King George II), played a huge role in the frontier life of the American colonies and was central to the westward expansion of that time. Its location made it a key player in the French and Indian War (1754–63), known as the Seven Years' War outside the United States. Frederick County stood as a defensive stronghold against both French and Indian incursions, drawing in settlers from diverse backgrounds—Germans, Scots, Irish, and more—creating a truly multicultural frontier community. The town of Winchester became the county seat in 1743 and quickly grew into a bustling market and military hub.[2]

Mason's Recorded Lineage

Mason's family, if you follow the Norfolk line, was thought to represent a long line of colonists, although records were not as well kept in those days. As with his birthplace, there are also some questions regarding the accuracy of Mason's lineage. Mason's great-grandfather has been identified as Lieutenant Francis Mason, born in 1594. Francis arrived in Jamestown with his first wife, Mary Dackman (Dickman), and daughter Anne in 1613. They were listed in the census of Elizabeth City, Norfolk County, Virginia, in 1623/4. The couple had a son, Francis, born about 1623. Around 1625, Francis (the father) married Alice (Ganey), with whom he had two children, Lemuel and Elizabeth. In 1637, Francis was a Justice of the Peace and a sitting justice in 1642. He served as a high sheriff in 1646 and died in 1648 at the age of 54.[3]

Mason's recorded great-grandfather, Colonel Lemuel Mason of Lower Norfolk, Virginia, was born in 1628. Lemuel was the son and fourth child of Francis Mason and his second wife, Alice. Francis died when Lemuel was just twenty years old, and Lemuel married his wife, Ann Seawell, the following year. Lemuel was a Justice of the Peace from 1650 until he died, a presiding justice from 1669 onward, a major in the militia from 1658 until 1665, and a militia colonel from then on. Lemuel died in 1702 at the age of 74. He had three sons, Lemuel, George, and Thomas, and seven daughters, Elizabeth, Frances, Alice, Mary, Dinah, Margaret, and Anne.[4] Mason's grandfather has been recorded as the middle son, George Mason, born in 1655. George served as a Justice of Norfolk in 1702 and Captain of the Militia in 1707.[5] He died in 1710 at age fifty-five, leaving his wife, Phyllis (Hobson) Mason.

As with the Norfolk connection, the military and civil service connections of the Norfolk Masons would have provided a logical foundation for Sam's future accomplishments. Both Draper and Rothert were of the belief that Sam came from the Norfolk elite. But try as we did, we could find no validation that overcame what appeared to be, at best, speculation and, at worst, shoddy research by well-meaning but amateur genealogists. And we will add that to the collection of historical misinformation in Appendix C.

Perhaps the most convincing information was the difference in social class. The Masons of Norfolk were from an elite bloodline, with pedigrees and generations of engagement in the region's social and economic fabric as landowners and merchants, and involved in local governance. Norfolk was an important agricultural and commercial area during the period, with prominent families often holding roles in trade, agriculture, politics, or the Anglican Church. The Mason family in the area that later became Winchester, originally called Frederick Town, was part of the wave of Scots-Irish and other settlers who moved into the Shenandoah Valley as some of the first European settlements west of the Blue Ridge Mountains. The Scots-Irish were descendants of Scottish Presbyterians who had settled in Northern Ireland (Ulster) before migrating to America in large numbers during the eighteenth century. They were known for their resilience and frontier spirit and often settled in the backcountry of the American colonies, including the Shenandoah Valley of Virginia.

The typical life of a Scots-Irish family involved subsistence farming, raising crops like corn, wheat, and flax, and maintaining livestock. They had strong community ties, an independent spirit, and a deep Presbyterian faith. On the frontier, families like the Masons built their homes, cleared land for farming, and participated in local defense efforts, as the area was on the edge of English colonial settlement and faced threats from both Indian tribes and occasional French incursions during the colonial wars. As more common folks, the Masons would not have been part of the wealthy planter class that dominated eastern Virginia. Instead, they would have been part of the more modest and hardworking class, contributing to the region's development through agriculture and trade. Winchester became a trading hub due to its strategic location on key routes between the Piedmont and the western frontier, so families like the Masons would have participated in local markets, trading their produce and goods.

Mason's father was Thomas Mason, born February 22, 1707.[6] Thomas' name has also been spelled Meason and Measor,[7] as family names during colonial times were spelled indifferently, often phonetically. Thomas' wife has been identified as Mary Meason, formerly Newton, who died in the Colony of Virginia in 1755, presumably in Frederick.[8] And that was another place where it got confusing. Thomas was thought to have sold land in Norfolk after Sam's birth and bought land on Mill Creek (now in West Virginia, about 300 miles northwest of Norfolk) in 1754, when Sam was a teenager, selling it five years later. It was speculated that the family then moved to what became Charles Town, West Virginia (about 180 miles northeast of Mill Creek, 230 miles northwest of Norfolk). Charles Town was founded in 1788 by the youngest full brother of George Washington. According to Coker (personal communication, January 21, 2020), some genealogists have determined that most of what was reported about Sam's ancestry was inaccurate.

Coker found that in 1938, Robert Torrence chronicled his family's history and erroneously connected the family of Sam Mason to the Masons of Norfolk. Coker noted the connection to Mason's father, Thomas Meason (Mason), was certain, and there have also been genealogical DNA tests that separated the Thomas Meason line from the others. Additionally, given Mason's criminal activities, some of his descendants might have intentionally tried to distance themselves from his bloodline. At the time of publication, Coker was straightening out the family tree (personal communication with M. Coker, June 4, 2025). Based on the research I have reviewed, I will explain confusing information and perspectives as we encounter them.

While I am neither a genealogist nor a historian, I am a researcher who spent many years as an investigator. Given the information Coker found and made available, I am confident that Sam's father was Thomas and that no connection to earlier generations can be verified. It appears that the Thomas who fathered Sam Mason had only one documented wife and that her name was Elizabeth.[9]

The other Thomas Mason, who married Mary, lived in Norfolk, Virginia, until he died between 1737 and 1740. Mary sold that property as a widow in late 1740.[10] To further validate the proposal that Sam's father Thomas was from Mill Creek in Northern Virginia, in 1995, Cecil O'Dell reported that "Thomas Mason (b.1706 c.) 'lived on the east side of Opechon [sic (Opequon)] Creek about 1736 or 1737,' and for several years afterward' near present-day Middleway, West Virginia."[11] Middleway is 7 miles west of Charles Town and 17 miles northeast of Winchester, Virginia. To contextualize (or contest) the notion that Thomas came from the Norfolk elite, we should consider that the Masons from that generation forward were ordinary folk or perhaps typical colonials.[12]

Mason's Verified Lineage

Thomas' will documented that he had twelve children.[13]

> Hannah, born May 3, 1737;
>
> Samuel, born November 8, 1739 (died 1803);
>
> Isaac (1743–1818);
>
> George, February 6, 1746;
>
> Rachael (Meason) Worthington, born November 6, 1749 (died 1779);
>
> Sarah (Meason) Briscoe, wife of George Cole Briscoe born February 15, 1751 (died 1779);
>
> John, born February 22, 1753;
>
> Thomas, born July 17, 1755;
>
> Joseph, born July 7, 1759;

Ann, born January 27, 1761;

Mary, born January 22, 1763;

Elizabeth (Meason) Fell, born May 11, 1765 (died c. 1831)

Thomas Mason was mentioned in several court documents in the Frederick County, Virginia area, supporting the idea that he was there before 1754, the earliest many Mason historians have placed the family in the area.
April 2, 1745. Served on a jury in a case of slander.[14]
November 18, 1752. Mentioned as a neighbor in a land transfer in Frederick County.[15]
March 27, 1753. Sold 85 acres on Mill Creek, a branch of the Opeckon.[16]
September 27, 1754. Registered a deed in Frederick, Virginia, for 370 acres of land from Thomas Low.[17]
In 1777, Thomas moved to Fayette County, Pennsylvania (about 45 miles south of Pittsburgh). Sam was stationed at Fort Henry, in present-day Wheeling, West Virginia, at the time. Thomas died at about age seventy, on March 15, 1779, in Westmoreland County, Pennsylvania (about 40 miles east of Pittsburgh), leaving Sam, who was then thirty-nine, 5 shillings. Isaac, Rachael, and Sarah also received the same nominal amount, with the notation that they had already received their portion. There was no such comment for Sam. The other siblings (Thomas, Joseph, George, and John, along with daughters Hannah, Ann, Mary, and Elizabeth) were identified as the recipients of a much higher (though not equal) portion of the inheritance. Records extended to the reading of his will following his death in 1779, but the list was limited to when Sam likely lived with him. See the extended documentation in Appendix D.

Geographical Reference

When Sam Mason was born, there were thirteen British colonies in North America that would later become the United States. The colonies stretched along the eastern coast, from New Hampshire in the north to Georgia in the south. The colonies were politically, economically, and geographically diverse. Each colony had its own government, with a governor appointed by the British Crown and a legislature elected by the colonists. Some colonies had more democratic systems than others, giving more power to elected representatives. The colonies' economies varied, but agriculture was the primary industry. Some colonies had large plantations with enslaved persons providing most of the labor, while others had smaller farms with free (not enslaved) labor. Trade between colonies and countries was also important; some colonies had thriving ports.

Historians' population estimates for the early eighteenth century suggest that the colonial population was 650,000 to 700,000. That figure included European settlers and many enslaved Africans, particularly in the southern colonies, where agriculture, especially cotton, tobacco, and rice cultivation, required large amounts of labor. Those population figures were approximations based on various historical records and calculations.

The area known as West Virginia did not become a state until President Lincoln proclaimed it as one midway through the Civil War on June 20, 1863. It was still a part of the Colony of Virginia in Mason's time, and it was largely rural, primarily used for hunting and farming by the European settlers and Indians. Relations between the two groups were often troubled, with conflicts over land and resources. The area was also a disputed territory between the French and the British, and both nations established settlements and trading posts along the Ohio River, which starts near and runs along the northern border of present-day West Virginia. The competition for control of the region (see the map at the beginning of the section) led to a series of conflicts known as the French and Indian War. The land was (and still is) mountainous and rugged, and travel was difficult. The settlers, primarily of English and German descent, were mostly farmers, and they had to clear the land of trees and brush for farming and build their own homes and infrastructure.

Influences and Culture

For readers who haven't been to the places we will go or haven't studied the time in which Mason lived, I will try to help familiarize you with that point in history. Using a combination of maps, research, and personal experience, I hope to help you imagine the times and areas so you can better relate to the folks who lived at this time in history. That's what it took for me, so I hope it will work for you. For help with that endeavor, reread or recall the section on imagination at the end of the introduction (you might want to bookmark it). Visit www.PirateSamMason.com for more tools!

Literacy

In mid-1700s America, the level of literacy was growing but varied significantly by region, gender, social class, and ethnicity. The northern colonies, particularly New England, had higher literacy rates due to the Puritan emphasis on reading the Bible, with up to 70–80 percent of men and around 45–60 percent of women being literate. In contrast, the southern colonies had much lower literacy rates, especially among the non-elite and enslaved populations.

Social class played a crucial role, with wealthier individuals having greater access to education and literacy. In urban areas, formal schooling was available, while in rural areas, literacy was often learned informally. Print culture expanded during that period, with newspapers, almanacs, and books becoming more accessible, contributing to the spread of literacy. Mason was literate and was one of the few in the culture who signed his name in lieu of a mark with an X, which needed to be witnessed by others.

Corrective eyewear, such as reading glasses, also became more available, which likely aided in literacy by allowing older adults or those with poor vision to read more easily. This increased the potential for a broader range of people to engage with written materials, further promoting literacy across different segments of society.

Food and Drink

In the 1700s, diets varied widely but had some common elements. Bread was a universal staple, ranging from delicate white loaves enjoyed by the wealthy to coarse, dark bread for the poor. Meats such as beef, pork, and mutton were common among those who could afford them. Venison, turkey, and other game meats supplemented rural and poor diets and were crucial, especially when combined with domesticated livestock. Fresh and salted fish were widely consumed, especially near rivers, lakes, and oceans, and by those who could not afford meat.

A variety of herbs and vegetables, many of which are part of the contemporary diet, were also grown in the early years of the United States. Herbs and vegetables played a crucial role in the daily lives of settlers, with culinary, medicinal, and practical applications reflecting a rich heritage of agricultural practices. Many historical sites we visited, especially the forts, had herb and vegetable gardens.

Herbs were particularly valued for their medicinal properties. Early American settlers brought knowledge of their uses from Europe, where herbs like sage, thyme, mint, and rosemary were staples in cooking and medicine. Sage was commonly used to treat digestive issues and sore throats, while thyme was used for soothing coughs, rosemary for memory, and mint served as a remedy for stomach ailments. Indian tribes also contributed significantly to the settlers' herbal knowledge. They used plants such as echinacea for infections, willow bark (which contains salicin, a precursor to aspirin) for pain relief, and yarrow for its anti-inflammatory properties.

Settlers grew various vegetable crops, often relying on seeds from Europe. The "three sisters" planting method, adopted from Indian agricultural practices, was widespread. That method involved growing corn, beans, and squash together, complementing each other's growth and maximizing yield. Corn provided a structure for the beans to climb, beans fixed nitrogen in the soil, and squash spread out on the ground, preventing weeds. Root vegetables like carrots, turnips, and onions were dietary staples, alongside peas and cabbage. Apples, pears, and various berries (wild strawberries, blackberries, raspberries, grapes, plums, and pawpaws, a native North American fruit) were commonly eaten fresh or used in pies and jams. Dairy products, including cheese and butter, were prevalent as well. Maple syrup, harvested by Indians and adopted by Europeans, was a popular sweetener. Pumpkins were versatile and used in stews, pies, and roasted dishes. There are several colonial-era recipes for food and drink in Appendix A.

Given the occasional scarcity of clean drinking water, various non-alcoholic beverages were essential. Milk, fresh from cows, goats, or sheep, was readily consumed, especially on farms. Apple cider was another staple, enjoyed in its non-alcoholic form as sweet cider, which was essentially fresh apple juice. Herbal teas or tisanes were also popular, brewed from various plant parts like leaves, roots, and seeds; mint, sage, and sassafras were among the favorite flavors. Freshly pressed juices from blueberries, raspberries, and blackberries provided a refreshing option in rural areas. In its traditional form, root beer was crafted from various roots, including sassafras, and was valued for its taste and its reputed health benefits. Occasionally, when lemons were available, lemonade was made and served as a special treat. When lemons were not available, a replacement was found in the native red sumac trees (smooth, winged, or staghorn), not to be confused with poison sumac, a bush.

Before refrigeration, folks preserved fruit drinks with sugar or honey and vinegar. Called a *shrub*, the drink could be prepared as a concentrate and added to water to flavor it. Similarly, hot chocolate was a luxurious beverage enjoyed by those who could afford the costly imported ingredient. All social classes enjoyed alcohol-based drinks such as ale and beer; wine was popular in grape-growing regions.

In colonial and early America, alcohol was a vital part of daily life and social culture, with consumption levels significantly higher than they are today. During that period, Americans drank about 5.8 gallons of pure alcohol per person each year, a stark contrast to the 2.3 gallons consumed on average today. Alcohol was often considered safer than water, which was frequently contaminated with pathogens like cholera, E. coli, and typhoid. This perception contributed to the widespread consumption of beverages such as beer, cider, and spirits, which were staples in the American diet. Wine, while popular, had to be imported from Europe due to early challenges in domestic production. Thomas Jefferson and George Washington were interested in viticulture (growing wine grapes), although Washington's efforts were perhaps more motivated by practicality than preference, as alcohol was considered a safer alternative to water. We will look more into wine in some of the tasting notes at the end of each chapter, with a lot of coverage on its relation to the early years of the United States in Appendix A.

In New England, apple cider was ubiquitous, thanks to the abundance of apple orchards. Beer, brewed both at home and in local breweries, was another common beverage. Rum was the most popular spirit, especially in the northern colonies, where it was produced from Caribbean molasses. Whiskey later gained popularity, particularly in frontier areas where grains were readily available. Taverns served as community centers where people gathered to socialize, discuss politics, and conduct business. The social acceptance of alcohol, along with its medicinal uses, was reflected in attitudes of the time. Even Puritan preacher Increase Mather regarded alcohol as "a good creature of God," underscoring its integral role in colonial life.[18]

The economic importance of alcohol was evident in its trade and taxation. The production of rum was crucial to the triangular trade (between Europe, Africa, and the colonies), and whiskey became an important commodity as the nation expanded westward. Government taxation of alcohol led to the Whiskey Rebellion, a significant insurrection in the early history of the United States from 1791 to 1794, about the time Sam's violent criminal activity was getting underway. The Whiskey Rebellion was primarily a protest against the unfair targeting of small farmers who distilled and sold whiskey from their surplus grain, essentially bootlegging.

President Washington led a federalized militia force into western Pennsylvania to quell the rebellion, showing the federal government's willingness and ability to enforce its laws. Strangely, Washington, demonstrating an understanding of the morale and health benefits of alcohol for his troops, included beer and spirits in their rations. Congress later supplemented that with a daily ration of rum, brandy, or whiskey, also recognizing the value of alcohol in maintaining the well-being of soldiers. The practice, alongside the public's high consumption levels, illustrates how deeply embedded alcohol was in the fabric of American life.[19]

During the colonial wars, including the French and Indian War, the regular army received provisions based on the victualing (food or provisions) requirements of the British government. The rations were *adequate* in caloric content but were *deficient* in essential vitamins, leading to potential nutritional deficiencies unless the soldiers supplemented their diets with garden-grown produce or purchased food. According to Pennsylvania's Militia Supply Act of 1755, for example, the weekly ration was 3 pounds (1.4 kilograms) of meat, 1 pound (455 grams) of fish, 10 1/2 pounds (4.8 kilograms) of bread, and 7 gills (82 centiliters) of rum.[20]

Colonial Clothing

In the mid to late 1700s, the clothing worn in the colonies and on the frontier was shaped by practical needs, climate, and social status. While colonial wear could be elaborate and made from imported materials, frontier clothing prioritized durability and practicality, reflecting the time's hardy and often harsh living conditions. In the colonies, men typically wore breeches, linen shirts, and waistcoats, topped with hats for everyday activities. They donned longer coats, silk waistcoats, and finer shirts for formal occasions. Women wore shifts, stays, petticoats, and overdresses, with aprons for daily chores. For special events, they dressed in gowns made of silk or imported cotton adorned with lace and ribbons. Accessories such as bonnets and shawls were standard, and children's clothing mirrored adult styles but was simpler.

On the frontier, the clothing was rugged and practical. Men often wore leather or homespun garments, including buckskin breeches and linen shirts, suited to the demanding life of the frontier. The hunting shirt, a loose frock reaching halfway down the thigh, was often worn, secured by a belt designed to rein in the extra fabric of the frock as well as allowing the wearer to secure their mittens, bullet bag, tomahawk, and sometimes a scalping knife. A pair of breeches or leggings was worn below the waist, and often, a pair of moccasins was worn on the feet. Women wore simpler, durable dresses made of homespun wool or linen designed for functionality. Both genders commonly used leather boots, woolen hats, and accessories like kerchiefs or woolen socks. Each of the sketches of Sam in the book was designed in period clothing. See the travel and tasting notes section of Appendix A to get more information.

Leisure Activities

As a teen and young adult in the mid-1750s, Sam might have listened to music played on a piano, guitar, violin, or flute. Much of the music from those times was classical or baroque music. However, opera and ballad opera, with spoken dialogue using popular tunes with new words, were also enjoyed during that time. Dramatic narrations, often concerning Jack and the Beanstalk, leading to Jack's adventure with a giant, consumed the leisure time of many.

Folk music was a vital part of everyday life, adding its unique cultural twist. Folk songs, which often addressed themes of love, hardship, and nature, remain known today, though they have evolved. One such song, "Greensleeves," was incredibly popular.[21] Another song from the period, "Early One Morning," told a tale of betrayed love.[22] Sea shanties and work songs were also integral, especially among sailors and laborers. Additionally, the legend of Robin Hood was often the subject of songs.

The music combined English, Scottish, Irish, and African influences in Colonial America. Songs were often adapted from European tunes and reimagined to reflect the new American influences. "Yankee Doodle," for instance, originated before the American Revolutionary War and was initially used to mock American soldiers, though it later became a song of American pride. Religious hymns were also significant, reflecting the strong religious sentiments of the time. Influential hymn writers like Isaac Watts and Charles Wesley produced works that were staples in church services and community gatherings.

Dancing in Colonial America during Mason's time reflected the diverse influences of the settlers. Dance was a central component of social life, crucial in community bonding, entertainment, and social gatherings. English country dances were popular, known for their lively and relatively simple steps that allowed groups of dancers to participate together. They often involved long lines of couples performing a series of figures as called by a dance master.

The Irish jig and Scottish reels (Mason was Scots-Irish) also found their place in colonial festivities. The African influence on dance in Colonial America was profound, though often underrecognized in historical accounts. Particularly in the southern colonies, African rhythm and dance blended with European dance, creating a unique hybrid style that laid the groundwork for future dance forms.

Many of the early settlers' sports and leisure activities reinforced survival instincts. Boys learned how to use a bow and arrow early in life; target practice with firearms was the logical evolution of such activity. Boys often learned how to imitate the songs and noises of birds and other forest animals, including the sounds of turkeys and young deer, to facilitate hunting such creatures. Tomahawk throwing, running, jumping, and wrestling kept young boys busy and prepared them for frontier life. Cockfighting was enjoyed in some of the larger cities. An American creation, organized horse racing along a quarter-mile track was enjoyed in the mid-Atlantic and southern colonies.

Cultural Insight

Essential to understanding the period was the existence of the *Renaissance Man*, a term used to describe the great thinkers living before, during, or after the fifteenth and sixteenth centuries who knew all that was learnable. It was characterized by an effort to revive and then surpass the ideas and achievements of their historical predecessors. That was what gave the colonies their uniqueness. In 1752, Benjamin Franklin, seen by many as a Renaissance Man, invented the lightning rod, which conducted lightning bolts harmlessly into the ground when placed at the uppermost point of a barn, church steeple, or other structure.

Also in 1752, Britain and its colonies, including the future United States, transitioned from the Julian calendar to the Gregorian calendar, correcting a growing misalignment with the seasons. The Julian calendar, introduced by Julius Caesar, had overestimated the length of the solar year, causing a drift of about eleven days by the eighteenth century. To address that, Britain skipped eleven days in September 1752—Wednesday, September 2, was followed by Thursday, September 14. The start of the legal new year was also moved from March 25 to January 1, in line with the Gregorian system, introduced by Pope Gregory XIII in 1582 and already adopted by much of Europe. The change caused confusion and resistance among the public, with some fearing they had "lost" eleven days of their lives. Nevertheless, the shift was necessary to bring Britain in sync with much of Europe and create a standardized calendar, which remains in use today.

While the 1750s did not see many groundbreaking American inventions, the period was marked by practical improvements and innovations in printing, shipbuilding, and agricultural tools that laid the groundwork for future advancements. As one of my reviewers summarized, this was not a colony of Indigenous peoples invaded by western Europe. That happened a century or more before. This was a colony of the best and brightest leaders with a population of farmers and hunters. It was unique in history and was the core of society at the time, and the root of our revolution.

People in those times often placed a high value on their relationships with others in their community. Working hard and being self-sufficient were highly valued, and many saw it as a moral duty. Patriotism and a sense of duty to one's country were also common values, particularly in the colonies still under British rule. People generally respected authority figures such as government officials, religious leaders, and parents. Slavery was still widely accepted in many parts of the colonies (and the world) during this period. Education was not compulsory, and most children were taught at home by their parents or private tutors.

The ethics and values of the period varied. Many people were deeply religious and saw their faith as a guiding force. During Mason's lifetime, the American colonies underwent significant religious transformations, driven by revivalist movements, evolving political contexts, and a growing sense of religious tolerance. As the colonies matured and later transitioned into the United States, their religious landscape shifted in notable ways.

The impact of the Great Awakening, with the fervent revivalism and emphasis on personal religious experience over formal church doctrine, reverberated throughout the colonies from the 1730s forward. Evangelical denominations, such as the Baptists and Methodists, gained ground, especially in frontier regions where traditional church structures were less influential. That spirit of revivalism would later resurge with the beginning of the Second Great Awakening in the 1790s, fostering emotional, conversion-driven worship that defined the new religious culture of the early United States.

Religious diversity was also a defining feature of the period. The colonies were home to a broad spectrum of Christian denominations, from the Puritans in New England to the Anglicans in the southern colonies, and various other groups such as Quakers, Lutherans, and Mennonites in the Middle Colonies. While some colonies, like Massachusetts, maintained established churches, others, particularly in the Middle Colonies, experienced a greater degree of religious pluralism. The growing diversity contributed to increasing religious tolerance, even as some regions retained established churches with limited rights for dissenters.

When interviewed later in life, Sam identified himself as practicing the Protestant faith. Many of his children did as well. We have no record of his living in that way or raising his children to follow it, though. The Protestant faith is a branch of Christianity that emphasizes the Bible as the sole authority, and followers believe that salvation comes through faith alone, not by good works or church rituals. Identifying as Protestant in the early United States generally meant adhering to one of the denominations that originated from the Reformation, which began in the sixteenth century with figures like Martin Luther and John Calvin. Those denominations had separated from the Roman Catholic Church for various theological, political, and cultural reasons. Identifying as Protestant also had cultural and social implications, often associated with independence, literacy (due to the focus on personal Bible reading), and a certain moral rigor.

As the American Revolution approached, Enlightenment ideas began to influence religious thought. Intellectuals and political leaders like Thomas Jefferson and Benjamin Franklin embraced Deism, a rationalist approach that rejected traditional doctrines and portrayed God as a distant, non-intervening creator. The philosophical shift away from organized religion was part of a broader trend among the elite, though it existed alongside the continuing strength of evangelical and revivalist Christianity.

The Colonial Home(stead)

Many of the settlers were farmers. Mason's boyhood home was likely agrarian (most people worked in agriculture). Hard work and self-sufficiency defined life on a colonial farm in America. Before sunrise, the daily routine began, with men heading to the fields to tend to crops and animals while women focused on household tasks like spinning, weaving, and cooking. Children were not exempt from labor; when old enough, they contributed to light tasks around the house or farm and sometimes even worked outside the family farm in places like blacksmiths or cooper shops. Colonial farms typically had a few domesticated animals like cows, horses, pigs, and chickens.

Early morning chores were essential, with men feeding and milking animals, preparing the soil for planting, and collecting firewood. Women maintained the household, washing clothes, cooking meals, cleaning, and caring for children. On larger farms, enslaved workers might take on the more labor-intensive duties, while children helped with simpler jobs such as weeding and gathering eggs. With twelve children, half of them boys, Thomas and Elizabeth Mason's home likely had plenty of workers. The twenty-eight-year span between the births of their oldest and youngest children would have provided many years of help with household chores.

Breakfast, usually consisting of cornbread, porridge, or meat, was shared by the family after several hours of morning work. As the day ended, families gathered for dinner, a hearty meal of proteins, grains, fruits, and vegetables based on availability. By nightfall, the family settled down for much-needed rest.

Bad Apples

In mid-1700s America, crime reflected the time's social, economic, and political conditions. Property crimes were among the most prevalent offenses. Theft was widespread, with burglary, pickpocketing, and livestock stealing frequently reported. In small, rural communities, the theft of animals or crops could have devastating consequences for the victims, threatening their very livelihood. Highway robbery, where highwaymen preyed on travelers along less-policed roads, occurred in many of the colonies, especially on isolated routes. Smuggling was also widespread, driven by the era's high taxes and trade restrictions. In the colonies, goods like tea, sugar, and rum were often smuggled to avoid the heavy tariffs imposed by the British government.

Crimes against persons, like assault and battery, were common outcomes of personal disputes that escalated into physical altercations, often occurring in taverns, domestic settings, or public spaces. Murder, though rarer, was met with severe punishment, usually resulting in the death penalty. Dueling also persisted as a socially acceptable means of resolving disputes among gentlemen despite its illegality in many regions. Dueling was often tolerated, particularly among the upper classes, as it was seen to defend one's honor.

Religious crimes like blasphemy and heresy were considered grave offenses against religious norms, and those found guilty could face fines, public humiliation, or imprisonment, particularly in Puritan communities. Sexual crimes, including adultery and fornication, were also criminalized, with harsh penalties like public whipping, branding, or fines. Witchcraft, though less common than in the previous century, still lingered as a crime, particularly in more superstitious or religiously strict communities.

Political crimes also held a prominent place in the mid-1700s. Treason and sedition were treated with the utmost seriousness, especially in the politically charged atmosphere of the time. Speaking out against the crown or colonial governments could lead to imprisonment or even execution, reflecting the era's heightened sensitivity to challenges to authority.

Law enforcement was rudimentary, relying on local sheriffs, constables, and militias to maintain order. In larger cities, night watchmen patrolled the streets, though their effectiveness varied greatly. Punishments for crimes were typically harsh and public, serving as both retribution and deterrence. Minor offenses were often met with fines, while more severe crimes could result in corporal punishment, such as public whipping, branding, or time spent in the stocks. Imprisonment was usually a temporary measure, used more for holding individuals before trial or punishment than as a long-term penalty. For the most serious crimes, such as murder or treason, capital punishment was the ultimate sentence, with hanging being the most common method of execution.

Virtually nothing was documented regarding Sam's early life. Draper erroneously noted that he was "connected by ties of consanguinity with the distinguished Mason family of Virginia and grew up bad from his boyhood." Rothert attributed Mason's criminal actions to the influence of frontier life and "not the family from which he sprang."[23] Those pioneer times, Rothert observed, "produced a variety of characters, and Samuel Mason rapidly developed into a product quite distinct from most men of the day."[24]

Travel and Tasting Notes

Frederick County (including Winchester), Virginia
Washington's Office Museum
Abram's Delight
See the Appendices for many more travel and tasting notes and the master timeline of our investigation and of Mason's life. Consider planning a visit to some or all of these locations.

Investigative Team

Bell, Coates, Rothert, Coker, Nicodemus, Lach, and Cabell were among the investigators who contributed to this phase of the investigation. For more on these team members, see the introduction—assembling the team.

2
THE BATTLE TESTED COLONIES (1754–76)

Let's set the scene: it was 1754, and what would soon become the United States was still a patchwork of British colonies. No official census had been conducted, but historians estimate there were about 1.5 million people living in those colonies. That number came from a mix of records and writings from the time and included European settlers and enslaved Africans.[1] While it's not as precise as the first official census taken in 1790, it gives us a decent snapshot of the population just before the American Revolution kicked off.

Home and Community Defense

In the 1700s, military service wasn't just a choice—it was a way of life, especially in Europe and Colonial America. In Europe, armies filled their ranks through a mix of conscription and voluntary enlistment. The lower classes typically made up the backbone of the forces, often joining for economic reasons, while the nobility sought out leadership roles and a shot at honor. Military training? It was no joke, with strict discipline and effectiveness as the foundation.

Meanwhile, life on the frontier meant you couldn't exactly count on a standing army to come to the rescue. Local militias were the answer, with every ablebodied man expected to serve part-time. Those militia members often carried on with their everyday lives but stayed ready to grab a musket and defend the community at a moment's notice. Think of them as the colonial equivalent of today's National Guard or volunteer firefighters—there when you need them, but otherwise just your everyday neighbor. Militia service was a critical piece of local defense against threats from Indian tribes, rival European powers, and even internal uprisings.

But it wasn't all part-time soldiers. During bigger conflicts, like the French and Indian War, regular troops were sent in as well. Those soldiers, often serving under more formal conditions, resembled the European armies they fought alongside or against. The British, for example, kept several regiments in the colonies and beefed up their numbers with local forces whenever a campaign demanded it.

Life on the frontier was tough, and settlers had to be prepared to defend their homes and communities against all kinds of threats, making military life a lot more integrated into daily survival than in the more established coastal settlements. It shaped the social structure of colonial life, offering opportunities for lower economic classes to advance while also facing the ever-present risk of death or injury. Serving in the militia brought communities together and gave veterans a place of respect.

Continental Versus Militia Soldiers

The *regular* or Continental soldiers and state militia were much different in Mason's time than the US Military and National Guard today. Over a decade after the Continental Congress declared independence in 1776, the individual states controlled the militia, not the federal government.[2] Before 1788, a colonel in the Continental Army had no absolute authority over a captain in the state militia. The self-appointed *commander* of a family fort, of which there were many, could identify himself as a colonel, even without proper military training.

Fort Necessity

Fort Necessity, located in present-day Farmington, Pennsylvania, was built in 1754 by British colonial forces under the command of a young George Washington. In the summer of 1754, Washington was a 22-year-old lieutenant colonel in the Virginia militia, tasked with leading an expedition into the Ohio Valley, a region of strategic importance where British and French colonial interests clashed. That mission marked Washington's first significant military engagement.[3]

Washington aimed to secure the Forks of the Ohio, a vital point where the Allegheny and Monongahela Rivers converge to form the Ohio River, against French encroachment. Arriving in the region, he learned that the French had already constructed Fort Duquesne (which preceded Fort Pitt in what is now Pittsburgh). Undeterred, Washington pressed on, constructing a temporary fortification named Fort Necessity. The fort was hastily built, consisting of a circular stockade of logs surrounding a small wooden storehouse, with earthworks and trenches for added defense.

Figure 2.1 Fort Necessity replica at the Fort Necessity National Battlefield. Fort Necessity was built in 1754 by British colonial forces under 22-year-old Lieutenant Colonel George Washington. Photo by ScottyBoy900Q [User], *FortNecessity*, 2006, Wikimedia Commons (https://commons.wikimedia.org/wiki/File:FortNecessity.jpg). CC BY-SA 3.0.

On May 28, 1754, Washington's forces encountered a French reconnaissance party led by Joseph Coulon de Jumonville. The skirmish that ensued, known as the Battle of Jumonville Glen, resulted in the death of Jumonville and several of his men, while others were captured. The incident ignited tensions between the British and French, leading to Washington's retreat to Fort Necessity to await reinforcements.

In late June 1754, French forces, seeking to retaliate for the earlier skirmish, laid siege to Fort Necessity. On July 3, Washington and his troops found themselves outnumbered and under heavy fire from the French and their Indian allies. Despite their efforts to defend the fort, Washington was forced to surrender after a day of intense fighting. The terms of surrender allowed his men to retreat, but they had to abandon the fort and their supplies. That defeat was a significant moment in Washington's early military career and highlighted the challenges faced by the British colonists in their struggle against French expansion in North America.

French and Indian War

The defeat at Fort Necessity marked the beginning of the French and Indian War, a larger conflict between Britain and France that spread to Europe as the Seven

Years' War. Despite the setback, the engagement provided Washington with valuable military experience and a deeper understanding of the complexities of frontier warfare.

Life in the American colonies during the French and Indian War was marked by uncertainty, hardship, and a profound transformation of their daily lives. The war, which lasted from 1754 to 1763, was somewhat mislabeled as a war between France and England, the two superpowers of the time. The war pitted the North American colonies of the British Empire against those of the French, each side being supported by various Indian tribes. The war disrupted trade routes and agricultural production, the lifelines of the colonial economy. Farmers struggled to work their fields with the threat of attack looming, and merchants' trading activities were severely hampered by naval blockades and the seizure of goods by privateers (government-supported pirates).

The Mason family was living in Frederick County during the war, on 370 acres of land, and later on 180 acres. It was likely they were farming, as many families

Figure 2.2 Private Sam Mason of the Frederick County Militia in a linen frock with a wool waistcoat and linen trousers—common dress for militia in the 1760s. Mason served under Washington in the British colonial forces. Sketched by Isuru Sandeep, with Fiverr.

did. Family members, particularly women and children, often had to fend for themselves as men went off to fight, leading to increased responsibilities. The Masons lived within the city limits of Winchester, originally named "Frederick Town" at its founding in the 1730s. Winchester, originally a Shawnee village, is situated northwest of the confluence of Opequon Creek and the Shenandoah River.[4] First sighted by Governor Alexander Spotswood in 1716, the northern (or lower) Valley attracted German and Scotch-Irish settlers from the 1720s. Acting on a land grant from Thomas, 6th Lord Fairfax, James Wood established a courthouse and renamed the town Winchester in 1743.

Many folks have assumed Sam's first taste of militia life came during the Revolutionary War when he served as a captain. But if Sam was born in 1739, he would have been nineteen years old in 1758, old enough to have served in the French and Indian War. So, what did that mean for Sam? Well, if he did serve in the war, that might explain why he was promoted to captain in the militia. He would have already been seasoned with both age and military experience under his belt. And Mason's name was found in the records. In 1760, Captain Thomas Speke listed him among the Officers and Men of the Frederick County Militia. It's another piece of the puzzle when we're trying to figure out how Sam's military life got started.[5] Many of the names listed on the Frederick County, Virginia, militia rolls from that war matched up with names found on land records and other local documents from the time.

Private Samuel Mason

Mason might have served under Colonel Washington at Fort Necessity, about 100 miles west of Frederick County. He was listed in the Frederick County Company roster in 1760 and was also on Captain John Stevenson's Roll under Frederick County.[6] He may have served as early as 1758, as he would have been 19 years old. In November 1760, Sam was court-martialed and fined 10 shillings for missing private muster.[7]

At some point, Sam stole some horses from Colonel John Hite (likely Johannes Henrich Hite), who was his Colonel in the Frederick County, Virginia militia as early as 1756.[8] Mason was chased down and caught, and during the pursuit, he was slightly wounded. He made restitution, but he had nonetheless earned a reputation for dishonesty by the age of twenty-two. It appears the theft from Hite was in the 1760s, which would conflict with prior notations that he was a teenager, though, as noted, some members of the investigative team, including Rothert and Lach, thought Sam was born in 1750.[9,10] The scene of the crime was the city of Winchester, in Frederick County, near his family home and not far from where he was serving during the war.

On September 5, 1762, Sam and Jonathan Clark incurred a debt of 4 pounds and 4 shillings to John Bozworth.[11] He was twenty-two years old at the time. Repayment appeared to be in the amount of eight pounds, eight shillings. No record of the cause of the debt was found, and very little information about Clark or Bozworth could be located. What was clear was that Jonathan Clark, who was on the debtors' note, was not the Jonathan Clark who was the older brother of George Rogers Clark, mentioned throughout the book.

Postwar Colonial Activities

Military casualties in the French and Indian War were high on both sides. British and colonial troops, often inexperienced and poorly equipped, faced the harsh

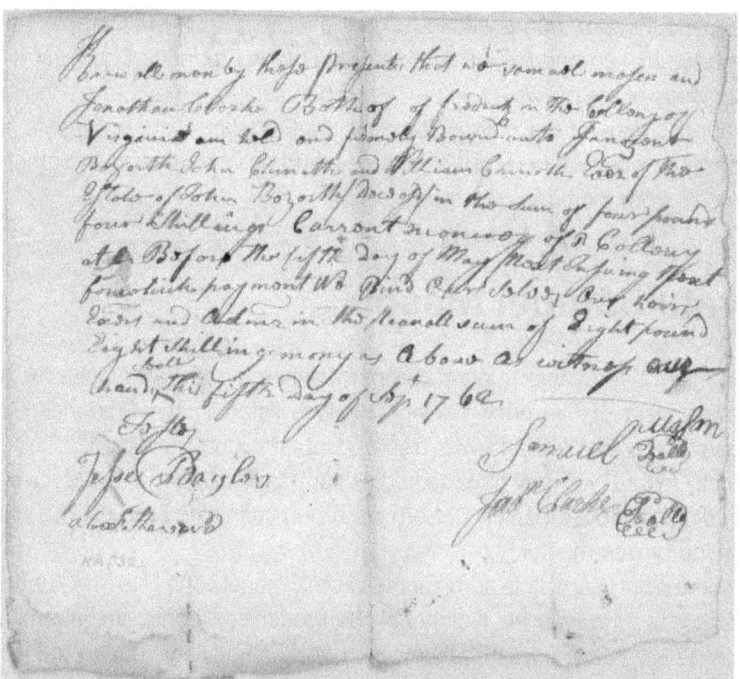

Figure 2.3 Samuel Mason and Jonathan Clark's debt of 4 pounds and 4 shillings to John Bozworth. September 5, 1762. Today's value would be about $600, depending on the specific conversion method used. *Samuel Mason and Jonathan Clark's debt to John Bozworth*, Ohio Company Papers, 1762, Historic Pittsburgh, University of Pittsburgh Library System (https://historicpittsburgh.org/islandora/object/pitt%3A31735061276352).

THE BATTLE TESTED COLONIES (1754–76)

realities of wilderness warfare, where traditional European tactics were often ineffective. Many soldiers fell not only to the musket fire of their enemies but also to disease, which swept through encampments with deadly efficiency. Over the course of the conflict, British forces lost thousands of men, with many more wounded or incapacitated by illness. French forces, though more accustomed to fighting in North America's rugged terrain, also suffered significant losses. The French, with their smaller population base in Canada, found it difficult to replace fallen soldiers. Their Indian allies, who played a crucial role in the war, also paid a heavy price. The war's end marked a significant decline in the power and influence of many tribes, as their French allies were defeated, and their lands were increasingly encroached upon by British settlers.

In 1763, the French and Indian War ended with a peace treaty between the British, French, Spanish, and Portuguese, known as the Treaty of Paris (not to be confused with the treaty ending the Revolutionary War in 1783, also called the Treaty of Paris). The treaty didn't stop the battle with the Indians, though; tensions did not subside, and the frontier was far from peaceful. Instead, a new series of challenges and conflicts emerged. The British government, seeking to prevent further conflicts with the Indians, issued the Royal Proclamation of 1763, which limited colonial expansion westward. That was resented and ignored by many colonists, who continued to move westward in search of new land. Their expansion often involved the clearing of land for agriculture, the establishment of new settlements, and the construction of roads and forts to protect the new outposts. Those activities often led to the displacement and dispossession of Indian tribes. Meanwhile, the fur trade remained a lucrative business, fraught with competition and conflict. Traders and trappers ventured deeper into Indian territories, which led to frequent skirmishes and hostilities.

As you can imagine, the years 1763 and 1764 were marked by intense and violent conflicts between the colonists and the Indians. The disputes were best demonstrated by what came to be known as Pontiac's Rebellion. Pontiac, an influential leader of the Ottawa tribe, led a force of various tribes in a significant uprising aimed at resisting British expansion into the Great Lakes region and the Ohio Valley. The rebellion effectively began in May 1763 when the Indians surprised the British and captured a series of forts along the frontier, including Forts Michilimackinac, Detroit, and Pitt. Settlements were not spared, and the attacks spread fear across Pennsylvania, Maryland, and Virginia.

The British response was initially slow but became increasingly harsh as they regained control over the territories. Two Delaware Indian delegates visited Fort Pitt in June 1763 and urged the British to abandon it. The British refused, and the delegates asked for provisions to help them return home. In an early American use of biological warfare, the delegates were given two blankets and a silk handkerchief infected with smallpox. That infectious disease begins with fever and headache and proceeds to an eruption of the skin that leaves pockmarks.[12]

Attacks and counterattacks led to significant losses on both sides, and by late 1764, the resistance had been mainly quelled, but the issue of land ownership remained. In the middle of 1764, Sir William Johnson, the British Superintendent for Indian Affairs, called a grand congress at Niagara, where he met with about 2,000 delegates from multiple tribes. The Treaty of Fort Niagara, concluded in July 1764, was a landmark agreement in which Indian leaders agreed to peace terms with the British. Fort Niagara was located on the Niagara River's eastern bank at the mouth of Lake Ontario.[13]

The treaty and similar agreements were crucial in stabilizing the region. However, it did not end all Indian resistance or fully address all grievances. Among the provisions of the treaty were: (1) release of all prisoners in Indian control; (2) all claims to English forts in the west were abandoned; (3) new forts could be constructed to protect traders, with surrounding land only enough to cover a cannon shot; (4) if an Indian killed an Englishman, the Indian would be tried by English law with a jury one-half Indian; and (5) the Indians gave up six hostages.[14]

Figure 2.4 Fort Niagara is in the upper left corner of New York State, overlooking Lake Ontario to the North and the Niagara River to the West. Niagara-on-the-Lake is across the river. Photo by Adithyavr [User], *Lake Ontario from Fort Niagara*, 2017, Wikimedia Commons (https://commons.wikimedia.org/wiki/File:Lake_Ontario_from_fort_Niagara.jpg). CC BY-SA 4.0.

British colonial authorities and later American leaders attempted to manage and mitigate frontier tensions through treaties and negotiations with Indian tribes. The treaties often involved many negotiations over land, trade rights, and military alliances. Sadly, colonial authorities ignored many agreements, leading to further grievances and conflicts.

Married with Children

In 1767, at age twenty-seven, Sam married Rosanna Dorsey in Frederick County, Virginia.[15] The Masons had eight children (six sons and two daughters). Their first child, Elizabeth, was born on the 29th (or 28th) of July 1767, and the next four were born every two to three years after that. Coker identified the following from the Daughters of the American Revolution (DAR) record of Martha Mae Latham Kimble, Coker's great-grandmother's cousin:

> The children of Samuel Mason and wife were eight. The old Mason Bible that Madie Briscoe McCloy (Mrs. Bertrand McCloy) has (now January 31, 1948 at the ranch near Angleton, Texas . . . . I, Elizabeth Gardner Naquin, Great-Great-great-grand daughter of old Samuel Mason, Junior, who was son of Captian (sic) Samuel Mason of Revolutionary fame am now at Madie's) is the one Samuel Mason, Junior, Husband of (Polly) Mary Searcy of Mississippi, bought at Fort Gibson, Mississippi in 1821 and on the fly leaf there is this.
> The Record of Samuel Mason, Seignor, and Roseana, his wife.

I.   Elizabeth Mason was born the 29th (or 28th) of July 1767.
II. Thomas Mason was born the 24th of October 1769.
III. John Mason was born 29th of April 1771.
IV. Isaac Mason was born the 31st of March 1774.
V.   Dorsey Mason was born the 12th of August 1776.
VI. Mary Mason was born the 3rd of February 1781.
VII. Samuel Mason was born the 3rd of December 1784.
VIII. Magness Mason was born the 19th of March 1786.

As you can imagine, family Bibles were often cherished possessions that served not only as religious texts but also as vital record keepers for many families. Bibles were used to document significant family events, including births, deaths, marriages, and other important milestones. For many families, the Bible was the primary record of their genealogy. In an era when official birth and death certificates were rare, especially in the American colonies, the family Bible provided a crucial source of documentation. Those records were often consulted for legal purposes, such as proving inheritance rights or establishing identity in legal disputes. The practice was especially common in Colonial America, where official record-keeping systems were often limited or inaccessible to many people, particularly in rural areas.

Living in Wheeling

Around 1773, ten years after the French and Indian War, Sam moved his family to Ohio County, Virginia (now known as Wheeling, West Virginia, about 60 miles southwest of Pittsburgh). Besides the first three of Sam and Rosanna Mason's children being born before that time, little was documented about their early married life. Ohio County, part of the frontier, was in the northwestern part of Virginia, near the Ohio River. The region was characterized by its hilly terrain and abundant natural resources, including rivers and forests. The area was primarily settled by pioneers moving westward. Many were of English, Scots-Irish, and German descent, seeking land and opportunities. The economy in the region was largely agrarian, with farming, hunting, and trade being crucial for survival. The Ohio River served as a vital transportation route for goods. By 1773, tensions were building between the colonies and British authorities, and settlers in the Ohio region were influenced by revolutionary ideas.

Eckert reported Mason's presence in Wheeling in April of 1774. He described Sam as "a large, rough-and-tumble man without social graces and minimal human compassion."[16] Mason was seen as a troublemaker and freeloader who was generally disliked. He settled near Shepherd's Fort in the region now known as Elm Grove to try to get a fresh start at the age of thirty-four. The family lived about 2 miles east of contemporary Wheeling, at Mason's Bottom, and owned three tracts on Wheeling Creek. Wheeling is in the uppermost part of West Virginia, where the state thins significantly to a peninsula and juts north into the borders of Pennsylvania to the East and Ohio to the West. Pittsburgh (founded November 25, 1758) and Columbus, Ohio (founded in 1812) are about 60 miles east and 120 miles west, respectively.

Forts in the 1700s

Unlike today, the fledgling United States was at war with multiple enemies on the North American continent. Many people lived in or near a fort for safety and treated those fortified dwellings like folks in a multi-story building should treat fire escapes. Unlike today's forts, typically large remote cities used for military training or strategic defense, forts in the late 1700s were smaller and often served as a place of defense and a residence for a smaller group of families. They were usually constructed near (and often became the foundation of) settlements or towns. Forts were primarily designed to protect local communities from attacks, including raids by Indian tribes or conflicts between European powers. They provided a haven for civilians during times of conflict and served as centers of community life, often as gathering places for social events.

Often, the husband of the family was a militia member, and family members supported him in those efforts. Families resided near or within the fort's walls for refuge and protection. When the number of people seeking safety in the forts increased, adaptations were made. The communal nature of the forts led to strong family and social bonds between neighbors. That helped them endure even the toughest frontier challenges.

Forts were typically constructed using local materials, such as wood, stone, sod, or earthworks (dirt and clay), and featured defensive structures like watchtowers and gates to deter potential attackers. In most instances, the entirety of the structure was made without a single nail or iron spike, as those items were not readily available. As military strategies evolved, forts became more specialized and focused on military purposes, leading to the development of the modern forts we see today. The military forts that Mason was connected to included Fort Pitt and Fort Henry. He also lived near Fort Shepherd, the soldiers from which supported Fort Henry.

Fort Pitt, Pennsylvania

Fort Pitt was a British fort built on the site of French Fort Duquesne. The fort's placement in the eighteenth century in present-day Pittsburgh provided a critical strategic location during the French and Indian War and the American Revolution. The fort and Pittsburgh were named after William Pitt, the British prime minister, from 1783 to 1801 and again from 1804 until he died in 1806. Fort Pitt was built on the confluence of the Allegheny and Monongahela Rivers, which formed the Ohio River.

During the French and Indian War, Fort Pitt was a significant target of French attacks, but they were unsuccessful in capturing it. The fort was also a key staging point for British expeditions against the French in the Ohio Valley. After the French and Indian War, the town of Pittsburgh grew up around the fort, eventually becoming one of the largest cities in the United States, as it is today.

By 1774, Mason was stationed at Fort Henry. Fort Pitt, with its larger garrison and greater resources, often provided critical support to Fort Henry. Supplies,

Figure 2.5 The Fort Pitt Block House was constructed in 1764. It was the only surviving structure of Fort Pitt, Pittsburgh's oldest architectural landmark. Photo courtesy of author.

reinforcements, and communications would be routed through Fort Pitt before reaching the more vulnerable Fort Henry. When Fort Henry faced threats or direct attacks, Fort Pitt troops or materials would reinforce Fort Henry, or the leaders would provide military guidance on how to handle the situation. The two forts were connected not just by their military purpose but also by the network of trails and river routes that linked them.

One mid-May morning in 1774, while at Fort Pitt for supplies, Mason saw an Indian coming out of the woods and approaching the settlement with his hand up, showing the sign of peace. Mason grabbed a rifle and shot the Indian, a young teenager from the Wyandot tribe, who had come to deliver a message. Mason was arrested and locked up for his actions. Shortly thereafter, a mob of settlers protested the arrest of a white man for killing an Indian. The mob broke into Fort Pitt, freed Mason from his shackles and left. Mason returned immediately to his home.[17]

Fort Henry, (West) Virginia

Built in June 1774, Fort Henry was initially called Fort Fincastle. It was named after Lord Fincastle, a title held by the eldest son of Lord Dunmore, the last Royal

THE BATTLE TESTED COLONIES (1754–76)

Governor of Virginia. The fort was established in 1774 during Lord Dunmore's War.[18] Fort Henry was not erected by any specific plan or design but was one of several similar forts built to protect settlers on the frontier. The need for a fortified shelter in the area was noticed simultaneously by the residents and the military authorities at Fort Pitt in the spring of 1774. Colonel Ebenezer Zane and John Caldwell began constructing the fort, which was completed with the help of Captain William Crawford, Colonel Angus McDonald, and 400 militia and regulars from Fort Pitt. Fort Henry was considered one of the most substantial structures of its time, and it has been said to have been planned by Captain George Rogers Clark, who was known to have been in Wheeling in the spring of 1774 before Lord Dunmore's War.[19]

The fort was rectangular, about 175 feet long by 125 feet wide (about a half-acre or just over a third of a football field), with four stockade walls of upright log pickets 8 or 10 feet high. Forts of that type had a blockhouse (defensive strong point) at each corner, extended a few feet beyond the lines of the walls so that a lateral fire could be directed against any who tried to scale the pickets. The second floor of each blockhouse was also projected beyond the first-floor wall so that the enemy could be exposed at every point outside of the fort. On the inside of the stockade were rows of cabins comprising the barracks for the garrison, the storehouses, and other areas.

Figure 2.6 Captain Mason was stationed at Fort Henry, in present-day Wheeling, West Virginia, prior to and during the Revolutionary War. Illustration from Wills de Hass, *History of the Early Settlement and Indian Wars of Western Virginia* (Philadelphia: H. Hoblitzell, 1851), 222. Via Internet Archive (https://archive.org/details/historyofearlyse00deha/page/n237/mode/2up?view=theater).

While the exact lines of Fort Henry could not be traced in the modern topography of Wheeling, the approximate site can be defined with certainty. In 1774, and for many years later, the ground between present-day Main Street and the Ohio River, at about Eleventh Street, formed a prominent elevation or bluff considerably higher than the highest point of the present hill. On the riverside, there was a steep decline, and on the south, the hill fell off abruptly to the lower levels of the bottomlands toward the creek. On the north and east, there was a gentler slope from the height chosen for the fort to the general levels of bench land between the river and the hills. An attacker could only partially assail from the river or the grain fields in the bottomlands to the south. The ground below the fort on the east and north was likewise cleared, and only a few scattered cabins protected an enemy approaching the fort from those directions.

The layout made the fort nearly impregnable from any ordinary attack. They would have been caught in a crossfire between the fort and the blockhouse. All the recorded attacks on Fort Henry came from the east, away from the river. Zane's blockhouse protected the fort's entrance since attackers had to pass by it to attack the fort. The cleared area was about 10 acres along contemporary Main and Market Streets, from the brow of the hill to a point above where the Suspension Bridge crosses, surrounded on three sides by forest and by the river to the west.[20]

Shepherd's Fort

Shepherd's Fort was located where Wheeling Creek splits (forks) to Big Wheeling Creek and Little Wheeling Creek in present-day Elm Grove. The site is now where the National Road joins Bethlehem Boulevard at Kruger Street. Shepherd's Fort, named for Colonel David Shepherd, Commander of Fort Henry, was burned to the ground by Indians in 1777. Shepherd's Hill, the residence built to replace the fort, was built by Shepherd's youngest son, Moses, on the site where the fort stood. The building was completed in 1798 and still stands.

Dunmore's War

Dunmore's War, a lesser-known but significant conflict, occurred in 1774 between the Colony of Virginia and several Indian nations, primarily the Shawnee and Mingo. The war was fundamentally about territorial disputes over the Ohio Country, a region of strategic importance and rich in resources, which both British settlers and Indian tribes claimed. As colonial populations expanded, settlers from Virginia and other colonies increasingly encroached on Indian territories.

THE BATTLE TESTED COLONIES (1754–76)

Tensions escalated due to those encroachments, leading to a series of violent incidents. One such incident involved the murder of the family of Mingo Chief Logan in 1773, an act that ignited a cycle of retaliatory violence between the settlers and Indian tribes.

Virginia's governor, Lord Dunmore, saw the ongoing skirmishes as a threat to the colonial claims and ambitions in the Ohio Country. In response, he orchestrated a military strategy to assert Virginia's dominance over the contested territory. The strategy involved a two-pronged military campaign: Dunmore from Fort Pitt and Colonel Andrew Lewis from Camp Union in modern-day Lewisburg, West Virginia. The pivotal moment of Dunmore's War came at the Battle of Point Pleasant, along the Ohio River near modern-day Point Pleasant, West Virginia, on October 10, 1774. Point Pleasant was located about 170 miles south of Fort Henry on the Ohio River.[21] Known by some as the first battle of the Revolutionary War, approximately 1,000 Virginia militiamen under Colonel Lewis fought against Shawnee warriors led by Chief Cornstalk, whom we will learn more about in the next chapter. After a long and fierce day of fighting, the Virginia militia emerged victorious.

Following the battle, Governor Dunmore continued to press westward, and his military pressure culminated in the Treaty of Camp Charlotte in October 1774, marking the formal end of hostilities. The Shawnee were forced to cede their claims to the lands south of the Ohio River, effectively opening up the region to further colonial settlement and exploitation. Following the battle, Fort Randolph was constructed in 1776 to defend against further Indian attacks and assert a colonial presence there. The fort was named after Peyton Randolph, the first president of the Continental Congress.

While it is possible that Mason or members of the militia in the Wheeling area served in Lord Dunmore's War, some historians might think it unlikely. The theater of Lord Dunmore's War was mainly restricted to the frontier areas of Virginia, less populated and developed than the eastern counties. Each county's militia was responsible for local defense and order, meaning their involvement in conflicts would typically be regional unless a widespread mobilization were ordered. Militia from the eastern counties were less likely to be mobilized and sent to the frontier, as the logistical challenges of moving and supplying large numbers of troops over long distances were significant, especially for a localized and relatively brief conflict.

But Dunmore's War seems to have been more large-scale and organized than the battles that preceded it. Based on Dunmore's planned route from Fort Pitt, west and then south down the Ohio through Wheeling, then southwest to Point Pleasant, along with his need to collect hundreds of fighters, we can imagine Sam and his fellow militia became part of that army.[22] He had militia experience from his service in the French and Indian War. He was in the Wheeling area of Fort Fincastle and had been since 1773, the year prior. Dunmore's strategy called for him to amass 1,500 fighters to match the 1,500 General Lewis brought from the southern approach to Point Pleasant. Additionally, as noted previously, Mason was at Fort Pitt a mere two months before the northern wing of fighters was assembled.

Revolutionary War

The American Revolutionary War lasted from 1775 to 1783. The war was the pivotal conflict between the thirteen American colonies and Great Britain. International involvement played a crucial role in the war, as France, Spain, and the Netherlands supported the American cause, significantly enhancing their chances of success against the British. Tensions had been mounting for years due to pushback against British taxation without representation, exemplified by measures like the Stamp Act and the Townshend Acts. The colonies increasingly sought greater autonomy and the right to govern themselves. The conflict ignited with the Battles of Lexington and Concord in 1775, marking the first military engagements of the war.

On the night of April 18, 1775, British General Thomas Gage ordered a detachment of about 700 British soldiers to march from Boston to the town of Concord, about 20 miles away. Their mission was to seize a cache of weapons and ammunition that colonial militias were reportedly storing there. However, colonial spies, including the famous patriot Paul Revere, had been monitoring British movements and quickly warned the local militias, known as minutemen, of the impending attack. As the British troops advanced toward Lexington, they encountered a small group of militiamen gathered on the town green in the early hours of April 19. The minutemen, vastly outnumbered, had no intention of starting a fight but stood their ground as a show of defiance. The tension was palpable, and a shot was fired in the confusion—though no one knows from which side. The shot, later called "the shot heard 'round the world," triggered a brief skirmish in which eight colonists were killed and several others wounded. The British soldiers continued their march toward Concord, having easily dispersed the Lexington militia.

When the British reached Concord, they found that most of the weapons and supplies they had come to confiscate had already been moved. Meanwhile, more colonial militias were gathering in the surrounding countryside. After a brief confrontation at the North Bridge, the outnumbered British soldiers found themselves under heavy fire from militia forces. They began their retreat to Boston, with militias firing on them from behind trees, stone walls, and houses along the road. What started as an orderly withdrawal soon turned into a chaotic retreat, with the British suffering significant casualties. By the time the British troops reached the safety of Boston, they had lost over 70 men, with more than 170 wounded or captured. The colonists suffered fewer casualties and proved their ability to stand up to the British army.

During the American Revolution, several colonies recognized the need for naval defenses against British forces, prompting the formation of their own navies. Virginia, with its vulnerable coastline and vital waterways, established its navy primarily to protect trade and support its militia.[23] That was part of a broader colonial trend, with Connecticut and other colonies creating similar forces.[24] Those state navies were tasked with defending their waters, disrupting British shipping, and supporting the fledgling Continental Navy, which Congress established in 1775 to coordinate national naval efforts.[25] The navies often relied on converted merchant ships and privateers, playing a key role in safeguarding American waters. Approximately 5–10 percent of Revolutionary War soldiers, mainly from maritime regions like New England, had prior experience with ships, contributing to the naval efforts.

On July 26, 1775, the Second Continental Congress established the office that would later become the United States Post Office Department. Benjamin Franklin of Pennsylvania took office as Postmaster General. We will see more about the post office in later chapters, as Sam had a special connection with one of the mail carriers.[26]

Virginia's governor Patrick Henry (known for his "Give Me Liberty or Give Me Death" speech) served from 1776 to 1779. During that time, the Wheeling fort was renamed to Fort Henry. In June 1776, Thomas Jefferson drafted the Declaration of Independence, a bold statement formally declaring the colonies' intention to break British rule. In September 1776, Colonel Dorsey Pentecost, the militia commandant in the West Augusta district, wrote to Colonel David Shepherd, appraising him of the decision to station detachments of militia at different places on the Ohio between Fort Pitt and the mouth of Grave Creek, and appointing Shepherd as commissary for victualing (provisioning with food and supplies) the militia employed in the service. In October of the same year, the state assembly divided the old district of West Augusta and created the three counties, Ohio being one, comprising nearly all the present West Virginia Panhandle and parts of Pennsylvania to the east.

Also in 1776, the first submarine was invented. David Bushnell's "Turtle" submerged by taking water into its tanks and reversed the process to rise. It moved using a hand-crank propeller. Bushnell had begun building underwater mines while a student at Yale University. He built the 8-foot-long wooden submersible large enough to accommodate one operator, with lead ballast to keep the craft balanced. The "Turtle" was used in an attack on Lord Howe's

Flagship "Eagle" in New York Harbor, but attempts to attach a mine to the Eagle's hull failed. The invention proved valuable, as we will see in the next chapter, as more battles involved bodies of water. Imagine that device in the hands of river pirates during or after the war! We will see more military engagement by Howe in Brandywine and Germantown, as well as other engagements as the war continued in the next chapter.

Travel and Tasting Notes

Niagara, Ontario Area:

> Fort Niagara, New York
> Prince of Wales Restaurant, Niagara-on-the-Lake
> Organized Crime Winery, Beamsville Bench

Pennsylvania:

> Fort Pitt Museum, Pittsburgh
> Fort Pitt Blockhouse, Pittsburgh
> Heinz History Center, Pittsburgh

West Virginia:

> Fort Henry Marker, Wheeling
> Good Mansion Wines, Wheeling
> Figaretti's Restaurant, Wheeling

See the Appendices for more detailed travel and tasting notes and the master timeline of Mason's life. Consider planning a visit to some or all these locations.

Investigative Team

Coker and Nicodemus primarily contributed to this phase of the investigation. For more on these team members, see the introduction—assembling the team.

PART II
1777-83

Figure 3.1 Wheeling, West Virginia; Marietta, Ohio; Kingsport, Tennessee; Knoxville, Tennessee. Sketched by Rotna, with Fiverr

It may be helpful to bookmark and reference Appendix A (additional travel and tasting notes), Appendix B (Timeline of Mason's life), and Appendix C (Historical Misinformation), as or after you read this chapter to help provide a foundation for the historical commentary.

3
WILD WESTERN VIRGINIA (1777-78)

Back in Mason's early days, there wasn't any official counting of the population in what would become the United States—at least not until the first census in 1790. But historians estimate that the colonies had about 2.7 million people at that time, which was double what it had been just twenty years earlier.[1] That number included European settlers and African slaves, though Indian populations weren't counted in the estimates. The population figures come from a mix of historical records and educated guesses by scholars. Even with the ongoing war, life in the colonies carried on as usual—or at least what people considered "usual"—though with a fair bit of caution and a strong focus on security.

Sam joined the Ohio County Militia, part of the Virginia State Forces, in 1777. Despite his less-than-stellar past behavior, he still managed to gain some respect in the community, enough to be seen as an upstanding citizen. In fact, the First Court of Ohio County even recommended him to Governor Patrick Henry for a commission as a militia captain. A few months later, when Ohio County's government was officially formed, Sam was selected to help build the first county road. According to a historical marker, the road stretched 6 miles to very near where Sam and his family had been living since 1773.

On January 6, 1777, records from the Ohio County Court (now West Liberty, West Virginia) showed Captain Sam Mason, Lieutenant Ebenezer Zane, James McConnel, and Conrad Wheat were tasked with determining the most direct way to lay out a road from Fort Henry to the first fork of Wheeling (presumably Creek).[2] The road was designed to connect Fort Henry with Shepherd's Fort, where Wheeling Creek forks into Big and Little Wheeling Creek. On March 3, 1777, the group reported that the best route would be from Fort Henry:

over the ridge to the lower end of Mason's Bottom; up the Creek Bank to wheet's Narrows; to the top and along the North Side o Wills Nobb to a Blas'd white walnut on Will's old road; then to the upper end of Wills field on the creek bank. Then up the creek bank to Hawkin's old house; then to a blas'd white oak on Williamson Road; then to the forks of Wheeling.[3] (Creek)

Indian Raids in Wheeling

During the spring of 1777, the Indian raids on the settlers of the Ohio Valley increased. The letters Mason wrote showed that he and his company were busy scouting the area and giving chase to the raiders. In May of 1777, Mason and his militia unit pursued some Indians who had robbed and killed a family near Pittsburgh. Mason and his men followed the murderers and frightened them so severely that the expedition was regarded as a success.

On June 8, 1777, Mason wrote a letter from Fort Henry to Brigadier General Edward Hand at Fort Pitt, advising that further defense of Fort Henry would be difficult as an attack was considered imminent. General Hand had also received word from Christian missionary David Zeisberger, originally from Moravia (now part of the Czech Republic), that an Indian attack on Fort Henry was imminent. Zeisberger was passing on intelligence from the Moravian Indians, who received it from Isaac Zane, brother of Ebenezer Zane.[4] General Hand was previously a leader in the Irish faction of the British army. Promoted to Brigadier General in March 1777, Hand became the commanding officer at Fort Pitt, responsible for fighting British Tories (Loyalists) and their Indian allies (more on them later).

While the local militia had been established two months prior, it had yet to be tested as a unit. Colonel Shepherd was named the commander, and Samuel McCulloch, who had served in Dunmore's War, was promoted to major and named second-in-command. Mason was among the six captains appointed, with four lieutenants and an ensign. Each captain began recruiting men to serve in their company, and the unit was organized quickly. Conditions in the newly formed Ohio County deteriorated, inspiring Colonel Shepherd to suspend the civil government and declare martial law.

On August 2, 1777, General Hand, at Fort Pitt, wrote to David Shepherd, warning him that the Indian situation was dangerous and ordering him to leave his fort and go to Fort Henry, 6 miles west. General Hand advised Shepherd to rally all the militia members between the Ohio and Monongalia Rivers.[5] Seven companies were ultimately dismissed within a few weeks when the raid failed to materialize as quickly as expected. Two companies, including Mason's, were

Figure 3.2 Captain Sam Mason writing to General Hand about needing reinforcements. An Indian attack on Fort Henry was imminent, and the soldiers were unsure of their ability to repel the attack. Sketched by Isuru Sandeep with Fiverr.

assigned to garrison (defend) the fort. The other company, led by Captain Joseph Ogle, was sent on a scouting expedition up the river and returned on the evening of August 31, 1777, reporting no signs of Indians.

First Siege at Fort Henry

Around 6:00 a.m. on the morning of September 1, 1777, the first siege of Fort Henry began as the sun rose over the horizon. Overnight, about 400 Indians, and a few Tories had set up an ambush. A Negro slave and a bondservant named Boyd were confronted by a few Indians at the crest of Wheeling Hill as they went to retrieve horses. The two attempted to flee, but Boyd was killed. When the slave returned to the fort to report the attack, Mason and a detachment of fourteen men, who had only arrived the night before, went to investigate the report, and one of them saw an Indian running from the area. Though a thick morning river fog lay over the region, someone spotted activity in a cornfield down near the mouth of the creek.

Colonel Shepherd ordered Mason and his soldiers to kill or disperse them. As Mason and his men approached the creek, the Indians (about 350 in number, though Mason hadn't yet realized it)[6] moved off to the east. Mason's company wheeled left and followed for another 300 yards when he and his sergeant saw two warriors materialize out of the fog. All four men fired their weapons, and Mason was the only one left standing. Seriously wounded, Mason found himself in the middle of several hundred Indians, including Mingoes, Shawanese, and Wyandotts, who had been waiting in ambush. All but two of Mason's men were massacred. A second and slightly smaller party of twelve soldiers, led by Captain Ogle, was also ambushed about an hour later as they went to aid Mason's group. Only five escaped. Mason made it to Wheeling Creek, where he hid among the roots of a sycamore tree, and later recovered from his wounds. After the siege, Mason was hailed as a hero for his part in the fort's defense. Significantly, the Indians suffered only three fatalities in that fight, and Mason was responsible for two.

In hindsight, many might suggest it was foolhardy to send out such a small contingent of soldiers, first to investigate the killing of a servant and then to back up the first group. But the context and geography are informative. At Fort Henry and in the area now known as Wheeling, mornings often brought a thick fog, given its setting along the Ohio River surrounded by Appalachian hills. The combination of river moisture and cool air creates ideal conditions for fog, which lingers until the sun strengthens. The persistent fog impacts daily life, particularly for those navigating roads or managing river traffic on the Ohio. It served as a natural concealment for the attack on Fort Henry. The investigative team witnessed the fog at the Fort Henry site firsthand and can attest to its total concealment ability, even well after sunrise.

Loyalist Simon Girty, who led the enemy force, boldly moved against Fort Henry. Once aligned with the American cause (he had served with Lord Dunmore alongside Captain Clark), Girty had become a Torie, defecting to the British side. As the sun rose to dissipate the fog, Girty approached the fort with a force of British soldiers and Indian warriors.[7] The settlers inside the fort, aware of the positions of the enemy troops, watched anxiously as Girty, known for his harsh tactics and deep familiarity with frontier warfare, appeared before the gates. He called for the fort's immediate surrender, noting that many of his (enemy) troops were waiting outside and promised leniency if the inhabitants complied but threatened destruction if they resisted. Despite the overwhelming power imbalance (at most a dozen troops were within the fort's walls at the time), the defenders of Fort Henry refused to yield to Girty's demands. Colonel Shepherd reported they had consulted with their families, and they would rather die fighting for their lives than trust Girty with their safety. As Girty started to reply, a gunshot from the fort halted the conversation.[8]

Not long afterward, Girty's troops rushed the fort, firing at the portholes from which defensive fire often came. The attack continued for many hours. Several follow-up surges were attempted, and all were met with sufficient firepower to repel them. The attacks continued until the following morning when reinforcements arrived. Major Samuel McCulloch, Fort Henry's second-in-command, led one of the groups to help defend the fort. McCulloch, known for his frontier skills and leadership, had been outside the fort with his troops when the siege began. As the last of his men returned to the fort, the attacking forces returned, and his route to the fort was cut off.[9]

McCulloch rode his horse away from the fort at full speed, leading the attackers away from the gates. With the enemy close behind, McCulloch spurred his horse to jump down a steep, almost vertical embankment. He and his horse miraculously survived the leap, evading capture. The jump occurred on a cliff known as Wheeling Hill, which overlooks where Fort Henry stood from the east in what is now downtown Wheeling. Realizing they had neither breached the fort nor captured McCulloch, Girty's forces fired a few more shots in the direction of the fort and departed the area. While it was estimated that dozens of the attackers lost their lives, none of the people in the fort were killed, and only one was wounded.[10] As you can imagine, the historical record again appears to be split on Girty's involvement in the siege. Nicodemus found that Girty was serving in the Pennsylvania Militia at Fort Pitt at the time he was said to have led the attack on Fort Henry. General Hand was no fan of Girty, it appeared, and accused Girty of being a British spy. Read more in Nicodemus' account.[11]

In another example of identifying historical misinformation, DeHass found some historical misinformation regarding whether Major *Samuel* McCulloch or his younger brother, Major *John* McCulloch, made the famed leap. Friends of the former had initially made convincing arguments, but the most notable distinction between the two was their date of promotion.[12] Samuel was commissioned a major in 1775 and was known then as a terror to the Indians. John was not commissioned as a major until 1795. That was long after the siege of Fort Henry. Samuel was killed on July 30, 1782, while the two were scouting the area for Indians. Samuel was shot and killed, as was John's horse. While John secured his brother's horse, escaping to the fort with a slight wound, the Indians disemboweled Samuel, dividing (and eating) his heart. One of the Indians later explained they did so because it would make them bold, like Major McCulloch. John and Samuel's sister Elizabeth was married to Colonel Ebenezer Zane.[13] See Appendix C for more examples of historical misinformation.

Figure 3.3 Major Samuel McCulloch, Fort Henry's second-in-command, led attacking forces away from the fort after the last of his men entered the fort. Illustration from Wills de Hass, *History of the Early Settlement and Indian Wars of Western Virginia* (Philadelphia: H. Hoblitzell, 1851), 358. Via Internet Archive (https://archive.org/details/historyofearlyse00deha/page/n237/mode/2up?view=theater).

Fighting Elsewhere

Battle of Brandywine

On September 11, 1777, just days after the attack on Fort Henry, General George Washington was working to protect Philadelphia from British capture. He positioned his troops along Brandywine Creek, about 30 miles west of Philadelphia and 290 miles east of Pittsburgh, mistakenly believing he had blocked all possible crossings. Under the cover of fog, the British moved into position, with part of Sir William Howe's forces crossing the Brandywine upstream.[14] Howe's troops unexpectedly attacked the Continental Army's right flank as the battle progressed. Despite efforts to reinforce that side, the Americans were ultimately overrun. Simultaneously, enemy forces pressured the remaining American units, leading to a collapse of Washington's line. Washington and the Continental Army retreated to the northeast. Although the defeat allowed the British to occupy Philadelphia, most of the Continental Army survived to continue the fight.

Battle of Paoli

On the night of September 20, 1777, the Battle of Paoli, also known as the Paoli Massacre, was fought. Following the defeat at Brandywine Creek, General Washington positioned his army between Philadelphia and Reading, Pennsylvania, to monitor British movements. General "Mad" Anthony Wayne was tasked with harassing British forces but mistakenly believed his camp was undetected. British General Charles Grey, utilizing surprise tactics, attacked Wayne's camp at night, leading to chaos and the routing of Wayne's division, resulting in 272 casualties, mostly prisoners.[15] Grey's troops, lacking flints in their muskets, relied on bayonets, earning him the nickname "No Flint" Grey. Wayne faced charges of misconduct but was acquitted after an investigation, though he acknowledged tactical errors. Eyewitness accounts of the brutal attack fueled American propaganda, depicting the British as merciless.[16]

Battle of Germantown

After capturing Philadelphia, General Howe stationed 9,000 troops in Germantown, a suburb of Philadelphia. Sensing an opportunity, Washington planned a double envelopment attack with his 8,000 Continentals and 3,000 militiamen. On October 3, he executed his plan, directing the forces to strike at dawn. However, darkness and heavy fog delayed their advance, compromising the element of surprise. Confusion arose as troops under General Wayne became separated in the fog and ran low on ammunition, leading to a retreat. Additional forces arrived in support but faced friendly fire due to miscommunication, causing further chaos. Thankfully, American artillery and determination prevented a complete disaster. Ultimately, Washington's army suffered about 700 casualties, with 400 captured, while the British lost over 500 men. Although the British won, the resilience of the Continental Army garnered admiration from European observers, particularly the French.

Battle of Saratoga

Not long after the attack on Fort Henry and the Battle of Brandywine, and on either side of the Battle of Paoli, significant activity was occurring a bit further (300 miles) north. The Battle of Saratoga, fought in September and October 1777, consisted of two significant battles: the Battle of Freeman's Farm on September 19 and the Battle of Bemis Heights on October 7. The American forces, led by Generals Horatio Gates and Benedict Arnold, fought against British General John Burgoyne, who aimed to secure a victory in New York and cut off New England from the other colonies. Burgoyne's plan relied on a coordinated effort with other British forces, but logistical challenges and slow reinforcements hampered his progress.[17]

In the first battle at Freeman's Farm, the British initially gained ground, but the Americans held their position. The second battle at Bemis Heights marked a decisive American victory. Arnold was said to have played a crucial role, leading a bold charge that broke the British lines. Burgoyne's forces were ultimately surrounded and forced to surrender on October 17, 1777. But there was another side to that story from an aide to General Gates. According to General James Wilkinson, Arnold, after clashing with Gates over matters involving the Battle of Freeman's Farm, was without a command on October 7. Nonetheless, he rode onto the battlefield and rallied the troops, ensuring victory at a key moment. While Wilkinson's recollection was generally believed by historians for over 200 years, it was ultimately disproven with historical documentation in a letter from a member of the New Hampshire Regiment.[18] We shall see more of Arnold and Wilkinson in later chapters.

The victory at Saratoga had far-reaching consequences. It not only boosted American morale but also convinced France to formally ally with the colonies, providing military support that would prove essential in the war. Although General Arnold made some traitorous decisions shortly afterward, the battle is often hailed as a pivotal moment that shifted the momentum in favor of the American cause, setting the stage for eventual independence.[19]

Siege of Fort Mifflin

With their victory at the Battle of Brandywine Creek, British forces under the command of General Howe occupied Philadelphia, forcing Congress to flee and further lowering American morale. However, despite British success, there was a logistical matter that the British had to face shortly after their occupation of Philadelphia. Several miles downstream, in the middle of the Delaware River, was Mud Island—home to the patriots' Fort Mifflin. The strategic position prevented British warships from landing in Philadelphia, hindering their ability to receive supplies from England.[20]

General Howe ordered a siege against the American position on September 26, 1777. Fort Mercer, located across the river in Red Bank, New Jersey, complicated matters for Howe. Between the forts on the river were nautical obstructions raised by the Americans, as well as the presence of a small American flotilla. On November 10, with the assistance of the Royal Navy, Howe began an extended bombardment of Fort Mifflin. After five days, the American position had become untenable, and the fort was abandoned on November 15. The fort's commander, Major Simeon Thayer, kept the American flag flying while escaping. By leaving it unclear whether the fort was occupied, the flag's presence gave enough time to row to Fort Mercer while the British wondered where they were. Less than a month later, Fort Mercer was also abandoned. The American forces who had garrisoned both forts joined the rest of Washington's army for their encampment at Valley Forge. And Howe gained free navigation of the Delaware River.[21]

Murder of Chief Cornstalk

In the last chapter, we learned about Lord Dunmore's campaign against the Shawnee led by Chief Cornstalk. The action effectively launched the Revolutionary War, with many of Virginia's military and militia taking part. Chief Cornstalk, whose given name was Hokoleskwa, was a prominent leader of the Shawnee Nation. He had emerged as a significant figure during the 1760s, when tensions between Indian tribes and European settlers were exceptionally high. As we saw earlier, his leadership and military prowess were especially evident during the Battle of Point Pleasant in 1774, during Lord Dunmore's War.

After the battle, Cornstalk sought peace with the American colonists, realizing the potentially devastating impact of continued conflict. He traveled to Fort Randolph in 1777 to warn the Americans of a potential alliance between the British and other tribes, which could have threatened American settlements.[22] Cornstalk and his son Elinipsico and other Shawnees were initially welcomed at the fort. However, the atmosphere of mutual suspicion and the volatility of frontier life soon undermined any hopes of lasting peace.

When two American soldiers were killed near the fort, presumably by Indians, the mood among the settlers turned vengeful, and Cornstalk and his companions were taken as hostages. He faced his fate calmly, even as he was brutally murdered. Cornstalk's murder on November 10, 1777, symbolized the ruthless and often treacherous interactions between European colonists and the Indians.[23] The story of Chief Cornstalk is remembered as a tale of betrayal and a testament to the courage and integrity of a leader who sought peace in the face of overwhelming adversity.

Weapons of the Time

During the latter part of the 1700s, firearms and knives were essential for many people's everyday lives, as they were used for hunting, protection, and warfare. Some of the weapons Mason and his fellow soldiers may have used at the time included:

- **Flintlock musket**: a smoothbore long gun fired by striking a flint against a steel striking plate, which ignited a small amount of gunpowder in the gun's pan, which in turn ignited the main charge in the barrel.
- **Kentucky Rifle**: a gun with a long barrel, for greater accuracy, and a smaller caliber bullet, making it more efficient to use.
- **Pistols**: a handgun often used as a secondary weapon for protection, hunting, and sometimes in duels.
- **Tomahawk**: an ax used by Indians and settlers for hunting, warfare, and everyday tasks.

Meanwhile, Back at Fort Henry

As was noted before, Mason's brothers, Thomas and Joseph, accompanied Lieutenant Colonel Clark on the Illinois Campaign in July 1778. As a result of Clark's military operations, the Colony of Virginia claimed territory from the Atlantic Ocean to the Mississippi River, including the area known as the Northwest Territory, now representing the states of Ohio, Indiana, Illinois, Michigan, and Wisconsin, as well as the northeastern part of Minnesota. Clark and his men traversed the area along the Ohio River in flatboats, and most of his men would have been skilled in operating the boats and using them during wartime confrontations. After the first attack at Fort Henry, Mason continued to serve the Patriot cause in the Western theater of the American Revolution. Still, his professional and personal actions

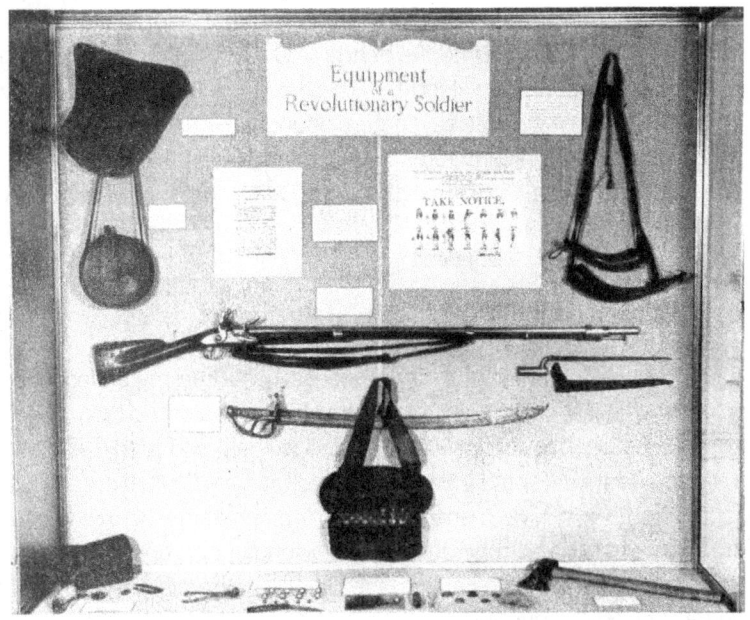

Figure 3.4 Revolutionary Weapons and Equipment. The equipment of the Revolutionary War soldier included a 1763 model Charleville musket, the regulation weapon of the French army. Most troops of the Continental Army carried one by 1779. A felt hat, wooden canteen, powder horns, and an ax are also displayed. Photo by US Department of the Interior and National Park Service, *Weapons and Equipment of Early American Soldiers*, National Park Service Popular Study Series, History No. 2 (http://www.npshistory.com/series/popular/2.pdf).

indicated his character may have flaws. On August 4, 1778, records from the Ohio County, Virginia Court show Mason was ordered to pay David McClure a fee for something Mason possessed.[24]

In September 1778, supplies came up missing from Fort Henry, and Mason was the chief suspect because, despite being a Captain, he had earned a reputation around town as a thief. Records from the Ohio County Court showed "An attachment . . . of . . . two potts, one frying pan, 2 wheels, 1 bed stead, 1 Churn, 1 Barrel, Twelve sheep, four cows & calves, & one hefer, in the hands of Samuel Mason." Mason claimed he had purchased the items and provided a witness to support his claim.[25]

The record also showed:

A Recognisance against Sam Mason, for disposing of & exchanging some of the Continental Stores at Fort Henry, Exhibited by Col David Sheepherd; whereupon the Defendant came into Court & acknowledged the Charge in part; whereupon this Court have Considered that Sam Mason afores be fined five pounds & Return into the hands of Col Sheepherd an equally good gun, or the value thereof; valued by Raesinb virgin & Joseph hoge, sworn for that purpose, valued at seventeen pounds; furthermore it appears to this Court that Sam Mason afores had exchanged his own property for the stores aforesd with a Ceryain V. Doulton, D.Q. master in the Continental service.[26]

Cultural Context

At this point, I will take a bit of editorial license based on my experience as a military criminal investigator. Over the years, I investigated dozens of soldiers from all ranks accused of theft. Most admitted to theft, and many were stealing property because they wanted it for personal activities or profit. But on occasion, we encountered a mid-level manager—usually a sergeant—who was accused of theft, often what the military identified as wrongful appropriation (temporary or partial stealing). In some instances, the practice was referred to by the self-defining term *tactical acquisition*.

For example, suppose you have a military unit that needs certain items to operate efficiently. In that case, whether it's uniforms, food, gas for the vehicle, or bullets for the gun, the process is to request those items from proper supply channels. What do you do if those supply channels are closed or closed to you? Many would suggest simply waiting, but a few *enterprising* leaders will "find a way" or "make it happen," knowing that it's all military property and it is *mission critical*. Some would even have a network of like-minded folks, allowing them access to more supplies despite the absence of paperwork.

Am I suggesting that Sam Mason didn't have a propensity toward criminality? Not a chance. There were claims that he stole horses from Colonel Hite in the 1760s, earning him a reputation for dishonesty. Early in his time at Fort Henry, almost fifteen years later, he was seen as a troublemaker and freeloader who was generally disliked. And then, four years later, supplies came up missing. Could it be a case of labeling gone wrong, where Mason was just in the wrong place at the wrong time? It could, but given his track record and our unique position looking back from the future, is it very likely? Perhaps that's a bit of a stretch. But context is essential, and an understanding of historic and contemporary military culture is imperative. That is especially true in the period we are studying when a man's ethical behavior was often evaluated based on his standing in society and with whom he associated.

Loyalist Tories

The Tories, also known as Loyalists, were European colonists who remained loyal to the British Crown during the American Revolution. They represented a significant portion of the population, particularly in New York, Pennsylvania, and the southern colonies. Tories believed that maintaining allegiance to Britain was essential for preserving order, stability, and especially their economic interests. They faced increasing hostility as the revolutionary movement gained momentum, with many being harassed, attacked, or forced to flee their homes.

Some Tories took up arms alongside British forces, while others provided support through intelligence and supplies. After the war, many Tories were ostracized or had their property confiscated, leading thousands to seek refuge in Canada, the Caribbean, or Britain, where they attempted to rebuild their lives. Despite their contributions, the Tories' loyalty ultimately placed them on the losing side of the conflict, leaving a legacy of division and displacement in the newly formed United States. We will see more Tories in the coming chapters.

Travel and Tasting Notes

West Virginia:

Zane's Island, Wheeling

McCulloch's Leap marker, Wheeling

Madonna of the Trail, Wheeling

Elle & Jack's, Wheeling

See the Appendices for more travel and tasting notes and the master timeline of Mason's life. Consider planning a visit to some or all of these locations. We had a blast!

Investigative Team

Earlier investigators who contributed to this investigation phase included Bell, Coker, Nicodemus, Roxby, and Wagner. For more on these team members, see the introduction—assembling the team.

4
MASON BOUGHT THE FARM (1779–80)

After being accused of theft—yet again—Sam Mason decided it was time to move on. He packed up his family and left Fort Henry, heading about 30 miles east to Buffalo Creek, which is now part of Buffalo Township in Washington County, Pennsylvania. On March 3, 1779, at the age of thirty-nine, Mason bought a 500-acre farm that sat right next to Samuel Williamson's land to the southeast. He purchased the property from Joseph Arnold. If you look at Washington County today, it sits right on the highway between Wheeling and Pittsburgh. Back in Mason's day, it was close enough to Wheeling—just 38 miles—that he could easily make the trip back and forth, which was convenient since he had started running a tavern just east of Fort Henry. It's likely that Mason left his family on the farm while he worked in Wheeling, tending to his tavern.

Mason's Tavern

For a few years, Sam ran his tavern, though business wasn't exactly booming. The reason? The Indian attacks had decimated much of the Fulton area north of Wheeling, so there weren't as many travelers passing through. Based on both documentary and physical evidence, it's believed the tavern sat about 200 yards west of where Generations Pub stands today, along the National Road in a ravine near Wheeling Hill. The location wasn't bad—50 miles southwest of Pittsburgh, where the Ohio River starts as the Allegheny and Monongahela Rivers meet. Wheeling, being on the Ohio River, made Mason's Tavern a potential stop for people moving goods downriver from Pittsburgh and the surrounding area.

Taverns in those days weren't just places to grab a drink—they were community hubs. Social, political, and economic life often centered around them. They were where locals met to swap news, dance, hold public meetings, and debate ideas as the American Revolution picked up steam. Take the Green Tree Tavern in Richmond, for instance. It was famous for its hospitality, often hosting military officers and local leaders. Then there was the Rising Sun Tavern in Fredericksburg, which, since its founding in the 1760s, had become a popular pit stop for travelers and a gathering place for locals. The Old Globe Tavern in Norfolk? Same story—it was the site of all sorts of community events and discussions. And there's Washington Tavern in Alexandria, which counted George Washington himself as a frequent guest and served as a hotspot for political and social gatherings.

And they weren't just for locals, either. Taverns also provided accommodation for travelers, soldiers, and merchants. Positioned along key roads and trade routes, they offered food, drink, and a place to rest. Many of those places also acted as makeshift marketplaces, selling everything from locally grown produce to imported goods.

Soldier Pay

In 1778, the Continental Congress voted to raise militias in Virginia and Pennsylvania to protect the western frontier. Each noncommissioned officer and soldier would receive twenty dollars and the same clothing as the Continental soldiers.[1] Due to funding challenges, however, they had to furnish their own blankets, rifles, and accoutrements. Soldiers in the Revolutionary War were paid in a variety of ways. The Continental Army, the main military force of the American colonies during the Revolutionary War, was initially financed by the Continental Congress, which issued paper money known as "Continentals" to pay the soldiers. However, the currency quickly became worthless due to inflation and a lack of public confidence in the government's ability to redeem it. Additionally, many soldiers were paid in kind, meaning they were given food, clothing, and other supplies as part of their pay. The lack of consistent pay was a significant source of discontent among the soldiers and contributed to desertions and mutinies.

Often, the only reward for serving as a militia soldier was the property they were able to take from enemies or the battlefield, and the reward paid by the government for Indian scalps. Scalp bounties were officially sanctioned by many colonial governments and were used as incentives to encourage colonists and sometimes allied Indians to attack enemy tribes. The practice was not only meant to weaken opposing tribes militarily and economically but also to instill fear. That aspect of history is often omitted from popular narratives but remains an essential reminder of the violent interactions that characterized the European colonization of North America.

Scalping is the forceful removal of the human scalp with hair attached. The victim may already be dead, but there are many examples of people being scalped while they are still alive. In several Indigenous cultures in North America, scalping was part of human trophy taking, which involves claiming human body parts as a war trophy, or for ceremonial purposes.[2] Colonies, territories, and states in what is now the United States used scalp bounties from the seventeenth through the nineteenth centuries. Massachusetts, for example, issued a bounty proclamation in 1775. The proclamation declared the Penobscot Indians enemies, rebels, and traitors to King George II and called on all "his Majesty's Subjects . . . to Embrace all opportunities of pursuing, captivating, killing, and destroying all and every of the aforesaid Indians."[3]

Bounty hunters were to be paid 50 British pounds for the scalps of living males twelve years and older, 40 pounds for the scalps of dead males aged twelve and over, 25 pounds for the scalps of women, and 20 pounds for the scalps of children under the age of twelve. The average annual salary of a teacher during the period was between 60 and 120 pounds.[4] As we will see later, Mason took the practice of collecting scalps far past the end of the Revolutionary War. He and his gang had about twenty scalps in 1803.

In May 1779, the General Assembly of Virginia, represented by Thomas Jefferson, advised George Washington: "Every soldier who enlisted into the corps of volunteers commanded by Colonel George Rogers Clarke, and continued therein till the taking of the several posts in the Illinois country, shall at the end of the war, be entitled to a grant of 200 acres of any unappropriated lands within the commonwealth."[5] The same Act granted bounties of 100 acres to all other Virginia volunteers who had enlisted or reenlisted to serve for the duration of the war. Western lands in present-day Kentucky and Ohio, which Virginia claimed based on its 1609 charter, were offered as an inducement.[6]

More recent documentation indicated Mason and his fellow veterans could have received even more. According to the Official Website of the Commonwealth of Kentucky, each state determined its veterans' land allotment. Legislation by the Virginia General Assembly indicated that Virginia paid the following bounties for service in the Revolutionary War, based on rank:

Sailor or soldier who served a three-year enlistment or to the end of the War—100 acres;

Noncommissioned officer who enlisted and served a three-year enlistment—200 acres;

Sailor or soldier who served throughout the War—400 acres;

Noncommissioned officer who served throughout the War—400 acres;

Subaltern-Cornet/Ensign/Lieutenant—2,000–2,666 acres;

Chaplain/Surgeon/Surgeon's Mate—2,666–8,000 acres;

Captain—3,000–4,666 acres;

Major—4,000–5,333 acres;

Lt. Colonel—4,500–6,666 acres;

Colonel—5,000–8,888 acres;

Brigadier General—10,000 acres+;

Major General—15,000–17,500 acres.

Where any officer, soldier, or sailor fell or died in the service, his heirs or legal representatives were entitled to and received the same quantity of land as would have been due the officer, soldier, or sailor had he been living.[7]

However, we have no record of Mason explicitly serving in the Regular Army, only the Virginia State Militia. While Virginians could acquire land through special military service in Lord Dunmore's War, the French and Indian War, and the Revolutionary War, routine militia service did not appear to qualify for special compensation.[8] To qualify for a land bounty, a soldier had to shift from short-term local militia duty and commit to serving for three continuous years in the State Line (within Virginia) or Continental Line (which served primarily in other states until the 1781 Yorktown campaign). For many families, the continuous commitment took a key worker away from the farm for three harvest seasons. After the military service, affidavits testifying that a person qualified for the bonus were submitted to the governor.[9] As we will see, it appeared Sam did receive a land bounty, but how he qualified for it was not clear.

Revolutionary Retirement

Military retirement systems are designed to provide financial security for service members who complete a substantial service period, typically after twenty years or more. The systems generally include a pension plan that offers a percentage of the retiree's base pay, often with adjustments for inflation and cost of living. Retirees often retain access to certain benefits, such as healthcare, military base privileges, and commissary access. The concept of military retirement has evolved to recognize the unique sacrifices and demands placed on military personnel. Modern retirement systems are structured to ensure that those who dedicate a significant portion of their younger years to military service are supported in their later years, acknowledging the physical and mental toll of military careers.

In the early years of the United States, the concept of military retirement was less formalized than it is today. During the Revolutionary War, the Continental Congress made provisions for pensions, but they were not always reliably funded or consistently applied. Early military retirement policies evolved slowly and were often influenced by the financial constraints and political climates of the times.[10] During the Revolutionary War, the Continental Congress promised pensions to encourage enlistment and reward long service. In 1776, a pension of half-pay for life was promised to officers who served until the end of the war and soldiers who were disabled in service. That was expanded in 1778 to include half-pay for seven years for widows and orphans of officers who died in service.[11]

Funding the pensions proved challenging. The fledgling government faced significant financial difficulties, leading to delays and inconsistencies in pension payments. Many veterans had to petition Congress for their promised benefits, and some received land grants instead of monetary pensions. After the war, pensions continued to be a contentious issue. The 1780s and 1790s saw numerous veterans petitioning Congress for their due, leading to the establishment of a more systematic approach to military pensions. The 1792 Invalid Pension Act provided for disabled veterans, establishing a precedent for recognizing and compensating service-related disabilities.[12]

Prepared to Retire

Although he had reached forty, Mason hadn't yet finished serving his country, and the war had not ended. He served in the expedition to destroy some Indian towns on the Allegany River, which runs from New York through western Pennsylvania, joining the Monongahela River in Downtown Pittsburgh. On August 11, 1779, Mason accompanied Colonel Daniel Brodhead and over sixty men in the Battle of Thompson Island, the only Revolutionary War battle fought in northwestern Pennsylvania. There was little documentation to support the classification as a battle, after which Brodhead reported an advance guard discovered thirty or forty of the enemy descending the river in canoes. Immediate action followed, in which five of the Indians were killed and several wounded. Brodhead's party suffered only slight wounds.[13] Brodhead and his troops returned to Fort Pitt on September 14, 1779. Not long afterward, Mason retired from active military service at forty, about the age when many contemporary service members retire.

While there were questions about his integrity while in the militia, Mason's success against the Indians made him famous among the civilians in his

Figure 4.1 Mason served briefly under Colonel Daniel Brodhead before retiring. He was part of the force that destroyed Indian towns on the Allegany River in northwestern Pennsylvania. Illustration from *Daniel Brodhead*, 2007, Wikimedia Commons (https://commons.wikimedia.org/wiki/File:Daniel_brodhead.jpg).

community. His good standing was not the perception of all, however, as a fellow Revolutionary War soldier described Mason as ignorant and unfit for command, although brave and good with a rifle. Another contemporary, George Edgington, would later write that Mason "settled on Wheeling Creek with a bad name from the start—[a] horse thief. He had two sons, one John and two sons-in-law, all of a feather."[14]

But like many contemporary criminals, Mason's daily activities weren't all criminally oriented. On November 1, 1779, records from the Ohio County Court show that "A Grand Jury for this County being Called, Samuel Mason was Sworn as Foreman," and fourteen others were sworn.[15] That was followed by an order that Samuel Mason "act as an over to make a Road from Jacob Wolfs to Thomas Wallers, and that he Summons the tithables within Three Miles Each side said Road to work thereon."[16] On December 11, 1779, Mason accompanied his neighbors James Clemens, Samuel Williamson, John Bogs, and John McBride, and applied for certificates of ownership for their land.

General Treason

As if the war wasn't complicated enough, things got even trickier further north. On September 21, 1780, American General Benedict Arnold secretly met with British officers. They weren't just discussing the weather; Arnold was planning to hand over West Point, New York, the very same site that would later become the United States Military Academy. Washington himself called it "the most important post in America." In return, the British dangled a tempting offer: a tidy sum of money and a prestigious position in their army.

Now, Arnold wasn't always a villain. In fact, for much of the war, he was a bold and capable leader of the colonial forces. In 1775, he helped capture Fort Ticonderoga and even led an ill-fated but daring attack on Quebec, earning him a brigadier generalship. He led troops in the campaigns at Lake Champlain, Ridgefield, and especially the Battle of Saratoga, where his bravery won him the admiration of General Washington.

Arnold had plenty of enemies within the military, though, and in 1777, five men of lesser rank leapfrogged him in promotions. You can imagine how that affected him.[17] Arnold had married a second time, and he and his new wife settled in Philadelphia, living extravagantly, and racking up quite a bit of debt. Between his growing financial troubles and that stinging lack of military promotion, Arnold was ready to betray the country he had once fought for so valiantly.

Luckily for the American cause, his plot was uncovered before West Point could fall into British hands. But Arnold didn't stop there—he went on to lead British troops in both Virginia and Connecticut, though his efforts for his new comrades never quite lived up to his earlier successes. As for his new life, it wasn't the dream he had envisioned. He eventually moved to England, living out his remaining years without ever receiving all the riches and glory the British had promised. Instead, his name became synonymous with treason and betrayal.[18] But know that if this book were about General Arnold, there would be several references here to quite a bit of historical misinformation.[19]

The Frontier on Defense

Mason's retirement from the militia did not end the battles around him, or the war several hundred miles south. The Battle of King's Mountain, fought on October 7, 1780, was a key turning point in the war. The Tory force at King's Mountain was commanded by Major Patrick Ferguson, a determined leader whose right arm had been shattered at the Battle of Brandywine, earning him the nickname "Bulldog" after he learned to wield his sword with his left hand. A few weeks before King's Mountain, Ferguson bluntly warned local revolutionaries that if they did not cease their rebellion, he would march over the mountains, hang their leaders, and lay waste to their settlements. That threat provoked a strong reaction from the backcountry forces, leading to a strategic collaboration between Colonels Isaac Shelby and John Sevier, who we will see in the next chapter, who decided to go on the offensive.[20]

Shelby and Sevier called a rendezvous at Sycamore Shoals (now in Tennessee) for September 25. On that day, they arrived with 240 troops each, joining 160 North Carolina riflemen and 400 Virginians. On September 30, the force was

Figure 4.2 Home of the Pioneer. A sketch depicting a typical pioneer home. Illustration from Wills de Hass, *History of the Early Settlement and Indian Wars of Western Virginia* (Philadelphia: H. Hoblitzell, 1851), 89. Via Internet Archive (https://archive.org/details/historyofearlyse00deha/page/n99/mode/2up?view=theater).

joined by 350 North Carolinians. By October 1, they camped just south of King's Mountain.[21]

Meanwhile, Ferguson fortified his position atop King's Mountain, writing to British General Charles Cornwallis that he could not be driven off. Early on the afternoon of October 7, the Americans arrived at the foot of King's Mountain and launched a four-pronged attack, surprising Ferguson and his men with their boldness and speed. Ferguson was killed during the attack, and Captain Abraham DePeyster, his second-in-command, raised a white flag to surrender. Unfortunately, several Tories were killed before the firing ceased, as some of the Americans continued firing, recalling the ruthless conduct of the British after a previous defeat.[22] Besides Ferguson, 119 men were killed, 123 were wounded, and 664 were captured, while the Americans had 28 killed and 62 wounded.[23]

On October 13, 1780, Colonel Brodhead, commander of Fort Pitt, sent a letter to Colonel Shepherd at Fort Henry, advising him to order a captain and twenty-five militiamen, including a subordinate (possibly a captain or lieutenant), and two sergeants to Wheeling.[24] By the end of 1780, a lieutenant, one sergeant, and fifteen privates were assigned to Fort Henry.[25] The frontier settlers seemed to be in an on-again-off-again relationship with their defensive posture. As we will see in the coming chapters, that was not a good idea.

Travel and Tasting Notes

West Virginia:

Ohio County Public Library, Wheeling

Generations Pub, Wheeling

Later Alligator, Wheeling

Tennessee:

Sycamore Shoals State Historic Park, Elizabethton

See the Appendices for more tasting notes and the master timeline of Mason's life. Consider planning a visit to some or all of these locations. Visit us at www.PirateSamMason.com and share your adventures!

Investigative Team

Earlier investigators who contributed to this investigation phase included Bell, Coker, Nicodemus, Roxby, and Wagner. For more on these team members, see the introduction—assembling the team.

5
LIFE AFTER THE MILITARY (1781–83)

In 1781, the Revolutionary War was still ongoing. Engagements like the Battle of Cowpens in South Carolina (January 17), the Battle of Guilford Courthouse in North Carolina (March 15), and eventually, British General Cornwallis' surrender at Yorktown, Virginia, on October 19, shaped the year. While the war technically didn't end until the Treaty of Paris was signed on September 3, 1783, things quieted down on the battlefield after Yorktown. No major battles occurred in the two years before the treaty.

On January 2, 1781, Colonel Broadhead directed Major William Taylor to send a lieutenant, a sergeant, a corporal, and ten privates to guard Shepherd's Mill, which was all that was left of Shepherd's Fort after it was burned down. They were there to protect the mill and the nearby settlements. But just three weeks later, Broadhead advised that the soldiers stationed at Shepherd's Mill would have to fend for themselves when it came to food until more supplies could be arranged.

Meanwhile, Sam Mason's family was settled on their property in the newly formed Washington County (now Buffalo Township, Pennsylvania) since 1779. His sixth child, Mary, was born on February 3, 1781. Even though Sam had retired from active military service, he still held his title as captain in the militia through May of that year. And, surprisingly enough, despite everything he had done, Sam still had some respect in the community. On July 15, 1781, he was elected as a Justice of the Peace for Washington County. Back then, justices of the peace were usually chosen either by local elections or appointed by elected officials. In Pennsylvania, judges were typically appointed by the state legislature or governor. It's likely that Sam's political connections, local reputation, and service during the Revolutionary War played a role in landing him that position. Sam also showed up on a municipal roll call on August 23, 1781, in Philadelphia as an elected public official for Donegal Township. The very next day, August 24, 1781, he was commissioned as an associate judge.

Law on the Frontier

In the 1780s, justices of the peace emerged as vital figures within the local legal and administrative systems. These officials were tasked with maintaining order, administering justice, and overseeing various local matters in their counties. Their responsibilities were extensive and encompassed a wide range of duties. Justices of the peace adjudicated minor cases, handling offenses such as petty theft and civil disputes, issues that would not warrant the attention of higher courts.

In addition to adjudication, they performed essential administrative functions, overseeing elections, managing public funds, and enforcing local laws and

Figure 5.1 Sam Mason, an associate judge in Buffalo Township in Southwest Pennsylvania, hearing a case in a frontier courtroom. Sketched by Isuru Sandeep, with Fiverr.

ordinances. They also had the authority to issue warrants for arrests and licenses for businesses and marriages, playing a significant role in regulating community affairs. Maintaining public order was another critical aspect of their role; justices were responsible for addressing disputes, supervising local militia activities, and responding to community disturbances.

Associate judges presided over local courts, hearing cases and ensuring justice was administered in their respective jurisdictions. As an associate judge, Mason would have been responsible for adjudicating various cases, including land disputes, criminal offenses, and matters of local governance. The role required a deep understanding of the law and a commitment to maintaining order and justice within the community.

A Thwarted Attack

On August 24, 1781, Colonel Broadhead, Commander of Fort Pitt, sent another message to the Commanding Officer of Fort Henry.

> Sir: I have this moment received certain intelligence that the enemy are coming in great force against us, and particularly against Wheeling. You will immediately put your garrison in the best posture of defence and lay in as great a quantity of water as circumstances will admit, and receive them coolly. They intend to decoy your garrison, but you are to guard against stratagem, and defend the post to the last extremity.
>
> You may rely upon every aid in my power to frustrate the designs of the enemy; but you must not fail to give the alarm to the inhabitants in your reach, and make it as general as possible, in order that every man may be prepared at this crisis.
>
> I am, sir, your most obedient servant,
>
> (SIGNED)
DANIEL BROADHEAD
COL. COMMANDING W.D. [1]

About ten days later, in early September 1781, over one hundred Indians suddenly appeared at Fort Henry. The fort's inhabitants were alerted to their presence in the area by a young boy, who reported the Indians had just killed a friend of his and taken another as a prisoner while they were gathering walnuts. The Indians demanded the fort's surrender, which the inhabitants politely declined, and the

Indians departed. Although there were several isolated attacks on the local settlers, significant incursions did not recur, at least for many months.[2]

Wartime Indian Relations

The relationship between the colonials and the Indians remained strained. One example of the strain was found in the slaughter of Moravian Indians, often referred to as the Gnadenhutten Massacre, which occurred on March 8, 1782. The Christian Lenape Indians involved in the massacre were part of a larger group of Delaware Indians that Moravian missionaries had converted (shared the gospel of Jesus Christ with)[3] in the mid-eighteenth century. The missionaries, mainly from the Moravian Church, established several settlements in modern-day Ohio, including Gnadenhutten, to live in peace away from the violent frontier.

As the Revolutionary War intensified, British-aligned Indian groups conducted raids into American territory. Although the Christian Indians remained neutral (or assisted the colonials, like when they passed on information from the Zanes to General Hand in 1777), they were often suspected of aiding the British, particularly after they were relocated closer to British-held territory in Detroit by British forces and other Indian groups. In early 1782, a group of Christian Indians who had been allowed to return to Gnadenhutten to harvest crops left from the previous year was found by Pennsylvania militiamen led by Lieutenant Colonel David Williamson. The militiamen, who were seeking revenge for raids conducted by other Indian groups, accused the Moravian Indians of participating in the attacks. Despite the Indians' protests of their innocence and their demonstrated Christianity, the militia held a Council of War and voted to determine their fate. The decision was made to execute them.

The next day, ninety-six Moravian Indians, including men, women, and children, were gathered in two buildings, one for men and one for women and children. They were brutally murdered with hammers and scalping knives; their bodies were piled in the buildings, which were subsequently burned. The Gnadenhutten Massacre shocked both the American settlers and the Indian communities.

Several factors might explain why the event occurred. The event was apparently driven by a climate of wartime tension, misdirected retaliation for earlier Indian attacks, and a mistaken perception of the Moravians as hostile. The militia's actions were likely influenced by deep-rooted prejudice, dehumanization, and possibly strategic concerns about limiting any Indian support to the British. The decision to execute the Moravians highlighted a failure of leadership and discipline within the militia, exacerbated by a desire for revenge.

Nicodemus added a bit more to the context, though, noting the Christian Indians who had been harvesting crops initially encountered raiding parties who were using the deserted towns as temporary campsites. Despite being advised against it, a few teenage girls from the Christian group traded food for a blood-stained dress taken from a girl whom the raiders had killed. When Williamson and the Pennsylvania Militia found the young girl wearing the blood-stained dress among the Christian Indians, Williamson assumed those Indians were responsible for the killings. As a result, although some militia members refused to take part, he confined them in the chapel and ordered their execution.[4] All because of a dress.

Second Siege of Fort Henry

The massacre of the Moravian Indians led to many retaliatory attacks against the settlers. Despite the potential for danger, the militia from Washington County was relieved of their duty at Fort Henry in April of 1782.[5] Fort Henry's commander, Colonel Ebenezer Zane, sent General William Irvine at Fort Pitt a letter not long afterward, reporting that Fort Henry was vulnerable to attack with only the five militia members assigned there.

The second siege of Fort Henry took place from September 11 to 13, 1782. A force of about 300 Wyandot, Shawnee, Seneca, and Lenape accompanied fifty Tory soldiers from Butler's Rangers, a provincial military unit. The siege was "The Last Battle of the Revolutionary War." The Indian contingent was led by George Girty, brother of Simon Girty, who led the previous siege against Fort Henry.[6] Many considered George more ruthless than his brother Simon, although the two were often mistaken for the other by enemies and likely also by historians. The British force, a company known as the *Queen's Rangers*, highly effective and known for its disciplined tactics and ability to carry out scouting and raiding missions, accompanied the Indians.

As the attackers arrived at Fort Henry that day, the defending force of forty men and boys led by Colonel Shephard prepared to protect sixty women and children from the surrounding area who had come to the fort for protection. Girty demanded surrender, promising all who would quit "the best protection King George could afford."[7] Shephard refused, resolving to fight to the death to protect the people in his fort. Though Girty chose not to attack until dark, he continued the dialogue throughout the day.

Despite the relatively few militia members assigned to the fort, the settlers were mentally prepared to handle the second siege because of the previous attack. Although the Indians had burned all the homes and buildings to the ground, the settlers' homes, including Colonel Zane's, had been rebuilt. Zane's home contained surplus ammunition and arms, and it had been decided to occupy it in case of another attack. Additionally, the soldiers had shored up their defenses and were even better prepared. A real cannon had replaced the wooden model that had been displayed two years before.[8]

At nightfall, Girty again demanded surrender and cautioned that refusal would result in a massacre. The folks at the fort taunted him in their refusal, challenging his integrity based on previous violent attacks following such assurances.[9] The first attacks aimed to destroy the fort and the surrounding area. Enemy forces attacked the fort and burned many buildings. On the first night, an Indian attempted to burn down Colonel Zane's cabin, but one of the defenders saw him and killed him just before the house was set on fire. The cannon was used heavily, fired sixteen times with such effectiveness that the Indians and Tories attempted to replicate the cannon out of a hollowed-out tree wrapped in chains. When they attempted to fire their makeshift cannon, it exploded, killing and injuring the Indians standing nearby.

Saving the Day

During the fighting the following day, the fort's supply of gunpowder dwindled, and it became critical for someone to dash across the open ground to Zane's cabin, where it was stored, to fetch more. As it was an especially dangerous mission, Colonel Zane asked his soldiers if one was willing to volunteer. As one of them responded, a female inhabitant of the fort suggested it was better that she go as if she were killed, she was more disposable than one of the men.[10] As she left the fort, there was a pause in the fighting, and the Tories and Indians just stared as she disappeared into the cabin. The woman was not as lucky on her return trip, though. As she wrapped the gunpowder in her apron and left the cabin to return to the fort, the attackers recognized what she had and opened fire on her. Nonetheless, she sprinted the 60 yards up the hill to the fort and made it safely inside, unharmed by the attackers. The powder allowed the settlers to defend the fort until help arrived. In the morning, the enemy fled as reinforcements took up the fight.

Tradition and early written records generally credit Elizabeth (Betty) Zane, sister of Colonel Zane, with that act of bravery. In 1802, a Philadelphia newspaper attributed the courageous act to her, and that identification has been consistently echoed in later retellings of the event. However, in 1849, an alternative account emerged, suggesting there may be another incident of historical misinformation. Mrs. Lydia S. Cruger, then eighty-four and the daughter of a militia captain, provided an affidavit stating her recollection of the incident. She claimed that it was Molly Scott who undertook the mission. Scott and her family were part of the defending force at the fort. According to Mrs. Cruger, the situation was somewhat different than what was told: the powder was already inside the fort, and the occupants of the Zane home needed ammunition. Molly Scott thus set out from the Zane residence for the fort. At the time of the siege, Mrs. Cruger was seventeen and said she assisted Molly Scott in retrieving the gunpowder.[11] Despite the alternatives, you'll find the event in Appendix C.

Historians disagree on the fate of Fort Henry following the second siege. Some have suggested that it faded from history after 1783, as it had become obsolete due to the departure of Indians from the area. However, there were many Indian attacks on the settlers in the area as late as 1795.[12] In fact, a settler named Daniel Whitaker reported surviving an Indian attack in December 1790 when he and his companions were hunting in Ohio Country (across the Ohio River from Wheeling into modern-day Ohio). He found safety at Fort Henry and reported that several occupants had greeted him upon arrival. Nogay was of the impression that Fort Henry existed in some form until closer to 1800.[13]

Not So Upstanding

There is no mention from any source of Sam Mason being at the second siege of Fort Henry. By 1782, Mason appeared to have become a successful, upstanding citizen, with records showing he paid taxes in Pennsylvania on his 500-acre farm, with two horses, four cows, six sheep, and four slaves. In the spring of 1782, while Mason lived on Wheeling Creek at the Narrows, Indians stole some of his slaves. Mason and a man named Peter Stalnaker went after them. The Indians hid when they realized they were being followed and shot and killed Stalnaker. Mason escaped without physical injury. However, he was deeply in debt. As we will soon see, that came to a head when the sheriff sold the farm to collect back taxes in 1785.

At some point following the Revolutionary War, which ended in 1783, Sam traveled to what is now eastern Tennessee and lived as a squatter in some cabins near the Holston River (a 136-mile river that flows from Kingsport, Tennessee, to Knoxville, Tennessee) along the Virginia-Tennessee border. The cabins belonged to General Sevier, a soldier and politician whom we encountered in the last chapter. Sevier played a prominent role in Tennessee's pre-statehood period and became the state's first governor, serving from 1796 to 1801 and again from 1803 to 1809. Mason and other individuals, including a fellow named Barrow, lived in the cabins until General Sevier told Mason that he and his gang needed to leave the area. That decision was made in response to items missing from the slave quarters while the residents were in church. As the Mason gang was not known to work or attend church on Sundays, they were investigated and found to have several of the stolen items.

Around that time, General Sevier owned quite a lot of property in Tennessee, including a house in Rocky Mount, near present-day Piney Flats. Sevier also owned property in Knoxville and New Market, about 1/3 of the way to Piney Flats, and owned a large tract of land known as Grassy Valley, now in Jefferson County. Sevierville, the county seat of Sevier County, was created in 1794, and both were named in honor of Sevier. Wagner found that Mason lived briefly in Knoxville when he squatted on General Sevier's land.[14] It was most likely, and fits with both Rothert's and Wagner's time calculations, that he traveled there in 1783 from the Wheeling area. East Tennessee is characterized by a varied topography that includes mountains, valleys, and rolling hills, significantly influenced by the Appalachian Mountains, which provide dramatic elevation changes and scenic views.

Sevier registered his land grant for Mount Pleasant in December 1778 but did not move from his home near Telford to Mount Pleasant until the fall of 1783. The Sevier family lived in the Mount Pleasant home until 1788. While other locations were known as Mount Pleasant, documentation by Colonel George W. Sevier, son of General Sevier, indicated that it was their property. The 640-acre plantation was later lost in a court case, and in 1970, the land was sold to the US Forest Service.

Knoxville began with James White's Fort on the Trans-Appalachian frontier in 1786. The fort was chosen as the capital of the Southwest Territory in 1790, and the city, named for Secretary of War Henry Knox, was platted the following year. Knoxville became the first capital of the State of Tennessee in 1796 and grew steadily during the early nineteenth century as a way station for westward-bound migrants and as a commercial center for nearby mountain communities.

Travel and Tasting Notes

West(ern) Virginia:

Zane Log Cabin, Wheeling
Zane's Blockhouse, Wheeling
The Betty Zane Monument, Wheeling
Pricketts Fort State Park, Fairmont

> The Log House 1776 Restaurant, Wytheville, (Virginia)
> The Bolling Wilson Hotel, Wytheville

Tennessee:

> The Carter Mansion, Elizabethton
> Rocky Mount State Historic Site & Museum, Piney Flats
> Netherland Inn, Kingsport
> James White Fort, Knoxville
> Ramsey House, Knoxville

See the Appendices for more travel and tasting notes and the master timeline of Mason's life. Consider planning a visit to some or all of these locations.

Investigative Team

Investigators contributing to this investigation phase included Bell, Nicodemus, Rothert, and Wagner.

PART III
1784–1801

Figure 6.1 Russellville, Kentucky; Henderson, Kentucky; Cave-In-Rock, Illinois; Metropolis, Illinois; Cairo, Illinois; Cape Girardeau, Missouri; Wolf Island, Kentucky; New Madrid, Missouri; Caruthersville, Missouri; Memphis, Tennessee. Sketched by Rotna, with Fiverr.

It may be helpful to bookmark and reference Appendix A (additional travel and tasting notes), Appendix B (Timeline of Mason's life), and Appendix C (Historical Misinformation), as or after you read this chapter, to help provide a foundation for the historical commentary.

6
FRAUD ON THE FRONTIER (1784–97)

By the mid-1780s, Sam Mason had packed his bags and bid farewell to Virginia and its neighboring areas, never to return. According to Bell, around late 1784, Mason found himself tangled up in several debt-related lawsuits.[1] Over the next few years, he and his sons shifted to real estate careers, selling bogus land titles to new settlers in the Marietta, Ohio, area—about 80 miles southwest of Wheeling. It seems Mason had already sold his farm in Buffalo Township, Pennsylvania, to his eldest son, Thomas, on June 3, 1785. Thomas was only fifteen at the time, born in 1769, which makes it likely that the sale to him was more of a futile attempt by Sam to avoid having the land snatched away. But not even that could fix his debt problem. The sheriff seized the land later that same year to settle Sam's debts, selling it to Daniel Leet. Unfortunately, the sale only managed to cover about half of what Sam owed in back taxes. That might explain why he decided to squat on Sevier's land in eastern Tennessee for a while.

Sam was likely separated from his family at times. He was a man constantly on the hunt for the next big opportunity (or at least the next money-making scheme). Along the way, he dabbled in farming, served as a judge, made and sold counterfeit money and land deeds, and, later, helped himself to the valuables of those traveling on boats and horseback. He had a knack for figuring out exactly what he needed to do to get what he wanted. Some of the gigs may have been temporary, but it's likely that Sam would set off alone or with only part of his household (likely his oldest sons), scouting for something promising, and then send for the rest of the family once he found a means to make a living.

Now, life in post-Revolutionary War America caused folks to have optimism and hope. England recognized the United States as an independent nation. The Revolutionary War and the founding of the United States brought about significant changes in the relationship between religion and government. Many colonists saw their fight for independence as part of a divine plan for freedom and justice, intertwining religious and political rhetoric. After the war, Jefferson's Virginia Statute for Religious Freedom in 1786 formally separated church and state by disestablishing the Anglican Church.

The ideas of religious liberty were enshrined in the new nation's Constitution. With the ratification of the Bill of Rights in 1791, the First Amendment codified the principles of religious freedom, prohibiting the establishment of a national religion and protecting the free exercise of religious beliefs. That reflected both the religious diversity of the new nation and the Enlightenment's emphasis on individual rights and reason. Religious life continued to play a central role in shaping social and political movements during the period. The same religious leaders who had supported the Revolutionary cause often turned their attention to postwar reform movements, including education, temperance, and the abolition of slavery. The religious revivals of the late eighteenth century set the stage for the broader societal changes that would come in the following century, illustrating the deep interconnection between faith, politics, and social reform in the early United States.

For the sake of this story, we'll use 1784 as a historical benchmark. From that point on, we'll no longer refer to the colonists as frontiersmen or Europeans—they're now Americans, plain and simple. Similarly, we'll retire the term Indians (a bit of historical misinformation on its own) in favor of Native Americans. And what were once Colonies will now be considered newly independent American states.

On the Red River

Mason moved from East Tennessee to western Kentucky, possibly to take a land bounty granted to him for his services during the Revolutionary War. It appeared Mason moved to a place on the Red River, south of Russellville, Kentucky, about 300 miles west of Mount Pleasant in East Tennessee, 400 miles southwest of Marietta, Ohio, and 50 miles north of Nashville, Tennessee, as early as 1781. It is more likely that he traveled there in 1784, as he was known to be in the Wheeling area in 1782 and was likely in East Tennessee sometime in 1783.

As with most of the other areas Sam and his family lived in, their new place had access to the major waterways, the early version of the interstate highway system. The Red River flows generally northwest from north-central Tennessee into south-central Kentucky. As a tributary, it connects with the Cumberland River, which flows northwest and eventually terminates at Smithland, Kentucky, where it flows into the Ohio River about 20 miles east of Paducah, in northwest Kentucky. Mason's second youngest son and seventh child, Samuel, was born

FRAUD ON THE FRONTIER (1784–97)

on December 3, 1784. Mason's youngest son and eighth child, Magness, was born on March 19, 1786. It was likely that both were born in what is now Kentucky.

In the 1780s, the area that would become Russellville, Kentucky, was in its early stages of development, as it wasn't officially founded until 1798. It was named after General William Russell, a prominent figure in Kentucky's early history. The fertile land and the many opportunities for farming and trade attracted the settlers to the area, which was still a part of Western Virginia until 1792, when Kentucky became a Commonwealth of the United States. Situated in Logan County, the area was part of the Virginia Military District, comprised of land bounties set aside for Revolutionary War veterans. The town was planned with a typical grid layout, common to many frontier towns of the time, with a central courthouse square as the focal point.

The distinction between *commonwealths* and *states* dates to the founding period. Four states—Kentucky, Massachusetts, Pennsylvania, and Virginia—chose to designate themselves as commonwealths when they drafted their constitutions. The term emphasized the idea of government based on the common good and the welfare of the people, a concept rooted in English political thought. Despite the difference in nomenclature, commonwealths are functionally equivalent to states, and the designation carries no special legal status.

The economy of Russellville in the 1780s, like much of the country, was predominantly agricultural—early settlers engaged in farming, growing crops such as corn and tobacco, and raising livestock. Goods produced on farms were traded in town, fostering a developing local economy. Settlers established churches, schools, and other communal institutions central to social life. Settlers dealt with the typical hardships of frontier life, including isolation, limited access to supplies, and the need for self-sufficiency in many aspects of daily life. Throughout the 1780s, Russellville grew steadily as more settlers arrived and the community developed its infrastructure and institutions.

In April 1789, Jeremiah Clemens, son of Mason's former neighbor James, visited Mason in western Kentucky, presumably to collect a debt. His father had warned him (Clemons) that Mason would try to maintain the advantage and perhaps even cheat him in the transaction:

> I must believe you to know Mason so well as to be particularly well acquainted with the policy he generally makes use of where he expects an advantage. Take particular care not to give up the judgment till you have a final satisfaction for the whole amount.[2]

Also, in 1789, the Pennsylvania court learned of Mason's location, so it sent a man named David Bradford to Kentucky to attempt to collect the remaining debt or arrest Mason and return him to Pennsylvania.

Debt Collection

The practice of debt collection in the fledgling United States was deeply rooted in the British legal system, which had a long history of severe punishments for debtors. The British approach to debt dates to the sixteenth century, when laws allowed for the imprisonment of debtors who were presumed dishonest and fraudulent. Over time, the laws evolved to distinguish between honest and dishonest bankruptcies, but the stigma associated with debt remained strong, and harsh penalties were common.

In the newly independent states, debt was just a part of life. People relied on credit to keep their businesses afloat and make ends meet. The states looked to British practices when it came to handling debt, and if you couldn't pay up, the consequences were harsh. But unlike personal misconduct, financial failure wasn't considered a moral failing. That distinction was important as the states were figuring out how their economies would work.

If someone couldn't pay their debts, they might end up working as an indentured servant, transferred from one creditor to another until they managed to clear what they owed. The practice had deep roots in Europe, where debtors in ancient Greece and Rome sometimes faced brutal punishments—even slavery. In seventeenth- and eighteenth-century America, if you couldn't pay your debts, you could end up in prison. That was common and continued all the way up to the 1850s. Bankruptcy laws at the time weren't designed to help—they were there to scare people into avoiding court. The Pennsylvania's Bankruptcy Act of 1785, for example, allowed for some serious punishments, like flogging or even mutilation, for those who went bankrupt.[3]

Over time, the way people thought about debt and bankruptcy began to shift. The challenges of the postwar period started to chip away at the idea that going bankrupt was a moral failure. Insolvency wasn't just for the reckless or irresponsible anymore—anyone could fall into financial trouble, no matter how hard they worked.[4]

The Land of Opportunity

In 1789, the United States faced significant challenges and opportunities. Having just emerged from the Revolutionary War and recently adopted the Constitution, the country faced political instability. The leaders had to establish a functioning national government under the new Constitution, and the challenge of uniting the thirteen newly independent states, each with its own interests and cultures, was daunting.

FRAUD ON THE FRONTIER (1784–97)

Another challenge was economic recovery. The nation was heavily in debt from the war and needed to establish a stable financial system. The economy was underdeveloped, with limited industry and infrastructure. Additionally, there was no uniform national currency, leading to economic confusion. Managing trade relationships and repairing damaged commercial ties, particularly with Britain, were essential for economic growth.

The country also faced external threats. The young nation had to protect its borders from European powers like Britain and Spain, who still had interests in North America. Relations with Native American tribes were also a concern, as westward expansion continued to create conflicts. George Washington was inaugurated in New York City as the first president of the United States on April 30, 1789. Washington's presidency marked the beginning of the US government under the new Constitution, which had been ratified the previous year to replace the Articles of Confederation. The country had ample land for agriculture, settlement, and expansion, which, combined with a growing population, set the stage for economic development.

In 1790, Mason was one of the petitioners asking Virginia to establish Logan County in western Kentucky. The request was made on behalf of the 100 or so Revolutionary War veterans who were living on Virginia military grants on land between the Green River (a tributary of the Ohio that runs through the middle of Kentucky from west to east) and the Cumberland. The area that became Logan County was known as "rogue's harbor." That was where the "outlaws-of-the-outlaws" came to hide.[5]

Western Kentucky had a mix of rolling hills, flat prairies, and fertile river valleys, influenced by both the Ohio and Mississippi Rivers. The diverse landscape was attractive for early settlers due to its agricultural potential. The area was initially forested with hardwood trees, which provided habitats for a variety of wildlife, including deer and birds, essential for the livelihoods of the settlers.

The early phases of the Industrial Revolution saw many inventions and the importation of British technologies. In 1790, the first US Patent was issued to William Pollard of Philadelphia for a machine that roved and spun (preparing for use as yarn) cotton, and in 1794, Eli Whitney patented the Cotton Gin to comb and deseed cotton bolls. His invention made the revolution of the cotton industry possible but never made him rich. Instead of buying his machine, many farmers built their own. In 1797, Eli Whitney contracted to manufacture 10,000 muskets for the US Army. At the time, a single person would make an entire musket without standardized measurements. Whitney divided the labor into several steps and standardized parts for the government contract to make them interchangeable.[6]

In 1790, the population of the United States was approximately 3.9 million people, based on the first census, and included both free persons and slaves. On

January 24, 1791, President Washington issued a decree stipulating the borders of the next capital district (the District of Columbia, or DC). The construction period lasted ten years, and the government, including President Adams, worked from Philadelphia until May 15, 1800, when they moved to Washington, DC.

A Fresh Start at Red Banks

In the early 1790s, Mason and his family moved to Red Banks (now Henderson), Kentucky, 100 miles north of Russellville and over 500 miles west of Pittsburgh. Some have suggested it was as late as 1794, though the census recorded members of the Mason family as early as 1792. See the trial summary for the interview of Derousse and Peltier, who recounted an encounter with Mason in 1791 on the river near Red Banks. The site's name was due to the reddish clay soil of the bluffs overlooking the Ohio River.

In those days, Red Banks was a lawless place populated by men who had come there to escape the law. The town of Red Banks, in the north-central corner of the state, was located where the traditional overland route from Natchez through Nashville met the Ohio River, and it became a gathering spot for outlaws. The area west of there to Fort Massac in modern-day southern Illinois (about 100 miles west along the Ohio River) had become much of the same. We will see more about the stretch of river between Red Banks and Fort Massac in the coming chapters. Mason and his gang used the whole river to their advantage.

Henderson was founded in 1797. It was established as a river port by the Transylvania Company, led by Colonel Richard Henderson, for whom the city (and the surrounding county) were named. Henderson quickly became an important center for trade and commerce, with the Ohio River providing access to markets in the East and the West. Henderson and the surrounding area were primarily agricultural in the late 1700s. The main crops were tobacco, hemp, and grains. The city also had many small industries, such as distilleries, tanneries, and sawmills.

Mason, now in his mid-fifties, lived in Red Banks with his wife, four sons, and a daughter. At Red Banks, Mason expanded his criminal activities to counterfeiting money and continued selling fake land certificates. Ever the community leader, Mason also helped establish the local government and served again as a Justice of the Peace, likely his last position as a public servant.

According to Bell, in 1794–5, Mason killed John Dodd, a prominent citizen who owned a tavern across from the courthouse in Washington County, Pennsylvania. Dodd had traveled to New Orleans in 1794 and was killed on his return trip. Jonathan Leet, brother of Daniel Leet, who bought Mason's foreclosed Pennsylvania property in 1785, identified Mason as the killer years later.[7] It was speculated that Mason had visited Dodd's tavern in Washington

FRAUD ON THE FRONTIER (1784–97)

Figure 6.2 Counterfeiter Sam Mason, standing at a Gutenberg printing press making counterfeit bills. Sketched by Isuru Sandeep, with Fiverr.

County while Mason was a judge. No additional information regarding Dodd's murder was available.

Mason's sister (perhaps Mary, the second youngest) also lived in the area for a time, having married another criminal and counterfeiter, John McElduff (Duff). Duff's history started in South Carolina, but his family moved to Natchez before the American Revolution. He had been familiar with the area along the Ohio River as early as July 1778, when Lieutenant Colonel Clark met Duff and a hunting party at Fort Massac, near present-day Metropolis, Illinois, on the north side of the Ohio River across from Paducah, Kentucky.[8] Duff was not a violent man by nature, and he was never known to have killed anyone. Duff was an associate of Philip Alston, the South Carolina counterfeiter.

Post-colonial Counterfeiting

Counterfeiting was a significant problem in the newly independent states, inspired by a shortage of official currency and a fragmented monetary system. They used British pounds, shillings, and pence as the official currency, but Spanish dollars and other foreign coins were also commonly used. Barter and trade were common, particularly in rural areas and among the lower classes. Gold and silver coins, as well as precious stones, were widely accepted as forms of payment.

Counterfeiting techniques were often rudimentary but effective due to the simplicity of currency production methods at the time. Forgers employed various strategies, such as imitating woodcut and engraving designs, creating hand-drawn copies, and substituting lower-quality paper for the distinctive material used in genuine currency. Some counterfeiters would artificially age their fake bills to disguise imperfections, while others experimented with ink to replicate the colors and textures of authentic bills. Some forgers altered the denominations on legitimate bills to increase their value or produced counterfeit coins by mixing lower-value metals with small amounts of precious metal. Despite the severe penalties for counterfeiting, including imprisonment and even death, the widespread use of paper currency and the relatively basic security features of the era made counterfeiting a persistent issue.

Each state issued its own paper money, creating an environment ripe for counterfeiting. The idea of making easy profits by counterfeiting money was logical, given the skill set learned by some criminals while on the British payroll. The British had intentionally and overtly used counterfeiting to degrade the value of the Continental currency until the end of the war in 1781. In 1790, the US Congress passed the first federal anti-counterfeiting law, which provided for the punishment of anyone who made, imported, or used counterfeit currency. The widespread issue influenced the decision by leaders like Alexander Hamilton to establish a federal mint and national currency to ensure a more stable and secure economic framework for the emerging United States.

The US Mint

The Articles of Confederation initially governed the new nation and did not give the federal government sufficient authority to regulate currency. That resulted in a confusing array of state-issued coins and foreign money circulating within the country.[9] The Connecticut Mint, established in the late eighteenth century, played a unique role in the early history of American coinage.

In 1786, Connecticut authorized the minting of its currency primarily to address the need for a stable medium of exchange during economic uncertainty. In 1787, the infant US government asked for bids to produce the first official US coins. One of the Connecticut Mint's owners, James Jarvis, apparently bribed the assistant US treasurer, William Duer, to get the contract.[10]

FRAUD ON THE FRONTIER (1784–97)

The quality of the coins was often inconsistent, and the mint struggled to maintain the production standards required by the federal government.[11] In 1792, when a debate broke out about whether the US government should build its own mint, Jefferson successfully argued in favor of a national mint.[12] The need for a standardized national currency had become evident, leading to the ratification of the US Constitution in 1788, which granted Congress the power "to coin Money, regulate the Value thereof." The Coinage Act of 1792, passed by Congress, laid the groundwork, and President Washington appointed David Rittenhouse as the first director.

The first Mint building was constructed in Philadelphia, with its cornerstone laid on July 31, 1792. The US Mint commenced operations in 1793, producing the first official US coins, which were copper cents and half-cents bearing the image of Lady Liberty. Over time, the Mint expanded its operations to include silver and gold coins, which helped stabilize the American economy. As the nation grew, additional branch mints were established in Charlotte, Dahlonega, New Orleans, San Francisco, Carson City, and Denver.[13] Those events likely inspired Mason to find other financial opportunities than counterfeiting.

Trouble in Paradise

Mason's daughter (records aren't clear whether it was Elizabeth or Mary) was dating a(nother) criminal named Kuykendall, who worked out of Diamond Island, a three-by-one-half-mile-long island off the Kentucky shore, about ten miles further west down the river, and the two married and eloped to the island. One day, Mason lured them back to Red Banks by promising a wedding celebration, and when his new son-in-law left to return home, he was shot and killed. Elizabeth later moved to Cape Girardeau, Missouri, where the Ohio and Mississippi Rivers intersect. Records regarding Mary were not found. Daniels suggested the daughter's marriage to Kuykendall pushed Mason to a full-time life of crime. While his younger years had some dishonesty and deception, Daniels speculated that Mason was shamed by how the two acted.[14] Other members of Mason's gang at the time included Henry Harvard, a man from Tennessee; Nicholas Welsh, a tavern keeper; and two men named Barrett and Hewitt.

The 1792 Census of Henderson County, Kentucky included *Thomas Mason, Sen., Thomas Mason, Jun., John Mason, Abner Kyrkendall, and Adam Kirkendall* in a list of the sixty-three Free Male Inhabitants between the ages of sixteen and sixty years of Charlston (Red Banks), Ohio a part of Logan County, taken the 19th Day of November 1792. T. Mason, Sr., and Adam Kirkendall were noted as captured by Native Americans.[15] As Sam's son Thomas was born in October

1769, he would have been twenty-three when the census was conducted. It was not likely that he had a son who was over sixteen years old. What was possible was that Sam assumed Thomas' name to avoid arrest or capture by the many groups who wanted to catch up with him. The report that Mason was captured would have kept the census takers from identifying him.

Constable Dunn

Recognizing the need to restore order, the Commonwealth of Kentucky (admitted to the Union on June 1, 1792) appointed Captain John Dunn, a veteran of the Revolutionary War, as the Constable of Red Banks. By 1795, tensions between Mason and Constable Dunn escalated to violence. Mason had requested that Dunn sign some papers, but Dunn refused. A few days later, Mason and four of his men attacked Dunn, throwing his body over a fence and leaving him for dead.[16] Dunn survived the assault but continued to face threats from Mason's family and associates. In another incident highlighting the violence of Mason's gang, they attacked and stole a female slave along with her two children from Hugh Knox, a resident of Red Banks who later became a judge in Henderson County.[17] Although Knox, with Dunn's help, initially managed to recover the slaves, Mason's gang retaliated by attacking Knox.

The conflict with Dunn intensified in 1797 when Mason's son, Thomas, openly threatened Dunn's life. When Dunn's wife enlisted Dunn's cousin, Thomas Durbin, to intervene, Thomas Mason shot and killed Durbin and fled the town. That same year, Mason moved his operations and his family to Diamond Island. The violence culminated later in 1797 when Dunn, accompanied by Thomas Smith, traveled to Knob Lick, Kentucky, about 150 miles west of Red Banks, about equidistant (about 100 miles each way) between Nashville to the south and Louisville to the north. As they crossed Canoe Creek, an associate of Mason, thought to be Henry Harvard, ambushed and killed Dunn.[18] In retaliation, a group of Regulators (more on them later) tracked Harvard to his father's house on the Red River, about 100 miles southwest of Knob Lick. That indicated Harvard may have joined the Mason gang before they headed to Red Banks, as the home was near the Kentucky-Tennessee border, close to where the Masons lived in present-day Russellville. The vigilantes found Harvard and killed him while he was hiding under a bed.

The Mason gang had made their headquarters at a local tavern in Red Banks. According to Mrs. William Anthony, daughter of Constable Dunn, Nicholas Webb, the tavern owner, was an accomplice of the Masons. After Dunn was killed, the Regulators caught up with another accomplice, a man named Hewitt, near

Diamond Island. While at least one of the vigilantes was inclined to kill Hewitt, they chose instead to disable his gun. Webb disappeared right after Dunn was killed and never reappeared.[19]

A man named Isaac May began operating as a criminal in the Red Banks and Diamond Island area about the time the Masons left. May, also known as Samuel May and James May by others, spent time with a woman who claimed to be his sister.[20] May stole some horses at one point, and the two fled toward Vincennes, Indiana, 60 miles north on the other side of the Ohio River. May was pursued and returned to Red Banks but escaped the following night. Peter Alston, the son of infamous colonial-era counterfeiter Philip Alston (who we mentioned earlier as an associate of Duff in Red Banks), may have used the alias James May.[21] We will encounter James May later in the book.

The ongoing violence and lawlessness had prompted the Regulators' vigilante response throughout the region, aiming to dismantle Mason's gang and their operations. Members of the community were fed up with the criminal element and organized sweeps to drive out or eliminate the gang members. Meanwhile, Mason and his followers relocated for the second time that year, 55 miles west on the Ohio River to Cave-In-Rock, Illinois.

Travel and Tasting Notes

Kentucky:

> *Bibb House, Russellville*
>
> *Logan County Courthouse, Russellville*
>
> *John James Audubon Museum, Henderson*
>
> *Farmer and Frenchman Winery, Henderson*

See the Appendices for more tasting notes and the master timeline of Mason's life. Consider planning a visit to some or all of these locations.

Investigative Team

Bell, Coates, Lach, Nicodemus, Rothert, Roxby, and Wagner contributed to this investigative phase. For more on these team members, see the introduction—assembling the team.

7
ESCAPE TO THE CAVE (1797–99)

In 1797, Mason moved his headquarters west to Cave-In-Rock in Hardin County, Illinois, to escape the Regulators. The Cave was a well-known landmark across the Ohio River from northwestern Kentucky. The entrance to Cave-In-Rock was visible a little above the Ohio River's high-water mark, close to the bank. The mouth of the cave appeared like a half-circle with a flat base. The cave was about 100 feet deep and almost uniformly 50 feet wide. For another perspective, a typical semi-truck trailer is about 8.5 feet wide and about 50 feet long, so the cave's width is equivalent to two rows of six semi-truck trailers placed side by side with barely enough room to exit on the sides. Imagine that the next time you see a truck stop. When Mason and his gang were based there, several tall trees grew in front of the mouth of the cave, partially concealing it.

Diverse landscapes, including rolling hills, fertile valleys, and river systems such as the Mississippi and Ohio Rivers, characterize southern Illinois. The varied terrain supported both agriculture and settlement. The area boasted rich forests, prairies, and wetlands, providing a habitat for various wildlife.

During the final years of the 1700s, the United States dealt with tensions with France, which led to the Quasi War, an undeclared naval conflict from 1798 to 1800. It was sparked by tensions between the two countries over trade issues and France's revolutionary government's hostile attitude toward the United States. During that period, French privateers attacked American merchant ships, and the government responded by authorizing the Navy to seize French vessels. That led to naval engagements, with both sides capturing each other's ships. John Adams served as the second president of the United States from March 4, 1797 to March 4, 1801, after serving as the first vice president under President Washington starting in 1789.

Figure 7.1 Cave-In-Rock, a spacious cave opening to the Ohio River. Many travelers and criminals had ties to the cave during Mason's time. It is now part of a state park. Photo courtesy of the author.

Wilson's Liquor Vault

At Cave-In-Rock, or Cave Inn as it was previously known, Mason took up his old trade in the hospitality industry but with a much deadlier twist. He outfitted the cave with a liquor supply and converted it into a tavern. Mason also took on aliases like other past and present criminals to avoid capture and identification.[1] Among the tricks Mason used to lure unsuspecting river travelers to stop was a prominent sign that read, "Wilson's Liquor Vault and House of Entertainment." Some investigators have suggested that Mason also went by the name Bully or James (Jim) Wilson, although others have suggested that Mason and Wilson were not the same person. Others have suggested that it wasn't Mason but James Ford who used the moniker for a bar at the cave. Ford operated a ferry across the Ohio River in western Kentucky and southern Illinois in the late 1790s and was said to secretly be a river pirate and the leader of a gang later known as the "Ford's Ferry Gang." Like Mason and his gang, he and his men hijacked flatboats coming down the Ohio River. Ironically, James Wilson (1742–98) was a Colonial American lawyer and political theorist who signed the Declaration of Independence and the Constitution of the United States. Wilson was known for promoting currency reform and pressing Congress to levy a general tax. One wonders if Mason left his counterfeiting career for the Cave Inn bar across the river with that knowledge! We added that to the collection of historical misinformation in Appendix C.

ESCAPE TO THE CAVE (1797–99)

As we saw, Mason had kept a tavern in Wheeling a few years prior, near where the Ohio River begins. He also made a tavern into his headquarters in Red Banks. Like those locations, Mason established his tavern in Illinois to be seen as a stopping or meeting point for folks moving merchandise down the Ohio. However, the Cave-In-Rock location was more strategic and fully supported his pirating operation. The site offered an excellent view of the river in both directions, thereby giving Mason and his associates early warning of both potential victims and Regulators sent to curtail his activity. The riverside bar and bordello combination proved irresistible for many travelers.

Mason's gang included two sons and any other men he could persuade to engage in river piracy with him. The "entertainment" at the cave was supplied by one of Mason's daughters-in-law, some female slaves, and other female consorts of his pirate gang. Some flatboats were lured to shore near the cave using a man or woman (posing as a stranded settler) to hail the boats from the riverbank as they passed. Others were lured by the anticipated break from the river and a chance to relax. While the women were keeping the boatmen busy and getting them drunk, Mason's gang members examined their cargo for anything of value. The pirates often offered to assist in piloting the boat through the shallow parts of the river ahead. Once aboard, they would run the ship aground to facilitate their crimes. They also chased boats and captured the crew if their assistance was

Figure 7.2 Pirate Sam Mason welcomes a flatboat approaching his cave hideout. He and his pirate gang offered to assist so they could run the ship aground and rob the crew. Sketched by Jekaterina Hagen, with Fiverr.

declined. Sometimes, they sank the boats; other times, Mason used his network of people along the Ohio and Mississippi Rivers to sell the boats and goods to crooked or unsuspecting merchants. While some of the crews were killed to ensure their silence, Mason frequently coerced/forced his victims to join his gang instead of murdering them. He always promoted himself as a robber who only killed when necessary.

The gang members and profits sometimes didn't return to the Cave-In-Rock hideout.[2] Rothert suggested that Mason had that revelation about the time he determined an attempt to capture him was likely to be made. Most probably, the pirates took their ill-gotten gains and had a spending spree in Natchez or New Orleans, as both locations had a well-known, seedy section occupied by prostitutes, card hustlers, swindlers, and the inevitable enforcers that were spawned by those trades. The Natchez location was known as *Natchez Under The Hill*. Its counterpart in New Orleans was known as *The Swamp*. Both were places where most people did not venture more than once. Rothert observed no record of Mason's whereabouts between 1798 and 1799, although many robberies occurred along the Mississippi River and nearby trails.[3]

> Samuel Mason, that is my name. I left Fort Henry seeking fortune and fame. I came from Virginia a long time ago, but now I am a pirate along the Ohio.

Those are lyrics to *Samuel Mason*, by Andrew and Noah Van Norstrand, from their 2010 album, *All the Good Summers*, on Great Bear Records. The song continues:

> Murder and robbery, those are my crimes. I'll lure you in with women and wine. Hurricane Island seals your fate, for from this shore there is no escape.

Hurricane Island is located on the Ohio River between Kentucky and Illinois.[4] It is 6 miles west of Cave-In-Rock and could have been connected to the river pirate activities happening there. There is no historical evidence supporting that, though. There was obviously more to Mason's life, but you can listen to the rest of this folk song in the podcast or on their album.[5]

The American River Pirate

Piracy has been a persistent problem throughout history, emerging independently in different regions as soon as maritime trade became a viable economic activity. Piracy was a significant issue for the ancient Greek, Roman, and Chinese civilizations. Those early pirates were often not just criminals but sometimes operated with the tacit support or active participation of local rulers and city-states, blurring the lines between piracy and legitimate maritime warfare in privateering.

While no longer as rampant or organized as during the eighteenth and nineteenth centuries, piracy continues even today in more modern forms. Criminal activities such as hijacking cargo vessels, stealing equipment, or engaging in smuggling still occur, albeit on a smaller scale. A recent example includes thefts from barges transporting agricultural goods and fuel, with criminals using small boats to board unattended vessels during nighttime.[6] Additionally, drug trafficking via river routes highlights the persistence of criminal activity on America's inland waterways. Modern forms of river piracy echo the historical tradition of exploiting vital river systems for illicit gain.

Between April and September 2010, Falcon Lake—a reservoir on the Rio Grande near Zapata, Texas—experienced a series of violent incidents involving armed individuals targeting American boaters. Those events included robberies at gunpoint, attempted interceptions, and the tragic death of David Hartley, who was fatally shot while jet skiing with his wife. The assailants, often armed and sometimes posing as law enforcement, were linked to the Los Zetas cartel, a notorious criminal organization operating in the region.[7]

Piracy and privateering are maritime activities that have historically stirred fear and fascination worldwide but differ significantly in their legal standing and operations. *Piracy* involves the unauthorized or illegal act of violence, theft, or detention on the high seas, typically for personal gain and without the backing of any nation-state. Pirates operate independently, recognizing no authority other than their own and targeting any ship they consider a viable target regardless of nationality. Pirates have long been romanticized in popular culture and are often seen as rebels who live outside the confines of society and acquire wealth and power through their bold exploits. That can appeal to people, as the idea of living a life outside of the norm and being able to chart your own course is something that many people find exciting.

Privateering, on the other hand, is a state-sanctioned activity. Privateers are private individuals or ships authorized by a government via a document known as a letter of marque during wartime. They are hired or contracted to attack and capture enemy vessels and bring them before admiralty courts for condemnation and sale. The practice was an effective form of naval warfare that allowed states to augment their naval power with private ships while making a profit.[8] Thus, while pirates and privateers engage in similar activities at sea, privateers operate under the protection of national authority, which lends their actions a veneer of legitimacy and legality. Devoid of such endorsements, pirates are often hunted relentlessly and punished as criminals by nations worldwide.

However, Mason and his contemporaries engaged in a distinctly American brand of piracy. Instead of the swashbuckling, romanticized pirate known for wearing an eye patch and a tricorn hat and talking with a distinct accent that takes a lot of practice to replicate, river pirates were often colonial soldiers turned frontiersmen who, in their way, were seeking the American Dream and a better way to provide for their families. Unlike some of the well-known sea pirates, Mason's operations were primarily river-based along the Ohio and Mississippi Rivers rather than on the high seas.

Mason's name was feared by those who traveled the rivers he controlled, much like how sea pirates were dreaded by ocean-going vessels. He, like other pirates, targeted travelers, merchants, and cargo, stealing goods and money, and much like Blackbeard (Edward Teach, born around 1680 in England), Black Bart (Bartholomew/John) Roberts, born May 17, 1682, in Wales), or Captain Kidd (William Kidd, born January 1645, in Scotland), gained a notorious reputation. River-based piracy involved different tactics and targets, and Mason led a gang of outlaws like the other pirates led their crews. However, we don't have much information about how he ran the gang like a democracy, as pirates (and several of the militia units in the colonies) were known to do.

Blackbeard started as a privateer during the War of the Spanish Succession, attacking enemy ships with government authorization. Black Bart began his seafaring life as a merchant sailor before being forced into piracy. Captain Kidd also started as a privateer, with a commission from the English government, and was hired to protect English interests and attack enemy French ships. When the war ended, many privateers turned to piracy.

Like many sea pirates, Mason established strongholds along the rivers, which served as a base for his operations. He was familiar with the concepts of ambush, command, and evasion from his time in the militia. Although he had been a judge, he lived outside the law, constantly on the run from authorities, and his life was marked by violence, betrayal, and the constant threat of capture and execution. Mason operated primarily in the *late* eighteenth century when the United States was newly independent and expanding westward. In contrast, many well-known sea pirates operated in the late seventeenth and early eighteenth century during the so-called "Golden Age of Piracy."

Sea pirate captains were often captured in naval battles or ambushes by government authorities. For example, Blackbeard was killed in a fierce battle with the Royal Navy off Ocracoke Island, North Carolina, on November 22, 1718. Black Bart's downfall came on February 10, 1722, off the coast of Gabon in West Africa, when, during a battle with the HMS *Swallow*, he was killed by grapeshot. Captain Kidd was arrested in Boston in 1699, sent to England, and tried for piracy and murder. He was found guilty and executed by hanging on May 23,

1701. His trial was highly publicized and politically charged. Mason's end came in 1803, in a much different ending from the fates of the others, as we will see.

Why River Piracy?

River piracy on the Ohio and Mississippi was prevalent in the 1790s for several reasons. First, the region was experiencing rapid growth and development during that time. As more people settled in the area to the west and south and trade increased, so did the number of boats that traveled on the river, providing the river pirates with more targets. Second, the region was sparsely populated, with little organized policing. That made it difficult for the authorities to track down and apprehend pirates. Third, the Ohio and Mississippi Rivers themselves were ideal for piracy. They were wide and winding, with many secluded coves and inlets where pirates could hide.

River piracy significantly impacted the development and safety of regions along the Ohio and Mississippi Rivers, affecting areas now known as Pennsylvania, West Virginia, Ohio, Indiana, Kentucky, Illinois, Missouri, Arkansas, Tennessee, Louisiana, and Mississippi. Native American involvement in river piracy, which preceded Mason and his contemporaries, varied across different tribes. Some tribes, like the Chickasaw and the Miami, engaged in piracy, driven by economic needs and as a form of resistance against the encroachment of white settlers on their lands. The Chickasaw, for example, attacked ships to acquire goods and retaliate against settlers. Conversely, tribes like the Shawnee cooperated with government forces, providing intelligence and support in campaigns against pirates such as Mason, demonstrating their opposition to piracy and its disruptiveness to trade.

River pirates used a variety of methods to attack and rob their victims, including ambushes, aggressive boarding, luring, and impersonation. River pirates like Mason had the advantage over river travelers, using small watercraft-like canoes at night for sudden attacks, boardings, and escapes. Flatboats and keelboats were the vehicles used to transport goods and people along the Ohio and Mississippi Rivers, and they were difficult to maneuver.

From the 1780s to the 1820s, the flatboat era marked a critical period in American river transport. The vessels were constructed from wood, a material chosen for its buoyancy and availability. Flatboats, usually about 20 feet wide and 40 to 100 feet long, were simplistic in design. That's between 800 and 2,000 square feet, or the size of a starter house in contemporary America. They relied on the river's current for propulsion, with oars and poles used mainly to navigate away from obstacles like sandbars. Due to their construction and the lack of a

Figure 7.3 Flatboats and keelboats were used to navigate the rivers in the late 1700s. Mason and his crew often used canoes or other smaller boats to approach and rob the sailors. Sketched by Isuru Sandeep, with Fiverr.

reliable strategy for returning upriver, flatboats were often dismantled at their destination and sold as lumber, reflecting a one-way utility.

Keelboats, on the other hand, featured a more robust build. They could carry more cargo as they were about fifteen feet wide and up to 120 feet long. That's 1,800 square feet, about half the size of a professional basketball court. For another comparison, contemporary river barges measure 35 feet wide and 195 feet long, with a deck space equal to about four keelboats. The boats had a pointed design at both ends, facilitating navigation in both directions, although traveling upstream was labor-intensive. That involved a crew of up to 100 men who used long poles to push off the riverbed or ropes to pull the boat against the current. The upstream journey could take three to five months from New Orleans to Louisville, a testament to the challenging conditions and physical demands.

The Notorious Harpes

Many historians have linked Mason to the Harpe brothers, though others disagree. The Harpe brothers, Joshua (Micajah or Big) Harpe (Harp or Harper) and Wiley

(Little) Harpe, were notorious late eighteenth-century criminals known for their extreme brutality on the American frontier.[9,10] Their criminal activities included the horrific murders of boatmen, whose bodies they would weigh down with rocks and dump into rivers after stealing their vessels and cargo. The Harpers (as they were initially known) were Scottish settlers who had settled in Cape Fear, North Carolina. The family remained faithful to the British Crown and were Tories, fighting on the side of the English during the early days of the war. Around 1779, at the ages of ten and twelve, the Harpe brothers watched their neighbors execute their parents. Not long after, the brothers joined the British armies and fought in several battles against the American colonists. Like Simon and George Girty, the Harpe brothers were allied with the British during the war, but their attraction seemed to be more with brutality and criminal acts than loyal service. They delighted in burning farms, raping women, and looting and ransacking the property of the would-be American colonists.

Postwar, their violent exploits continued in Tennessee and Kentucky, where they were infamous for ambushing travelers and committing atrocities against both settlers and Native American communities. The brutality of the Harpes was such that they even fell out with other criminals. While there is some disagreement among historians, the Harpes were said to have joined Mason's gang briefly in 1799 at Cave-In-Rock. Their excessive cruelty during a robbery, where they tortured a man by forcing him over a cliff on a blindfolded horse, was said to have led Mason and his crew to eject them from the group.

Their legacy included a mixture of horror at their crimes and the almost mythical status of their savage acts. A letter carrier named John L. Swaney, whom we will meet later, reported he knew the Harpes in Knoxville, where he (Swaney) was a race-rider.[11] The Harpes were financially ruined after losing a lot of money betting on a race, Swaney recalled. That night, he said they killed and robbed an old man 2 miles west of Knoxville and fled to Kentucky. There, they embarked on a spree of robbery and murder. A posse was formed to capture them, resulting in Big Harpe's death. Little Harpe escaped but was later believed by some to have been hanged in Greenville, Mississippi, after reuniting with the Mason gang.[12] There is more detail later in the book in the collection of historical misinformation—Appendix C.

Frontier Policing

In the 1790s, policing was informal and often for-profit, relying heavily on part-time personnel and voluntary night watches tasked with monitoring community morals, such as gambling and prostitution. Those systems, starting in cities like Boston (1636), New York (1658), and Philadelphia (1700), were often inefficient due to the inattentiveness and poor conduct of the watchmen. As urban centers expanded, those systems became inadequate. In the Southern United States, police forces evolved differently, driven by the need to support the slave economy. Starting with the formation of the first formal slave patrol in the Carolina colonies in 1704, those forces focused on preventing slave escapes and revolts.

The establishment of the United States Department of the Navy in April 1798, with operations beginning in earnest in 1799, marked a significant step in strengthening the American naval presence. The Navy was established in response to the Quasi War with France. The Quasi War ended in 1800 with the signing of the Treaty of Mortefontaine, also known as the Convention of 1800. The establishment of the Department of the Navy likely had a limited direct impact on river piracy. While the Navy was responsible for patrolling the nation's coasts and protecting maritime trade, river piracy was primarily an inland issue. However, the increased naval presence may have deterred some pirates from venturing out to sea, where they could be intercepted by Navy ships.

The United States Coast Guard has a long history, tracing its roots back to the founding of the Revenue Cutter Service in 1790. At its core, the Coast Guard is responsible for ensuring the safety and security of the nation's waterways, patrolling rivers and coastlines to maintain the safe navigation of vessels and protecting the environment from pollution and other threats. The Coast Guard also plays a vital role in law enforcement, with the authority to arrest individuals for violations of maritime laws. In the early years, the Coast Guard played a crucial role in suppressing piracy in the Caribbean and the Gulf of Mexico. Had the Coast Guard been deployed inland in Mason's day, this book might have had a different ending.

On the frontier, where policing attempts were largely ineffective, groups of men, often composed of the same hardened individuals who served in the militia during wars, formed bands known as Regulators. Those vigilantes, who were not particularly concerned with legal formalities, were proficient with rifles and quick to employ ropes in their quest for justice. Their activities began making life dangerous for outlaws and criminals like Mason and his gang, who were quite active along the Ohio River. The Regulators used their combat experience to counter Mason's aggression, and conducted patrols, set up ambushes, and engaged in armed confrontations, employing military-style tactics to restore order.

Fort Massac

With river piracy increasing the dangers of river travel, several forts were built on the frontier. Two of those defensive positions were in Illinois on the western end of the Ohio. European explorers recognized the site's history as a defensive location as early as 1540. During the French and Indian War, the French erected Fort De L'Ascension in 1757. It was later rebuilt and renamed Fort Massiac in 1759–60 to honor the French minister of colonial affairs.

The fort was only attacked once when it repelled an assault by a group of Cherokee. After the French and Indian War concluded in 1763, the French abandoned the fort, which the Chickasaws then destroyed. The British, who claimed the area, anglicized the name to "Massac" but did not rebuild the fort, leaving the area vulnerable. During the Revolutionary War in 1778, Colonel Clark captured the Illinois Territory, including Kaskaskia, for Virginia and the fledgling United States, without a battle, near the site of the fort.

Recognizing its strategic importance, President Washington ordered the fort's reconstruction in 1794, ensuring it safeguarded US military and commercial interests in the Ohio Valley. In Mason's time, Fort Massac likely acted as a deterrent against criminal activities along that stretch of the Ohio River. Mason's familiarity with the Ohio and its strategic significance was well-established from his service during the French and Indian War, Lord Dunmore's War, and the Revolutionary War, suggesting his movements along the river were well-informed.

There was another defensive military position in the immediate area, Cantonment Wilkinson, a short-lived US Army camp established in late 1800 after Mason moved his headquarters out of the area. The camp was in present-day Pulaski County in southern Illinois, approximately 45 miles west of Metropolis and Fort Massac. Preparing for the possibility of war between the United States and both France and Spain in the late 1790s, President Washington and Alexander Hamilton asked General Wilkinson, who we last saw in the Battle of Saratoga, to secure the Mississippi River and New Orleans from the Spanish, who were expected to ally with the French. Despite a treaty with France and the death of Washington in 1799, Hamilton proceeded with the plans. It briefly became one of the largest military bases in the United States, peaking at about 1,500 soldiers. It was abandoned by 1803, with the troops moving to Fort Massac. We will learn more about General Wilkinson later in the book.

Colonel Fluger

In the annals of river piracy along the Ohio and Mississippi Rivers, Colonel Fluger, also known as Plug, carved out a notorious legacy eerily like that of Mason. Said to have been born in Rockingham County, New Hampshire, Fluger quickly rose to prominence in the local militia, only to fall into disgrace and imprisonment due to his debts. Upon regaining his freedom, he ventured westward, settling near

Fort Massac. Plug established a fearsome river pirate gang there, including his girlfriend Pluggy and a loyal associate nicknamed "Nine Eyes."

The gang specialized in a cunning and ruthless tactic: Stealthily board docked flatboats at night, tamper with their structural integrity by removing caulk or boring holes, and partially plug the openings to delay sinking. When the boats began to take on water, they rushed in under the guise of rescuers, only to rob the vessels of their valuable cargoes. That ploy proved lucrative until the gang targeted a decoy boat, a trap set with armed men hidden below deck. In the ensuing chaos, many of Plug's crew were killed, and he was captured, beaten, and nearly left for dead, saved only by the timely intervention of Pluggy.[13]

Despite the colorful tales of Colonel Plug's exploits, there is scant historical evidence of his military service or existence. He may have been an embellished or entirely fictional counterpart to Mason, or possibly an honorary colonel, a title sometimes given as a mark of distinction in Kentucky and Tennessee. No Fluger, Flueger, or Pflueger surnames, as many spelling variations exist, can be found in the New Hampshire US census records or the Rockingham County military muster rolls.[14] Whether fact or fiction, the legend of Colonel Plug remains a vivid chapter in the folklore of America's riverfront outlaws.[15] If Plug did exist, he was one of several military veterans who used their skills to rob and steal from others after the war. If he did not, perhaps he was the everyman example for river pirates, depicting all the attributes of those who chose the profession. I suspect, given his rumored activities, that his story was based on Mason's. Regardless, you will find him, along with the other examples of historical misinformation, in Appendix C.

Travel and Tasting Notes

Illinois:

Cave-In-Rock
San Damiano Retreat
Garden of the Gods
Golconda Restaurant
Fort Massac, Metropolis

Kentucky:

Purple Toad Winery, Paducah
Freight House Restaurant, Paducah

ESCAPE TO THE CAVE (1797-99)

See the Appendices for more travel and tasting notes and the master timeline of Mason's life. Consider planning a visit to some or all of these locations.

Investigative Team

Asbury, Coates, Lach, Roxby, Rothert, Nicodemus, and Wagner were among the investigators who contributed to this phase of the investigation. For more on these team members, see the introduction—assembling the team.

8
PIRATING THE MISSISSIPPI
(1799–1801)

The ongoing effects of the Industrial Revolution, which began in the late eighteenth century in Great Britain, continued to transform societal structures and economic practices worldwide, bringing a new chapter not only in urban environments but also on the American frontier. The revolution's innovations in technology and industrial practices found fertile ground in America, where vast tracts of land awaited transformation by the plow and the steam engine.

In 1800, the United States was still young, and Washington, DC, became its new capital that spring. The country was still primarily agrarian, but the growth of textile mills and factories in the northeast gave a glimpse of the future of industrialization, and many people moved to Ohio, Kentucky, and Tennessee. President Adams was the first president to reside in the newly built White House in Washington, DC, moving in during November of 1800. Thomas Jefferson became president in 1801. His administration was characterized by his philosophy of limited government, reducing the federal government's power, expanding individual freedoms, focusing on reducing national debt, and advocating for an agrarian-based economy.

The Ohio River was the primary transportation route for settlers and traders moving westward into the new territories, and it was also a significant source of food and resources for the people living along its banks. Like the Ohio, the Mississippi River was often treacherous, with strong currents, sandbars, and shifting channels. In addition to the natural hazards, travelers also have to contend with the threat of attacks from Native Americans, as the Mississippi River was also a contested area, and tensions between American settlers and Native Americans were high. The journey was long and arduous and often took weeks or even months, depending on the destination and the conditions of the river, compared to the same journey now, which takes hours or, at most, a few days.

International Boundaries

Possibly inspired by the Regulators, in the latter part of 1799 or 1800, Mason moved his operation west down the Ohio River and south down the Mississippi River into Spanish territory. He continued robbing travelers in the United States along the Mississippi River with the idea that if caught, he would be a Spanish citizen who had not committed crimes in Spanish territory. During Mason's time, the Spanish controlled the lands west of the Mississippi River in the Louisiana Territory.

Before the Louisiana Purchase in 1803, Spain and France primarily controlled the Mississippi River and its tributaries. Spain controlled the region currently in the extreme southern parts of the country, including present-day Florida, Louisiana, and parts of the Southwest. In contrast, France controlled the area to the north of the newly independent states, including present-day Illinois, Indiana, and Wisconsin. When the peace treaty between England and the United States was signed in 1783, there were no more than 12,000 settlers in the western part of the country. Contrast that with the combined populations of Ohio, Kentucky, Tennessee, and Mississippi (much of which Mason haunted) in 1800, which was 380,772. The combined population of those states now is over 26 million based on 2023 estimates.[1]

On March 29, 1800, at age sixty, Mason applied for and received a passport to the Spanish-held western bank of the Mississippi River in New Madrid, Missouri. Mason was able to receive a passport when Dr. Richard Jones Waters, who had treated his wife while in Red Banks, vouched for him (see Dr. Water's interview in the trial summary for more). The passport would allow him to purchase land in Spanish-held territory, concentrate his operations on the eastern (American) riverside, and use the western bank as a haven. Mason was granted the passport by Don Henri Peyroux de la Coundreniere. The passport allowed him to travel to Natchez to arrange business affairs and then select a place in the New Madrid district for his family to settle, having sworn loyalty to the Spanish authorities.

Mason's Passport—Translated from French

New Madrid, March 29th, 1800

Whereas Samuel Masson, Esqr. has expressed a wish to settle in this district and wishes to arrange his business affairs, We, Don Henri Peyroux, Captain of the Armies of His Majesty, Civil and Military Commander of this Post and

District of New Madrid, hereby grant permission to said Samuel Masson to proceed to Natchez per boat, and on his return from there, said Samuel Masson may select a suitable place in this District for himself and family. He, Samuel Masson, having by oath attested his loyalty and fidelity to us, we pray that no hindrance be placed to his proposed journey.

—HENRI PEYROUX

Mason's Safe Space

Mason's use of the Mississippi River as a buffer between US territory and Spanish-controlled Louisiana was a brilliant move. By committing his robberies and murders east of the river in the United States and then retreating west into Spanish-controlled, French-owned territory, Mason essentially created a safe, or buffer, zone for himself and his gang. US law enforcement couldn't pursue him across international lines, which gave him a distinct advantage. That wasn't just a matter of crossing state lines—Mason was navigating two entirely different legal systems, which made him nearly untouchable. It's an early example of how criminals used geopolitical divides to their benefit long before more modern criminals adopted similar strategies.

Take John Dillinger, for example. He operated during the 1930s, and while he didn't cross international borders like Mason, he still used the fragmented law enforcement system to his advantage. Dillinger was robbing banks left and right, but after each heist, he'd flee to another state. Local police had no jurisdiction to chase him across state lines, so he could keep going for quite some time. He wasn't dealing with international politics, but the gaps in state-level law enforcement allowed him to stay ahead of the game—at least until the FBI stepped in.

Then there was Bonnie and Clyde, who used a similar strategy in the same era as Dillinger. They were notorious for robbing banks and small stores across multiple states, always keeping on the move. Like Dillinger, Bonnie and Clyde took full advantage of the poor coordination between state police forces. They'd commit a crime in one state and be miles away before local authorities could react. It was all about being mobile and innovative and staying ahead of the law, just like Mason.

A more recent example was Whitey Bulger, who, as an Air Force Veteran, was also a military-trained gang member. Bulger and his gang controlled Boston's underworld in the 1970s and 1980s, but when he got wind of a looming indictment, he fled. Unlike Mason, who used Spanish territory as a refuge, Bulger hid in various places, evading capture for sixteen years, when he was arrested in California. In a way, his tactic was a lot like Mason's: commit crimes in one jurisdiction and hide out in another, where law enforcement couldn't easily reach him. The difference was that Bulger's flight came after his crimes, while Mason's life across the river was part of his daily operation.

Mason's criminal activities hit frontier communities hard. Mason wasn't just robbing people—he was shaking the foundations of early American commerce. Dillinger, Bonnie and Clyde, and Bulger caused plenty of damage too, but their crimes didn't hit national trade quite the way Mason's did. Dillinger and Bonnie and Clyde terrorized banks and businesses, causing fear and instability during the Great Depression, but their impact was more regional. Bulger controlled a significant piece of Boston's criminal underworld, also causing a regional impact.

So, while each of these criminals used a version of the buffer zone tactic, Mason's strategy of crossing an international boundary stands out. He wasn't just staying one step ahead of local law enforcement; he was exploiting the very nature of US and Spanish relations to keep himself untouchable. Mason's buffer zone was woven directly into his operations, making it a cornerstone of his criminal empire.

Wolves on Wolf Island

Mason moved his pirate operations to Wolf Island.[2] According to Missouri folklorist Margot McMillen, the name of the island stemmed from the large number of wolves in the area in the late eighteenth and early nineteenth centuries.[3] The wolves have long since disappeared, but the name remained. Wolf Island's strategic position made it ideal for launching pirate attacks on river traffic, located about 100 miles southwest of Cave-In-Rock and 50 miles southeast of Cape Girardeau, Missouri, near where the Ohio and Mississippi Rivers meet. Wolf Island simultaneously provided an excellent offensive and defensive position like the Cave-In-Rock location. As a large island after a slight bend in the river, it served as a natural break and would have been quite confusing for the uninitiated attempting to traverse the island, as it was about as wide as the river at that spot. The location provided Mason and his gang easy access to the river, allowing them to attack boats and retreat with their loot effectively.

Wolf Island's location between Missouri and Kentucky has led to a long-standing dispute over its ownership, culminating in a US Supreme Court case.[4] Despite Missouri's presentation of historical maps, Kentucky's testimony from residents swayed the court to award the island to Kentucky. Over the years, Wolf Island experienced changes in size due to sedimentation and erosion. The island covers about 5,000 acres, close to 8 square miles, although the size fluctuates with river conditions. Mason's reliance on the buffer zone strategy indicated that Wolf Island was considered part of Missouri (Spanish territory) during his time. How appropriate that he landed there for a time, given the way he and his gang preyed on travelers and other folks on the frontier!

New Madrid, Spain

New Madrid was 42 miles (68 kilometers) southwest of Cairo, Illinois, and 30 miles (40 if you travel by river) below Wolf Island, north of an exclave of Fulton County, across the Mississippi River in Kentucky. Native American hunters and European American merchants made the settlement a location for processing the bounty of hunts, including bears and buffalo. Mason's operations would have passed New Madrid in both directions, although he never lived there as expected when his passport was issued. As we will see soon enough, New Madrid marked the beginning of Mason's end.

Spanish settlers renamed the settlement New Madrid around 1780. They welcomed American settlers but required them to become subjects of (i.e., swear allegiance to) the Spanish crown. In addition, they had to agree to live under the guidance of the appointed impresario (manager), Colonel George Morgan, an American Revolutionary War veteran from New Jersey. Morgan recruited several American families to settle at New Madrid, attracting a few hundred people to the region.

Settlement in the 1790s and early 1800s remained relatively low due to the physical geography of New Madrid. The Mississippi frequently washed away the town's river banks, and a Spanish fort was washed away. New Madrid was a diverse frontier settlement of about 800 people. New Madrid, Missouri, was known primarily for the massive earthquakes in 1811–12. The first earthquake, on December 16, 1811, affected an area of 600,000 square kilometers. Although there were few man-made structures then, chimneys were broken, and the ground shook violently. The earthquake could be felt as far as New York City!

Eastern Missouri featured a diverse topography characterized by rolling hills, river valleys, and prairies. The region is primarily defined by the Mississippi River, which provided a crucial waterway for transportation and trade as the eastern boundary. The landscape includes several hills and bluffs, particularly near the riverbanks, offering elevated views of the surrounding areas. Dense forests were prevalent in many parts in Mason's day, particularly in the northern areas, providing resources like timber and wildlife, while there were more prairies to the west.

Figure 8.1 Pirate Sam Mason straddling international borders. Mason attempted to avoid capture and arrest using a clever strategy. He lived in one country's jurisdiction (Spain) and worked in another (United States). Sketched by Jekaterina Hagen, with Fiverr.

The Mighty Mississippi

In the late 1700s, the Mississippi River flowed as a major artery through North America, carving its path through vast wilderness and serving as a vital lifeline for trade, transportation, and settlement. Originating from Lake Itasca in present-day Minnesota, the river travels southward for approximately 2,320 miles before emptying into the Gulf of Mexico. The upper Mississippi River, stretching from Minnesota to the confluence with the Missouri River near St. Louis, Missouri, has a faster-flowing current. The landscape includes numerous bluffs, islands, and rapids, particularly in present-day Iowa and Illinois.

Meeting the Mississippi near Cairo, the Ohio River further increases the river's flow. Navigating the Mississippi River during the 1790s presented numerous challenges. The river's meandering course created hazards for boats and flatboats, including sandbars, snags, and shifting channels. Seasonal flooding was common, reshaping the landscape and sometimes creating new channels. The vast floodplain was dotted with swamps and bayous, complicating travel and settlement.

Native Americans had used the river as a crucial trade route long before European exploration. By the late 1700s, European and American settlers recognized its strategic importance for trade and transportation. The Spanish controlled the lower Mississippi, including the vital port of New Orleans, while the French, and later the Americans, established settlements and trading posts along its upper reaches.

Robbing Colonel Baker

In the spring of 1801, Colonel Joshua Baker, a wealthy merchant and planter from Hardin County, Kentucky, headed to New Orleans, Louisiana, arriving in mid-summer. He had made several such trips, going down on flatboats and returning on horseback along the old Natchez Trace.[5] He and his crew sold the livestock and produce they had brought to the market, and in early August, Colonel Baker, Mr. William Baker, and Mr. Rogers of Natchez headed home on their horses, along with their profits and provisions. They set out with five pack mules riding excellent horses. When they stopped for the night, they hid their money and did without fire or water to remain undetectable by roving gangs.[6]

The group encountered no significant issues until they arrived at the ford across what was then known as Twelve Mile Creek, now called Baker's Creek in Hinds County, Mississippi, approximately twenty miles west of Jackson and sixty miles from the Big Bayou Pierre River.[7] When they rode into the creek to let their horses get a drink, several land pirates (also known as highway robbers or highwaymen[8]) appeared as they climbed the steep incline to exit the creek and demanded they surrender their money and all their property. The pirates robbed Baker of his horses and $2300 in cash he had made from selling the livestock and produce.[9]

The September 14, 1801 Kentucky Gazette included this information:

As soon as they had dismounted and gone to the water four men appeared, blacked, between them and their horses and demanded the surrender of their money and property, which they were obliged to comply with. Mr. W. Baker was more fortunate than his companions. A pack-horse, on which was a considerable sum of money, being frightened at the appearance of the robbers, ran away, and they being in haste to escape could not pursue. Mr. W. Baker recovered his horse [pack-mule] and money. He, however, lost his riding horse, etc.[10]

Colonel Baker and Mr. Rogers found help and went after the gang, hoping they could apprehend them. They stopped at a creek to let their horses and mules drink water. Mason and his men jumped out of the bushes on the opposite side as they got off their horses. Baker and his associates, realizing they had been trapped again, immediately surrendered. Mason made them drive the pack mules over to his side of the creek, where two of his men took charge of them but permitted Baker and his companions to keep their riding horses and side arms. Colonel Baker then rode to Grindstone Ford, about 40 miles away, and got more help to pursue the outlaws.[11]

The posse followed the robbers' trail to Pearl River, near Jackson, Mississippi, and learned that Mason had crossed the stream only a few hours before. Among the pursuing party was Brokus, a quadroon (mixed-race) Native American. Brokus swam down the river to determine the route Mason's men had taken. As he climbed up the bank, one of the robbers jabbed him in the chest with a gun. Believing he had been shot, Brokus lost his grip and fell back into the river. After recovering from the shock, he swam to the opposite shore. At some point, Mason appeared and informed Colonel Baker that he would never get his money back. That statement seemed to be accepted as the final word on the matter, leading to the abandonment of the pursuit of the robbers.[12] While that was an acceptable recollection of the incident, as with so many other parts of the story, there are a few variations when told by others.

Rothert found a contributor to the Natchez Galaxy in 1829, wrote a short article reporting when Colonel Baker reached the river, he and the members of his party took the saddles off their horses and prepared to rest. Two of them went in the river to bathe. As they reached the bank, Mason rushed them and captured them. He advised them he was ensuring his own security against danger. He demanded their arms and ammunition while holding a rifle to their heads. Colonel Baker returned to Kentucky, and reports of the daring robbery on the Natchez Trace and his unsuccessful attempts to capture Sam Mason circulated throughout the country.

Mason's First Trial

Mason's gang robbed many other travelers in the wilderness following the Baker robbery. Ultimately, Mason was identified as the one responsible for robbing Baker and was arrested and thrown in jail along with his son John. The two were tried for the crimes shortly after that. Rothert suspected it was more likely that John Mason, Sam's son, happened to be in town when he was accused and arrested than it was that an officer brought him in from the country.[13] Coates speculated Mason may have been among friends when he was recognized by a witness to the Baker robbery, thus launching a seven-day trial sensation in Natchez and a nightmare for Mason.[14]

The Masons were represented by a defense attorney, Wallace, who performed his defense role so well that many in the community publicly supported the accused criminals. Coates advised he won the sympathy of the populace but not of the magistrates. The two Masons were sentenced to thirty-nice lashes and twelve hours in the town pillory (a device, sometimes called stocks, used for public humiliation and punishment in which the head and arms are secured while the person remains standing).[15] The punishment of "thirty-nine lashes" held particular significance as a severe yet common form of corporal punishment used to publicly humiliate and physically discipline the offender, reinforcing social and legal boundaries within the community. Rooted in Roman, British, and early American practices, less-than-lethal punishment was often employed as a judicial sentence for crimes considered serious but not capital, such as theft, fraud, or disorderly conduct.[16] During the administration of the lashing, the Masons cried out "Innocent" each time they were struck, according to Coates. After they were released from the pillory, they shaved their heads, stripped off their clothing, and rode their horses through the streets, yelling like Native American warriors until they were out of sight.

But again, there were conflicting stories regarding the punishment. Rothert suggested that only John Mason was arrested and whipped, and if there were two who received the punishment, the other was another member of the gang, not Sam. Rothert also reported the prisoner(s) were not released after the sentence. Instead, they escaped from the jail with help from other gang members.

Rothert noted explicitly that one of the jurors suggested in open court that John Mason should be hung for his crimes. Not long after the trial, that juror was riding toward the Trace. Just past the town limits, Sam Mason, armed with a tomahawk and a rifle, stopped and confronted him. The man pleaded for his life. Mason asked if he had ever done the man any harm or if the man ever heard of Mason murdering anyone. After the man responded no to both questions, Mason told him he wasn't worth killing, then rode away.[17]

Figure 8.2 Author demonstrating use of stocks with replica from Red House in Cape Girardeau. The demonstration did not include a lashing. Photo courtesy of the author.

While embarrassing, the sentence the Masons received was lax by the standards of the time. In 1801, the use of the death penalty in America was widespread and applied to a range of serious crimes. While the exact application depended on state laws, murder, manslaughter, arson, rape, forgery, and horse stealing (second offense) were commonly punishable by death. Over time, the scope of the death penalty was narrowed.

Travel and Tasting Notes

Illinois:

Fort Defiance, Cairo

Missouri:

Red House Interpretive Center, Cape Girardeau
Cape River Heritage Museum, Cape Girardeau
Trail of Tears State Park, Cape Girardeau
Cape Rock Park, Cape Girardeau

36 Restaurant & Bar, Cape Girardeau

River Ridge Winery, Scott City

Kentucky:

Wolf Island

See the Appendices for more travel and tasting notes and the master timeline of Mason's life. Consider planning a visit to some or all of these locations.

Investigative Team

Investigators contributing to this investigation phase included Asbury, Nelson, and Wagner. For more on these team members, see the introduction—assembling the team.

PART IV
1802–04

Figure 9.1 Memphis, Tennessee; Vicksburg, Mississippi; Natchez, Mississippi; New Orleans, Louisiana; Nashville, Tennessee. Sketched by Rotna, with Fiverr.

It may be helpful to bookmark and reference Appendix A (additional travel and tasting notes), Appendix B (Timeline of Mason's life), and Appendix C (Historical Misinformation).

9
ENOUGH IS ENOUGH (1802–03)

On February 10, 1802, Mississippi Territorial Governor William Charles Cole Claiborne sent a letter regarding river piracy to Manuel de Salcedo, his Spanish counterpart in New Orleans. Claiborne had recently been appointed as the governor and advised Salcedo that he had received notice of a robbery, presumably that of the Baker party, and that he didn't know whether the persons who committed the act of piracy were Spanish subjects or American citizens. The two agreed to work together to address the problem.

Adding Insult to Injury

Undeterred by the loss of his money and failure to capture Mason, Colonel Baker resumed his annual journey the following year. Sometime in early 1802, Baker headed back down the river from Kentucky to the market. His flatboat was loaded with merchandise and armed with guns to protect his cargo and to ensure his safety on the dangerous return trip over the Trace. Sometime in April 1802, when his boat reached a point below Walnut Hills, he again encountered Mason and his pirate gang. Mason's crew boarded Baker's flatboat to rob him.[1] Baker and his crew fought off the attack, but several men on both sides were wounded.

Baker wrote a statement about the attack and forwarded it to Governor Claiborne. While Baker's written statement has not since been found, upon receipt of it, Governor Claiborne sent out three official letters from the capital of Mississippi Territory. Claiborne was aware that outlaws like Mason had long infested the frontier and realized the necessity for action, as only force was likely to stop such an attack. A member of Mason's gang later verified the strategy. John Sutton (Setton), who testified during Mason's trial, reported that Mason planned to stop flatboats and beat or kill the master (captain), steal anything of

Figure 9.2 Governor William Charles Cole Claiborne of Tennessee, governor of Mississippi. Head-and-shoulders portrait, right profile. Claiborne was the governor of the Mississippi Territory and worked with the Spanish government to stop Mason and his pirate gang. Illustration by Charles Balthazar Julien Fevret de Saint-Mémin, *William Charles Cole Claiborne, head-and-shoulders portrait, right profile*, 1798, Library of Congress (https://www.loc.gov/pictures/item/2007675942/).

value, and then burn the boat. They then took the stolen property and sold it to several storekeepers in the area.[2]

Governor Claiborne enlisted the assistance of the one man he knew he could trust to investigate the Mason gang. Along Bayou Pierre north of Port Gibson, Mississippi, on the edge of Choctaw Territory, lived Daniel Burnet, a colonel in the territorial militia and the owner of more than 1½ square miles (960 acres) of wilderness. Port Gibson was roughly equidistant between Vicksburg to the north and Natchez to the south along the Mississippi River. Colonel Burnet lived in a small cabin on the Trace (before it was named Natchez) where travelers heading north or south could get out of the weather and sleep for the night on Burnet's floor. Burnet also provided transport across Bayou Pierre on his flatboat ferry. Governor Claiborne wrote Burnet, asking him to investigate the pirates who made their headquarters near Walnut Hills (now Vicksburg, Mississippi, about 70 miles north of Natchez and 200 miles north of New Orleans).[3] Governor Claiborne reported that the gang was led by Samuel Mason and included members of Mason's family and other outlaws.[4]

To Daniel Burnet.
Town of Washington April 27th. 1802.—
Sir,
I have received information that a set of Pirates and Robbers, who alternately infest the Mississippi River and the Road leading from this District to Tennessee,

rendezvous at or near the Walnut-Hills, in the County of Claiborne;—a certain Samuel Mason & a Man by the name of Harp, are said to be the Leaders of this Banditti;—they lately attempted in a hostile manner to board the Boat of Colo: Joshua Baker, between the mouth of Yazou River, and the Walnut Hills, but were prevented by Colo: Baker's, making a shew of Arms, and manifesting a great share of firmness.—These Men must be arrested ; the honor of our Country, the Interest of Society, & the feelings of humanity, proclaim that it is time to stop their Career; —

The crimes of Harp, are many and great, and in point of Baseness, Mason is nearly as celebrated:—While these Sons of Rapine and Murder are permitted to Rove at large, we may expect daily to hear of outrages upon the Lives & properties of our fellow Citizens.—The Militia of your Regiment not being organized, I presume it would not be in your power, to execute (strictly) a Military Order, I shall therefore only request, that you will immediately endeavour to procure 15 or 20 Men as Volunteers^ and place yourself, or some confidential Character at their Head. —

This little force will then proceed to the Walnut-Hills, & after making due examination & enquiry at that place, they will examine the woods in the neighborhood of the Mississippi as high up as Yazou ;—If you should fall in with Mason & his party, you will use all the means in your power to arrest them, or any of them, and I desire, that the person or persons arrested, may immediately be conveyed under a strong Guard to Natchez.—I hope that the honor of taking these Lawless Men will be conferred on the Citizens of your Neighborhood ;

—Should they Succeed, I promise them a very generous reward.—

I have written to Lieutenant Rennick upon this subject, & it is probable, he will give you all the aid in his power.

With great Respect & Esteem.
I am Sir,
your Hble—Servt:
WILLIAM C. C. CLAIBORNE

P.S. For your information, I have enclosed you the Statement made by Colo: Baker to me, of the late attempt made to Rob' him.

W. C. C. C—COLO : DANIEL BURNETT—

The governor also alerted Lt. Rennick with the 3rd US Regiment at Walnut Hills and the commander of US troops on the Natchez Trace at Bear Creek, Tennessee, to be on the lookout for the gang. Claiborne ordered that any reports of mischief "being done or attempted" in the wilderness should be aggressively investigated.[5] He wanted the outlaws terrorizing travelers along the Mississippi River and Natchez Trace brought to justice, even if it meant killing them.[6]

Historical Context

From 1802 to 1803, the United States experienced significant political, social, and territorial developments. The country's leadership was negotiating for the Louisiana Purchase, which would double its size and extend its territory westward to the Rocky Mountains. Spain controlled the territory from 1763 to 1800 as part of the Treaty of Fontainebleau following the Seven Years (French and Indian) War. In 1800, Spain traded the territory back to France in the Third Treaty of San Ildefonso. Spain hoped to maintain a favorable alliance with France, which was rising as a dominant power in Europe under Napoleon. The treaty was intended to secure Spanish interests while navigating the political landscape of the time. After trying to regain control of Saint-Domingue (present-day Haiti), where a slave rebellion was underway, Napoleon gave up on his North American colonies, agreeing to sell the territory to the United States in 1803 as part of the Louisiana Purchase. Tensions with Native Americans continued due to westward expansion, leading to displacement through treaties. Slavery was deeply rooted in many, mostly southern states, with the importation of enslaved Africans continuing until it was banned in 1808.[7]

In 1802, at sixty-two, Sam Mason moved to Little Prairie, Missouri, a settlement founded in 1794 by Francis Lesieur, who was also involved in starting New Madrid. Mason reported they had intended to live in New Madrid but ended up in Little Prairie by accident. Both locations were in Spanish territory. The gang lived in Little Prairie (now Caruthersville, Missouri) while conducting business in two remote locations (again, not in his backyard). His River Pirate Headquarters was 285 miles south of Little Prairie at Stack Island and fifty miles north of Walnut Hills, near the Arkansas-Mississippi-Louisiana border. His Land Pirate Headquarters was 340 miles south of Little Prairie and 75 miles south of Stack Island, known also as Crow's Island or Island 94, at Rocky Springs on the Natchez Trace. Like other islands along the Mississippi, Stack Island washed away shortly after Mason's day due to the New Madrid earthquakes or some other natural cause.[8] Rothert related that one of Mason's robberies at Stack Island was a traveler with Governor Claiborne's letter. Mason and his gang were said to have enjoyed the notoriety that recognition by the territorial governor brought.

The village of Little Prairie prospered initially, growing from a population of 78 in 1797 to 103 by 1803. In the southeastern part of Missouri, the community included Fort St. Fernando, which was laid out over approximately 200 arpents (a French unit of land measurement equal to about 0.85 acres), with each lot approximately an arpent in size.[9] The region was part of Spanish Louisiana, and Spain governed it following the conclusion of the French and Indian War in 1763 under the terms of the Treaty of Paris. The area was sparsely populated, with a landscape characterized by swamps, forests, and the Mississippi River floodplain. The settlement of Little Prairie itself consisted of a few farms and homesteads, with the economy primarily based on subsistence agriculture, hunting, and trading. The inhabitants of the region were a mix of Native American tribes who had lived in the area for centuries, French settlers who moved from other parts of French Louisiana, and Spanish administrators or military personnel. The late eighteenth century was a period of relative stability in the region under Spanish rule, which tended to be less rigid than French or British colonial governance.

Mason's Operation

In May 1802, Mason's pirate gang was at the mouth of the White River, about 150 miles above Stack Island and 300 miles above Natchez. A traveler wrote to a Cincinnati newspaper in June 1802 that they were approached by two boats with six well-armed men in each who allegedly wanted to purchase rifles. According to the writer, the group was led by Mason. At the time of the second Baker robbery, Mason's headquarters was near Rocky Springs.[10] That was about 50

Figure 9.3 Land Pirate Sam Mason. Mason and his pirate gang robbed travelers along the Natchez Trace from Natchez, Mississippi, to Nashville, Tennessee. Sketched by Jekaterina Hagen, with Fiverr.

miles northeast of Natchez and 20 miles south of Vicksburg along the Trace. Mason had also lived about 20 miles northeast of Natchez, near what is now Fayette, Mississippi.

Mason's gang had an established method for robbing boatmen on the river. Coates related the story of a merchant named Owsley (Aurely in transcripts), who was hailed by some men on the shore while traveling slowly down the river. They claimed to need rifles and would give a reasonable price for them. Owsley provided some rifles to the group, and no sooner than the deal was agreed upon, he saw the business end of the loaded guns. He and his crew were ordered onto a small boat and pushed away from shore.[11] Similar stories were plentiful despite multiple rewards offered for Mason's capture. See the trial summary later in the chapter for more.

Mississippi had a diverse landscape. In the western part where Natchez was and is lay the Delta Region, known for its fertile alluvial plains along the mighty Mississippi River. The area was predominantly flat, making it ideal for agriculture, particularly the cultivation of cotton, which would later become a cornerstone of the state's economy. The rich soil and abundant water supply attracted settlers who recognized the potential for farming in that lush environment. To the northeast, following the path of the Natchez Trace, the Hills Region emerged, part of the Appalachian foothills. That area featured a more varied elevation, with ridges and valleys influencing the settlement patterns and lifestyles of those who lived there. In the southern part of the state, the land was flatter and marked by marshes and wetlands, shaped by the proximity to the Gulf.

Natchez was part of the Mississippi Territory, established by the United States Congress in 1798 from land ceded by Georgia and South Carolina. Initially founded by French colonists in the early eighteenth century, Natchez was an important port on the Mississippi River and a significant center of commerce and government in the territory. In 1817, the western part of the Mississippi Territory, including Natchez, became the state of Mississippi when it was admitted to the Union as the twentieth state. The eastern part eventually became the state of Alabama in 1819.

Mr. Swaney, the letter carrier for the Natchez area who was acquainted with the Harpes in Tennessee, was also familiar with members of the Mason gang. He reported finding the young wife of Tom Mason along the Trace on foot one day, carrying a baby.[12] She advised that the rest of the family had abandoned her, pregnant, in the wilderness, not far from the Chickasaw Native American Nation.[13] Swaney helped the young Mrs. Mason get to Natchez by alternating walking, riding his horse, and carrying the young child. She told him the others had fled across the Mississippi River into Spanish territory.

Swaney carried the mail on horseback from Nashville to Natchez and frequently encountered and conversed with Sam Mason. Swaney began his mail-carrying duties around 1796 or 1797, shortly after the United States Post Office Department was established, and continued for nearly eight years.[14] The journey from Nashville to Natchez was approximately 550 miles, through a rough path that became the Natchez Trace, which wound through woods and cane brakes (dense thickets). Swaney left Nashville on Saturday at 8:00 p.m., and the mail was due in Natchez in ten days and four hours. Being a skilled horseman, he often arrived early. The round trip took three weeks. He carried a few letters, government dispatches, newspapers, half a bushel of corn for his horse, provisions for himself, an overcoat or blanket, and a tin trumpet.

Starting from Nashville, he passed the last white man's house at midnight and reached Gordon's Ferry on the Duck River (51 miles from Nashville) by Sunday morning for breakfast.[15] John Gordon, trader, soldier, and friend of future president and Tennessee resident Andrew Jackson, had opened the ferry there and shared the profits with the Chickasaw Chief, who controlled ferries on Native American land according to a treaty. Swaney then rode 80 miles to Colbert's Ferry on the Tennessee River, arriving before nightfall. George Colbert operated that ferry from 1800 to 1819. His inn offered travelers a warm meal and shelter during their journey on the Trace.[16] The location is just south of the Tennessee-Alabama border near present-day Florence, Alabama.

In their conversations, Swaney learned Mason lived near Cross Plains in Robertson County, Tennessee, at some point before moving to Natchez. Cross Plains was about 30 miles north of Nashville and situated on the Red River, so it was likely that Mason was familiar with the area, as it was within 20 miles of Russellville, Kentucky, and the area Mason moved to after leaving East Tennessee twenty years earlier.[17] Swaney, interviewed many years later at his home in Sumner County, Tennessee, 10 miles east of Cross Plains, said Mason was a well-mannered and modest man who, contrary to his notorious reputation, assured Swaney he (Mason) only sought money, not lives.[18]

Mason's gang often terrorized boatmen and travelers returning from Natchez and New Orleans, ambushing them along the Natchez Trace. One of their first significant robberies (before Baker) was of Kentucky boatmen at Gum Springs (presumably Tennessee, south of US Hwy 64 near Hwy 43N, below present-day Columbia). Caught by surprise, the boatmen fled in panic, leaving all their belongings behind, which Mason's gang seized. Arriving at the deserted camp the following day, Swaney alerted the scattered boatmen with his bugle. The frightened and poorly clothed boatmen decided to pursue the robbers. Armed with sticks and knives, they tracked Mason's gang but were eventually ambushed. Mason's men, hiding behind trees, threatened to kill the pursuers, causing them to panic again. The pursuit ended with the biggest of the Kentuckians, who had retrieved his hidden gold coins, leading the retreat. He later used his last dollar to help his comrades with new supplies.[19]

The Darker Side of Natchez

Mason often met with a fellow named Anthony Glass at King's Tavern in Natchez. Glass was Mason's fence for stolen property, and he would get word to Mason when prospective targets were preparing to make the trip up the Trace. Glass and his brother Andrew were Tories, like the Girty and Harpe brothers, who moved to the Natchez area from Pennsylvania soon after the American Revolution and established a plantation.[20] Glass, perhaps also spelled Gass, was known in town as a prosperous and honest merchant with a well-stocked general store.[21] During one of his interviews, Mason recalled a robbery of Glass and an associate along the Natchez Trace, in which Glass and his companion were deprived of several horses, saddles, and some money. Near the location of the robbery, a sign on a tree was discovered afterward, which said, "Done by Mason of the Woods."

Glass, according to Sutton, was a conspirator of the Masons. Thus, the robbery he reported may have been staged. Glass rose from poverty in Nogales to financial success as a businessman in Natchez after being associated with the Masons. Sutton noted that Mason's strategy was to sell stolen goods to Glass, who would pay cash for half their actual value and never betray the gang. Coates suggested Glass arranged for Mason's lodging at Walton's tavern while in town and introduced Mason to the folks in Natchez as a wealthy planter from upstate. Glass was later known for more admirable activity and documented an important part of American history.[22]

King's Tavern was established in the 1780s in the oldest standing building in Natchez, Mississippi. The building was constructed in the 1760s with wood from flatboats. Initially, it was a blockhouse (defensive strong point) for nearby Fort Panmure, built as Fort Rosalie by the French in 1716. After the Revolutionary War, the blockhouse became available for purchase, and in 1789, Richard King, a postmaster, established a tavern and an inn in the building.[23] The building served multiple purposes—a tavern, an inn, and a home for the King family. It quickly became a popular stop for travelers navigating the Mississippi River, offering a much-needed rest stop.

Natchez Under-the-Hill, located at the base of the bluffs in Natchez, less than a mile from King's Tavern, was a notorious river port along the Mississippi River. In the late eighteenth and early nineteenth centuries, it was known for its bustling, rough atmosphere with saloons, gambling houses, and brothels, attracting a lawless crowd, contrasting with the genteel society atop the bluff. At Natchez Under-the-Hill, Mason and his gang found fertile ground for their criminal endeavors. The area's reputation for vice and disorder provided cover for their operations. They often frequented the taverns and establishments there, blending in with the other disreputable characters.

Figure 9.4 King's Tavern was established in the oldest standing building at the southern tip of the Natchez Trace in Natchez, Mississippi. Mason often met his criminal business associates at the tavern. Photo courtesy of the author.

Hiding in Plain Sight

On January 11, 1803, Ignace Belan and Pierre Dapron reported several men acting suspiciously on the outskirts of Little Prairie, Missouri (about 30 miles south of New Madrid, 90 miles north of present-day Memphis, and 380 miles north of Natchez). An inquiry began, and others, including George Ruddel, reported that they had seen eight men and one woman in the group, and they had arrived in Little Prairie about a week prior. They rented 10 acres of land and a cabin from a farmer named Lesieur and maintained an armed lookout at the cabin door. And just like that, the location of Mason's new hideout was no longer secret! It was possible that Mason's new neighbors were Kentuckians and were aware of who he was and what he was capable of from his time along the Ohio River.

Early on January 13, 1803, Militia Captain Don Robert McCoy (McCay, Mackay) met with Corporal Felipo Canot and twelve of his soldiers in Little Prairie to plan the sunrise arrest of Mason and his gang. As they met, Mason surprised them and asked about their inquiry into his activities. Instead of attempting to arrest him, Captain McCoy played it cool. He asked Mason and the members of the gang who were with him to show their passports. He then asked Mason to meet at a nearby cabin a little later with all the gang members so he could inspect their papers after he took care of business in town. McCoy advised Mason that if all their papers were in order, he (McCoy) could report back that everything was in order. Mason agreed, and not long afterward, McCoy and an orderly rode up to the cabin and found Mason's whole family awaiting his arrival. He asked Mason if everyone was there, and when he was assured they were, he ordered their arrest. Unbeknownst to Mason, the cabin had been quietly surrounded, and armed militiamen filed in to arrest them all.

Mason's Second Trial

The official record of the arrest of the Masons at Little Prairie and their trial at New Madrid was preserved in the Mississippi Department of Archives and History. The document was found among historian J. F. H. Claiborne's papers. Although faded and difficult to read, the manuscript provided a thorough record of the events from the Masons being spotted at Little Prairie to their subsequent trial in New Madrid. The commandant at New Madrid who ordered the Masons to be captured and tried, Don Henri Peyroux, the same authority who provided Mason his passport, did not understand English, the only language spoken by nearly all the witnesses who appeared before him. So, the trial was conducted in French and later translated into English by someone working for the Mississippi Department of Archives, according to Rothert. The following is a summary of the proceedings. For a more detailed dialogue, consult the transcript translation and digitization.[24]

Summary of the Trial

The transcripts recorded the testimony of fifteen witnesses concerning members of the Mason gang, thought to be hiding in Little Prairie. The witnesses, including eight who knew the Masons and seven prisoners, swore to tell the truth. Their statements were recorded in French and then read back to them in English for confirmation before they signed off on the accuracy. Given that it was a translation from French into English, several words and names were inconsistently spelled or unclear. What you see below is the best attempt to synthesize that.

The first testimony was from Pierre Dapron, who reported that Ignace Belan had seen four suspicious individuals at Little Prairie, though they hadn't attempted any robbery. The second testimony was from George Ruddell, who noted that eight men and one woman had occupied a house in Little Prairie without the owner's consent, arousing local suspicions. Ruddell suggested that those individuals might be part of the Mason band, which had likely split into smaller groups to evade capture by the militia actively searching for them.

Summary of Mason's Arrest and Imprisonment

On January 11, 1803, Dr. Henry Peyrouf, commandant of New Madrid, ordered Dr. Pierre Antoine Laforge and Dr. Robert McCoy to investigate and arrest individuals mentioned in earlier declarations. An interpreter, Dr. Jean Charpeutier, was assigned to assist in the process. Upon arrest, their belongings would be inventoried and transported to New Madrid. On January 12, Laforge and McCoy traveled to Little Prairie, where Lieutenant Francois le Sieur confirmed the presence of Samuel Masson (Mason) and his family. However, due to the late hour, the arrest was postponed.

The next morning, on January 13, news arrived that Mason and his group were preparing to leave. They met with Mason, who claimed innocence and agreed to visit le Sieur's house to clarify matters. Later that day, with the militia hiding nearby, Mason and his companions were arrested and placed in handcuffs. Present were Samuel Mason, his sons (Thomas, John, Magnus, and Samuel Jr.), John Taylor, and Marguerite Douglas (wife of John), along with her three children.

Summary of Property Inventory (January 1803)

On January 14, 1803, at 2:00 p.m., McCoy and Laforge, along with witnesses and an interpreter, began the inventory of the property belonging to Mr. Mason (father) and the other prisoners. The inventory included various personal items such as blankets, garments (including wool, cotton, and cashmere), razors, linen, and clothing packed in bundles. Noteworthy items included cashmere waistcoats, a blue cloth coat, gloves, socks, and other textiles. Also among the property were "bundles of hair to the number of 20 . . . most of them looks to have been cut on human creatures . . . not cut voluntarily and could be the acts of some murders" (twenty human scalps).

On January 15, additional items were found, including a gold watch marked "Benson of London" and a pair of silver buckles. The most valuable discovery was US banknotes totaling significant sums, including bills from the Bank of the United States dated between 1795 and 1798, and personal papers belonging to Samuel Mason. Property titles from Tennessee belonging to Mason were also inventoried. After delivering the requested blankets and bedclothes to the family, the inventory was signed and closed at 1:00 p.m.

The day after their belongings were inventoried, Samuel Mason requested the return of some essential items for his group as he sought to settle accounts with local citizens in Little Prairie, which was allowed. On January 16, Mason and the other prisoners were escorted to New Madrid for their trial, which started on January 17. Captain McCoy testified that he had frequent discussions with

Mason, who insisted on his innocence concerning any crimes on the Spanish side of the Mississippi. Mason expressed a willingness to provide information on other criminals to help clear his name. He also denied involvement in specific robberies, although he appeared nervous when informed that a victim was soon to testify. During the inventory, questions about the source of numerous banknotes led to an evasive response from members of Mason's gang, claiming the money was found in a bag. Don Joseph Charpentier testified similarly to Captain McCoy, adding that Samuel Mason claimed his only fault was a past prison stint for debt.

Mason Senior's Testimony

On January 18th, Mason told officials that he was a native of Pennsylvania and a Protestant. After swearing on the Bible to tell the truth, Mason was asked about his place of residence, which he replied was in Bayou Pierre, near Natchez. He added that he had sold his land there to a Mr. Bryan before arriving at Little Prairie.

When asked about other property, Mason mentioned he had claims to land in the Monongahela area as an heir to his brother, who had died childless.[25] Mason admitted to having no valid passport aside from one issued to him by New Madrid authorities in 1800. He explained his delay in settling on Spanish land, claiming he had been occupied with personal matters and preparing for settlement, but bad weather had diverted him to Little Prairie.

Mason was then questioned about his family's movements over the past three years, during which he said he had been reuniting his scattered family, including bringing back one of his sons. He explained that they had subsisted on income from his plantation, cattle, and his children's labor, supplemented by occasional hired work. Mason also denied possessing any other papers aside from those already found in his baggage.

Regarding a certain Philip Briscot (Briscoe), mentioned in his papers as being in business with Mr. Portell, Mason revealed that Briscot was his son-in-law and resided at Natchez. When confronted with accusations about his own involvement in various crimes, Mason claimed innocence, asserting that he had not committed any offenses on Spanish soil and was also innocent of crimes attributed to him in the United States.

Mason explained that their original plan had been to travel to New Madrid to request land for settlement. He acknowledged telling Mr. le Sieur that they might settle at Little Prairie if the land was suitable, though they had not intended it at first. When asked if others were expected to join him, Mason said two of his sons were coming from Monongahela, and he was expecting his son-in-law and daughter from Natchez. He denied knowing of anyone else joining them but admitted that he told le Sieur some friends might come if they learned of his location.

Suspicion was raised regarding Mason's failure to establish himself on Spanish land despite having permission for three years. Mason suggested that he could provide reputable people, such as his sister and others from Cape Girardeau, to vouch for him. He mentioned several names, including Mr. Ramsey and General Harrison.[26] Mason said he would seek land in New Madrid when he arrived.

The interrogation then turned to rumors of business dealings with local figures, including Harrison, Water, and Reagan. Mason denied making those connections but admitted he would have visited Harrison and Water as old acquaintances. When asked if Water, who had a good reputation, would vouch for him, Mason said he wasn't sure but would inquire.

Pressed on why no reputable people were available to support his claims, Mason explained that he had always conducted his affairs independently. He also denied having significant dealings with Dr. Water despite knowing him from America. When accused of involvement in various crimes, including river robberies, Mason expressed willingness to name the individuals involved in exchange for clemency. He insisted he had not participated in any crimes himself but had knowledge of them.

Mason recounted that around May of the previous year, two men had visited his sons' camp and informed them of a robbery on a flatboat after carbines were bought by his son-in-law, Philip. Mason named some of the robbers, including Wigger and Gibson, and explained that they had returned to Little Prairie and divided the stolen goods with Philip and Fulson. The stolen items, he claimed, were sold to Bassette and Fulson, who took them to Makookdochee to trade for horses.

Mason claimed he had written to both the commandant of the armies and the Governor of Natchez to inform them of those facts. When asked about Taylor, an alias for Sutton and a man implicated in the robbery, Mason denied ever meeting him but had heard that Taylor had bought some of the stolen goods. Mason also mentioned that Taylor had given samples of the merchandise to another man, Koiret, to verify whether the items were stolen, which led to an investigation authorized by the flatboat's master, Aurely (Aolery, Oarely, Owsley).

Mason continued by offering additional information about other robberies, proposing to act as a denouncer in exchange for a pardon. He emphasized his innocence and argued that his enemies had hindered his efforts to clear his name in both Natchez and Arkansas. He stated that he had come to this post to justify himself, considering himself a Spanish subject after being granted permission to settle.

Mason revealed that Taylor was also known by various other names, including Sutton and Wells. Recognizing the importance of that statement, the commandant decided to suspend the interrogation to question Taylor next. The session ended near 1:00 p.m., with Mason confirming that his statement was truthful, and he had nothing to add or alter.

Sutton (Setton/Taylor)'s Testimony

On January 18, 1803, the second prisoner, initially identifying as John (Jean) Taylor, appeared for questioning and revealed his true name as John Sutton, an Irishman and Catholic. Swearing on the cross to tell the truth, Sutton was first asked if he had anything to disclose before the interrogation began. He stated that he had been approached to act as a denouncer of crimes by both authorities and Samuel Mason's family. He described an incident at Mr. Charles Colins' house in Nogales, where Mason had tied him up and threatened him with a knife to prevent him from revealing any crimes. Sutton claimed that Mrs. Colins and her two sons could verify the attack.

Sutton then recounted how Mr. Koiret, who was investigating robberies on behalf of the American government, had come to Nogales and found both Sutton and Mason at Colins' house. According to Sutton, Mason tried to stab him with a knife he took from Sutton's belt, but Sutton managed to jump back and save himself. Mason then called for his son John, who tied Sutton up for several hours to keep him from speaking to Koiret.

When asked what information he had been prevented from sharing, Sutton revealed that Mason had restrained him to stop him from denouncing three robberies. One involved the theft of $2,500 in gold, silver, and banknotes from a man named Baker. Philip, Fulson, Gibson, and others from Little Prairie and the St. Francois River committed the robbery. The second robbery occurred on the Mississippi River at the Chaquetas Cross-Road, where a flatboat owned by a man named Aurely was pillaged. Mason had tried to coerce Sutton into claiming that Philip had purchased carbines from the flatboat before the robbery. Sutton confirmed that Philip had indeed bought two carbines in the presence of several people.

The third robbery Sutton mentioned involved Philip, Gibson, Fulson, and others, who stole horses, saddles, and porte manteaux worth about eighty-five dollars from a group while traveling from Kentucky to Natchez. Sutton recalled that one of the victims was named Campbell but could not remember the names of the others involved.

Sutton continued by recounting that John and Thomas Mason, along with their father, took him to a Justice of the Peace named Williams, where Sutton was forced to hand over a paper without signing it. Sutton believed he could justify himself in the future. When asked how long he had been in the company of the Mason family, Sutton replied that he had arrived in the area in 1797 with Major Guyou's troops. He had worked in various locations, including New Orleans and Makatoche, before meeting Mason in May the following year.

Sutton explained that he worked as a sawyer and carpenter in New Orleans and hunted with Native Americans, including the Chaquetas. He later traveled to Arkansas, where he was arrested by an American officer as a deserter but was soon released. He continued working and hunting, traveling between settlements until he was arrested again by the commandant of the Arkansas post, who imprisoned him for twenty-eight days. After his release, Sutton worked for about a month before Gibson secured passports for them to hunt on the White River. Sutton and Wigger then sold their furs to Fulson at Little Prairie.

Sutton claimed he met the Mason family while traveling and was forced to stay with them as a prisoner. The Masons had taken his money and clothes and even burned some of his belongings. Sutton remained with them until their arrest. When asked why he did not leave with Wigger, Sutton said he had been engaged to help transport Mason's mother (perhaps Mrs. Mason, his wife) to the settlement near the St. Francois River. He also mentioned that Mason claimed rights to the land.

When asked what the Masons did during their time together, Sutton explained that Samuel Mason had been sick with rheumatism for quite a while and spent much of his time in Natchez trying to clear his name. Sutton stated that he had been with the Masons since May 1802, and they had not harmed anyone during that time. When asked if anyone in the country could vouch for him, Sutton mentioned Mr. Andre Scot, Mrs. Conrad, and Jacob Wheate and noted that Mr. Dorsery knew him at Nogales and had traveled with him to New Orleans.

Sutton was then asked if the Mason family had ever invited him to participate in robberies. He admitted that they had asked him to steal horses from Natchez, although he never actually saw the horses. When questioned about how many horses they had when he met them, Sutton said they had three, and Mason's crippled son had two more.

When asked if he knew the origin of the horses or who sold them at Little Prairie, Sutton replied that he did not know. He explained that the Masons had intended to ask for land at New Madrid but had been diverted to Little Prairie by bad weather. Sutton admitted that he had concealed his identity, calling himself John Taylor at Mason's urging, though he did not know the reason for it, suspecting it was part of one of Mason's schemes.

Sutton was asked if he knew about a camp on the Yazoo River, but he denied any knowledge of it. When questioned about whether Mason had borrowed a pickaxe at Little Prairie, Sutton said he was on the other side of the river at the time but assumed it was used to repair a smoking chimney. He also mentioned that the Masons stayed on the opposite side of the river for four days due to bad weather.

The commandant asked about a story involving a man painted in black who had committed a robbery in the United States and written "Mason man of the woods" on a tree. Sutton said he had heard the story from Koiret, who mentioned that it was linked to a robbery involving Mr. Glass and Campbell. While Sutton did not know the full details, he suspected the Masons were involved.

Sutton recounted that Samuel Mason had discussed a potential robbery of a large amount of goods, which he planned to sell to Mr. Glass, a merchant in Nogales, at half price. Sutton observed that Glass had become wealthy despite once being poor, and he believed the riches were due to Mason's dealings.

When asked about a robbery in June, Sutton said he had no knowledge of it, as he was traveling with Mason's sons at the time. He also mentioned that John Mason had been imprisoned and beaten, but he did not know how Samuel Mason had escaped from prison. Sutton claimed that he had been forced by Samuel Mason to act as a denouncer, but he believed it was John Mason who had committed the robbery in question.

Sutton denied knowing anything about the $3,200 in banknotes found at Little Prairie, saying he saw them for the first time when they were drying out the notes. When asked why he had initially claimed the notes were found in the woods, Sutton explained that Mason advised him to take responsibility, believing it would not cause him harm, so he did.

Sutton went on to recount stories told by Samuel Mason about committing numerous crimes during the last war, including killing two officers, Barra and Brown, near Cumberland and robbing horses from wedding guests with the help of Barrat and Wood. Sutton added that Mason also claimed Barrat and Brown had killed a family on the Clinch River.

When asked about Barrat's whereabouts, Sutton said he had last seen him at Little Prairie and St. Francois, where he had been introduced to Barrat by Mason. Sutton confirmed that Mason had proposed stealing horses from Bayou Pierre and attacking flatboats to steal goods, which would then be sold to Glass at half price. Sutton noted that although he had not agreed to participate in those plans, Mason never gave him the opportunity to escape, constantly keeping him under close watch. Sutton expressed suspicion that the banknotes inventoried at Little Prairie might have come from a trade between Mason and Mr. Glass. He explained that Mason had mentioned having more money than he originally thought, suggesting the notes were part of that transaction.

When asked if Mason's sons were involved in discussions about robberies, Sutton confirmed that they were. John supported his father's schemes, while Thomas often disagreed, leading to arguments. Sutton admitted that he was not on good terms with any member of the Mason family, including John's wife, who shared their criminal mindset. He recalled an incident where Barrat threatened to report the Masons, and John's wife pulled out a knife, threatening to stab him, saying, "Thou shalt not go and denounce my father, my husband, and my family." Thomas, however, suggested they part ways peacefully.

When asked if John Mason's wife was hiding money or faking illness, Sutton said he did not know but speculated that her illness was a ploy to receive assistance from Dr. Water, one of her acquaintances. Lastly, Sutton was questioned about Harpe, a man connected to the Masons. He responded that he had heard of a Harpe who had been killed in Cumberland and knew Harpe had a brother, though he had never met him. Sutton also noted Mason's connections at Pierre Bayou and suggested some deals involving horses were made there. Sutton confirmed that everything he had stated was true and had nothing to add or alter.

Mason's Senior's Follow-up Testimony

On January 20, 1803, the commandant of New Madrid, along with witnesses and an interpreter, continued the interrogation of Samuel Mason, who was again sworn in on the Holy Bible. Mason was asked to provide further details about robberies on the Mississippi and elsewhere. He began by accusing Sutton, Wigger, and Gibson of jointly committing a robbery in April of the previous year against Glass and other travelers. The robbery resulted in the theft of gold, silver, banknotes, three horses, and a brass-barreled pistol. Mason explained that Gibson had initially hesitated to approach the travelers, leading to the group almost abandoning the plan before ultimately going through with the attack.

After the robbery, the group encountered the injured travelers the following day. One man had been shot in the leg, and Sutton gave him five dollars to ensure he received help from the Chicachas' chief. The group then continued on their way, writing "Samuel Mason, the man of the woods" on a tree and declaring their intent to continue robbing for the rest of their lives. Afterward, they built a canoe to navigate the waters to Little Prairie on the St. Francois River, where they had planned the robbery. The money was divided among Philip, Sutton, and a man named Patterson, who lived in Little Prairie and was aware of their activities. Mason mentioned that Patterson's family wore some of the stolen goods.

Mason continued, saying that Basset had joined the group at Pierre Bayou after stealing horses from the Arcs. Basset warned them that foreign troops from both the Spanish and American sides were pursuing them, but Wigger and Sutton reassured the group that they were not suspected. Mason recounted how Wigger and Sutton later met his sons, John and Thomas, and discussed the details of the robberies. Wigger, wanting to clear his name, considered denouncing the crimes but ultimately left the group instead.

Mason believed the meeting between Wigger, Sutton, and his sons occurred in late May or early June. Around that time, John Mason was accused of a robbery that occurred 45 miles from their settlement. Colonel Baker led a party to arrest John, who was imprisoned in Natchez. Rumors spread that John had escaped with help from friends, though no one knew the exact details of the escape.

Mason expressed that he, along with his sons, believed John was innocent and feared his rearrest. They attempted to gather information on the true culprits and suspected Basset's family knew the robbers but refused to implicate John. After the second robbery, which occurred on both the American and Spanish sides of the river, the Mason family hid in the woods, avoiding travel by river for fear of encountering French or American forces.

When asked about the robbery against Baker, Mason recounted that Wigger and Sutton had commented to John Mason that they were all engaged in similar criminal activities. Sutton detailed how the stolen money had been divided among Basset, Gibson, Sutton, and Philip, with Sutton hiding the gold in his lead sack for several days. That led to arguments between Basset and Philip, as Basset believed he had not received his fair share. Tensions caused Basset to distance himself from the group.

Mason also mentioned that Sutton had kept two pairs of pistols, later divided between Basset and Gibson, and that Basset had taken a large grey horse. However, a mare that ran off into the woods could not be recovered. Mason explained that $500 from the stolen money was set aside to purchase goods from flatboats, with the intent of later robbing the boats to recover both the goods and the money.

The group involved in those robberies, according to Mason, included Basset, Fulson, and Philip. Fulson boasted of having 500 Native Americans at his disposal who would follow his orders if needed. Mason noted that Fulson seemed to command a significant group of Native Americans, specifically from the Shaquetas, though Mason believed others were involved as well.

Mason then recounted how Gibson had been one of the first to commit a robbery on the road to Natchez, stealing several horses and a large sum of money from a man named Brown. Gibson was eventually caught and imprisoned but managed to escape, later joining forces with Philip and other associates. Mason added that both Sutton and Wigger had deserted from the American army, fled to the Chaquetas, and committed crimes there before joining the Chickasaws. Wigger was imprisoned but later escaped, and both men were hidden and supported by Fulson and Basset.

At that point, it was 1:00 p.m., and the interrogation was temporarily suspended. Before concluding, Mason confirmed the truth of his previous statements after they were read back to him by the interpreter.

At 3:00 p.m. that afternoon, Mason returned to continue his interrogation. He again swore on the Holy Bible to tell the truth. Through the interpreter, Mason explained that when Sutton and Wigger met his sons, they possessed a saddle and a pair of pistols, which his sons purchased. Mason's family kept the clothing and other goods from Sutton, believing they were part of the items stolen from Aurely.

Mason then recounted a trip to a magistrate named Dawn, located about 12 miles south of Nogales, where Sutton handed over the pistols and confessed to being involved in the robberies of Aurely and Glass, for which John Mason had been falsely accused. Sutton had intended to turn state's evidence, but the magistrate could not administer an oath due to the absence of a sheriff. Sutton was scheduled to testify the next day, but Mrs. Glass, Basset's sister, persuaded her husband not to proceed, and they planned to hand Sutton over as a deserter instead. Learning of that, Sutton fled into the woods before joining the Mason family as they prepared to leave the area.

When asked if John Mason had been whipped during his imprisonment in Natchez, Mason responded that he had heard rumors of it. He also acknowledged hearing rumors that John's brothers had broken him out of prison, though he was not certain. Mason was then asked if he knew of any additional robberies or crimes on the river or land, to which he replied that he had already revealed everything he knew.

Mason was questioned about a murder involving a slave carrying money for his master, but Mason claimed to have no knowledge of such an event, though he vaguely recalled hearing something about it from a soldier at Little Prairie. He stated that no one from the post had informed him of the crime.

When asked about the origin of the $3,200 found during the inventory at Little Prairie, Mason explained that part of the money had come into his possession accidentally, while another portion belonged to Sutton, though he was unsure where Sutton had obtained it. He insisted that he had never attempted to spend the money, despite knowing it was legitimate.

Mason was then pressed on how the money came into his possession. He claimed that while traveling with people who had many banknotes, he unknowingly took some of the notes without attempting to exchange them. That occurred at Pierre Bayou, where those individuals resided.

When asked about additional banknotes found among his daughter-in-law's clothes, Mason claimed he was unaware of their existence, though he knew there were many banknotes in circulation at the time. He was also asked who had given him the banknotes, and he responded that one man was named

Phules, but he could not recall the names of the others, describing them as travelers he had met on the Monongahela.

Mason provided no further details on the banknotes and confirmed that everything was true and signed the document alongside the witnesses and the interpreter.

John (Jean) Mason's Testimony

On January 21, 1803, John Mason, the third prisoner, appeared before the commandant of New Madrid, along with assisting witnesses and an interpreter. John stated he was a native of Pennsylvania and a Protestant. After swearing on the Bible to tell the truth, he answered questions about his background. John explained that he had come from Nogales and lived at a settlement in Natchez but no longer owned property there due to issues that arose regarding his conduct.

When asked about his intentions in traveling to Little Prairie with his family, John stated that they intended to settle on Spanish land if granted permission. That included his father, his wife, children, brothers, and a stranger named Taylor. He added that three or four additional families might join them if allowed, including a man named Briscot (his uncle according to his father) from Natchez and two of his brothers, one living in Kentucky and the other near Ohio.

John explained that they arrived at Little Prairie by accident, having lost their way, and stated their original intent was to settle at the St. Francois River. He acknowledged that his father had received permission to settle three years ago but had not acted on it due to unforeseen events. When reminded that the Commandant of the Arcs was the authority for granting land there, John stated that they had come to Little Prairie to seek permission to settle because others were already living in the area.

When asked if he had acquaintances in the region, John said no but expressed his willingness to live as an honest man and hoped to obtain land. He mentioned that he knew people in Illinois and Cape Girardeau, including Dr. Water, Mr. Wheates (an acquaintance since childhood), Mr. Samuel Bradley, and his aunt, who was married to a man named Thompson at Cape Girardeau.

John denied knowing Philip, Fulson, or Gibson personally but had heard of them in a negative context from a young man traveling with him. He also acknowledged hearing about a man named Taylor Metes Cherogui, though never in a bad light.

When asked about any robberies on the Mississippi, John confirmed that a man named Philip had purchased carbines from a flatboat, but he only knew about the robbery itself from what two men—who introduced themselves as

Wells—had told him. One of the men, whose real name was Smith Gibson (also known as Drunk Smith), had been involved in stealing $4,000 worth of fine dry goods, which were taken to Little Prairie and later hidden. The goods were rumored to be sold for horses, though John did not know if the sale took place.

Regarding the horses brought to Little Prairie, John explained that four of them had long belonged to his father, while the others were purchased. His father bought a large horse from a man named Taylor from Opelousas, and his brother Magnus purchased a smaller horse from someone on Bayou Pierre.

John admitted that his family had camped at the Yazoo River due to high waters, which caused their horses to wander. They stayed there for about a month. While two of his brothers stayed at the camp, John traveled to the River of the Arcs to find out who had committed the Baker robbery, for which he had been wrongfully accused.

John identified two men—Wigger and Sutton—who admitted to being involved in the robbery. They compared horses and realized they could easily be mistaken for one another. Sutton even promised to serve as a state's witness to clear John's name but was unable to swear his oath before a magistrate named Dawn because he was a deserter. Mr. Glass, present at the time, refused to proceed with Sutton's testimony, leading to Sutton hiding in the woods.

When asked about the accusations of living a nomadic lifestyle, John explained that after the Baker robbery, he and his family were forced into exile in the woods. He admitted to being imprisoned and punished for the robbery but claimed he left the prison after paying part of the required fees and could not afford the remainder.

John said he had heard of other robberies involving Wigger, Sutton, and Gibson. Those individuals also told him that Gibson, Sutton, Philip, and the Bassets (father and son) had divided the money from the Baker robbery, each receiving $500, with the intention of using the funds to buy goods from flatboats. However, plans fell apart after Basset had a disagreement with his partners.

John denied knowing about any murders, stating that neither Wigger nor Sutton had mentioned such events. He acknowledged hearing that the money from the Baker robbery was divided and intended for future purchases but did not know further details.

When questioned about the pursuit of two messengers last summer, John explained that he, his brother, and Sutton had chased after a boat with two Frenchmen, thinking they might be helpful in clearing his name. However, when they reached Nogales, they realized the men were not of use.

John also denied painting himself black and writing "Samuel Mason, the man of the woods" on a tree, saying he had only heard rumors about it. Regarding the banknotes found in the porte manteaux, John stated they belonged to Sutton.

He claimed ignorance of the banknotes found in his wife's clothing, suggesting they might have belonged to his father.

When asked where Sutton and his father obtained the banknotes, John said he did not know where his father got them but suggested that Sutton may have stolen them from travelers on the roads. He also explained that some of the merchandise found at Little Prairie belonged to his brother Thomas, while some belonged to Sutton.

At the end of the interrogation, John had nothing more to declare. He, like his father, requested not to be handed over to the American government. After his declaration was read back to him, John confirmed that everything he had said was true, with nothing to add or erase.

Thomas Mason's Testimony

On January 21, 1803, Thomas Mason, the fourth prisoner, appeared before the commandant of New Madrid. Thomas stated that he was a native of Pennsylvania and a Protestant. He swore on the Bible to tell the truth in response to the questions and declarations.

When asked about his residence, Thomas explained that he lived at Bayou Pierre and owned no property. As the eldest son, he was asked why he had not settled down, to which he responded that he was a farmer who had worked on different lands. Over the past three years, he had traveled to the West to collect for his brother, selling flour and whiskey at Bayou Pierre. He later made a crop at his father's land at "Stone to Sharpen" on Bayou Pierre. He added that his father had an accident last fall, and since then, he had stayed by his side, sometimes on the American side and sometimes on the Spanish side. He also mentioned traveling further up than the White River.

When asked if he had stayed with his father at the Yazoo River, Thomas confirmed that they had stayed there for about a month. He explained that their arrival at Little Prairie was accidental, and bad weather delayed them. Their original intent had been to travel to New Madrid. When asked if he had any friends or acquaintances at New Madrid or Cape Girardeau, Thomas mentioned he had some acquaintances and believed he might have relatives in Cape Girardeau.

Regarding robberies on the river or roads, Thomas confirmed hearing of robberies on the Mississippi River and a public road. He recounted that when he first heard about the river robbery, he was on the Yazoo River. The person who was robbed, Aurely, had seen men near a camp by the River of the Arcs selling arms to a man named Philip. Aurely's boat was robbed the next day by three men: Gibson, Wigger, and Wells, the latter later revealing his true name as

Sutton. Thomas learned the information from Sutton and Wigger, who claimed that Philip had signaled them to attack when buying arms from the flatboat.

Thomas explained that the stolen goods were taken to Little Prairie on the St. Francois River, where they were divided among Philip, Fulson, and Gibson, with Basset trading part of the stolen merchandise for horses. He also mentioned the robbery of Baker, for which his brother John had been accused.

When asked for more details about the robbery, Thomas said that Wigger and Sutton had told him that Fulson, Gibson, Philip, and Basset's son carried out the robbery. Wigger and Sutton sometimes claimed they were present, and at other times, they said they were not. Sutton had even tried to testify before a Justice of the Peace, but his oath was not accepted due to his status as a deserter. Fearing complications, Sutton fled before Mr. Glass, the militia captain, could take his oath.

Thomas added that his brother John had received permission from the governor of Natchez to bring someone willing to act as a state informant to Judge Dawn in an effort to clear John's name. When asked about rumors that he had helped his brother escape from prison in Natchez, Thomas denied any involvement, stating that the prisoners themselves had broken out of the prison.

Thomas was also questioned about a story involving someone painting themselves black and writing "Samuel Mason, the man of the woods" on a tree. He said that Wigger and Sutton told him they were present when it happened, but they did not hear John say he had been mistreated. However, they were there when travelers were fired upon, and one was wounded in the leg, with Gibson also present.

When asked why he and his comrades pursued two Frenchmen on the river above Nogales, Thomas explained that they believed the Frenchmen were connected to the crimes for which John had been accused. He, John, and Sutton pursued them, hoping to obtain information.

Thomas denied knowing a man named Musique or the Duff brothers in Illinois but had heard that one of them had been killed by the savages. He also denied knowing anything about the theft of a negro from St. Louis or from a Mr. Lecompte. When informed that his family had been accused of stealing a negro woman from a Mr. Maxwell, a priest at St. Genevieve, Thomas claimed no knowledge of the incident.

Regarding the banknotes found in a bag, Thomas explained that part of the notes belonged to Sutton, who said he had taken them on the road, and the other part belonged to his father. He denied knowledge of the banknotes found in his sister-in-law's clothing, stating he hadn't paid attention to them.

When asked about the various pieces of goods inventoried, Thomas said that some belonged to Sutton, and the rest were his. He also explained that some of the horses at Little Prairie had long been owned by his father, while others had been purchased.

Regarding the sale of whiskey, flour, and merchandise to Mr. Briscot in Natchez, Thomas explained that his father had arranged the sale, fearing creditors, to protect his property. He said his father and brother had sold their improvements and used the proceeds to buy horses, keeping some money for themselves. Thomas said his father had made a bargain in his absence, possibly using a horse as payment and obtaining the balance on credit. He believed the merchandise was purchased from a German man, though he was not present for the transaction.

At the conclusion of the interrogation, Thomas had nothing further to declare. After his statement was read back to him, he confirmed that everything was true, with nothing to add or erase. The interpreter affirmed that the declarations were accurately conveyed in English, and Thomas signed the document along with the commandant, witnesses, and interpreter.

Marguerite Mason's Testimony

On January 22, 1803, Marguerite Mason, wife of John Mason, appeared before the commandant of New Madrid. She confirmed she had been married for about eight years. Marguerite corroborated that her family intended to come to the city but ended up at Little Prairie due to bad weather and a mistake in their route. She also confirmed that her husband had been involved in trouble in Natchez, prompting the family to seek settlement on Spanish land.

Regarding the three-year delay in using the permission to settle, Marguerite explained, as others had, that her father-in-law asked her husband to delay their move to benefit from land her husband had been working on. She confirmed hearing of robberies involving Baker and Rogers, noting that her husband was wrongly accused. She reiterated what had been said about the involvement of Sutton and Wigger.

Marguerite explained, like others, that the family kept Sutton and Wigger with them in hopes of identifying the real robbers and clearing her husband's name. However, they eventually let Wigger go, and Sutton stayed with them, though his declaration was weak due to his status as a deserter. She noted that they feared traveling by river due to hostility toward the family, which forced them to stay in the woods and reach Little Prairie.

Marguerite also confirmed, as others did, that the family was prepared to flee when the detachment arrived because they anticipated being arrested. However, she added that they intended to clear their names and were unsure why the horses were saddled.

On the matter of the banknotes found in her belongings, she denied knowingly placing them there, suggesting it may have happened accidentally while gathering her things. She did not know how Mr. Mason obtained the banknotes but believed Sutton had some in his belongings.

Regarding the dry goods found, she explained that some linen belonged to Thomas and had been traded from Mr. Glass' store, adding that Sutton had facilitated the trade. She confirmed her statement was true and had nothing to add or change. Marguerite marked the document in lieu of signing.

Samuel Mason Junior's Testimony

On January 22, 1803, Samuel Mason Jr., the sixth prisoner, appeared before the commandant of New Madrid. He confirmed that he was 18 years old, born in Pennsylvania, and Protestant. Samuel Jr. swore on the Bible to tell the truth.

When asked about his family, he stated that he had lived with his father except when working on a plantation with his mother at Bayou Pierre. He rejoined his father and brothers after his brother John was accused of robbery, and his father took the family into the woods. Samuel Jr. explained that he had left his mother three months earlier at his father's request to settle on Spanish lands, though his mother could not join them due to illness.

Samuel Jr. claimed to have heard about robberies on the public road but denied having specific knowledge. He recalled hearing from a man named Aurely about a robbery involving Philip, who had purchased guns from a flatboat before being robbed by the same group. However, he did not know the names of the robbers and had no knowledge of Sutton being involved.

Regarding his family's horses, Samuel Jr. said two were purchased using effects from his father's house, and the others were bought from various men, including Taylor, Uper, Duet, Collins, and a "savage." He noted that his father did not know many Indians or speak their language.

Samuel Jr. explained that his family came to Little Prairie because they planned to settle at Punesdcoiet's River, having already purchased livestock and corn. He said he did not know where the banknotes found in their belongings came from but believed his father had bought the merchandise at Nogales.

After confirming that his declarations were accurate, Samuel Jr. affirmed that he had nothing to add or change. Unable to sign, he marked the document.

Magnus Mason's Testimony

On January 24, 1803, Magnus Mason, the seventh and youngest prisoner, appeared before the commandant of New Madrid. Magnus, a sixteen-year-old

Protestant, confirmed he was born in Pennsylvania. He swore on the Bible to tell the truth.

Magnus stated that he had lived part of the time with his father in Kentucky and later at Bayou Pierre near Natchez. He recalled that his father left Natchez about two winters ago and had spent time in a camp on the Yazoo River, where his brothers John and Thomas had stayed with him while Magnus lived with his younger brother at his sister-in-law's.

Magnus explained that his father remained at the Yazoo River camp to investigate the robbery for which John was accused. He mentioned that he traveled with his father up the river to meet his brothers between the Arcs and White Rivers to see if they had discovered anything about the robberies. They returned with two strangers, one of whom, Sutton, admitted knowing the robbers and being one of them.

Magnus listed the names of robbers he had heard from Sutton, including Philip, Gibson, Fulsom, Basset, Wigger, and Belley. Sutton also told him that Philip had bought guns from a man named Aurely and later sent the others to rob him. Magnus confirmed that he heard Aurely discuss the robbery at Nogales.

Regarding other robberies, Magnus said Sutton had mentioned robbing travelers on a public road, where Sutton wounded a man in the leg. He also heard about a robbery involving a man named Baker, and Gibson admitted to Sutton that he had part of the money from that crime.

When asked about the horses taken to Little Prairie, Magnus listed various sources, including purchases from men named Florence, Hedry, Collins, Armstrong, and Taylor. He denied any knowledge of the banknotes found in his father's belongings.

Magnus stated that the family's intention at Little Prairie was to settle and identify the robbers involved in the crimes for which his brother John had been accused. He denied knowing anything about murders.

After his declaration was read to him, Magnus confirmed that it was true, with nothing to add or erase. As he could not sign, he made his mark.

Dr. Waters' Testimony

On January 24, 1803, Dr. Richard Jones Water, captain of the cavalry of the New Madrid militia, appeared before the commandant to provide his testimony regarding his interactions with Samuel Mason and his sons. Dr. Water clarified that he had never been well acquainted with the Mason family and had only crossed paths with them briefly.

Dr. Water first met Samuel Mason around 1791 or 1792 at Red Bank on the Ohio River. He described a second encounter about a year later when he stopped at Red Bank for supplies. At that time, Mason's wife was ill, and Dr. Water provided medicine and merchandise worth $70, of which Mason only partially repaid him. The outstanding debt remained unresolved when Dr. Water sought compensation in 1798 from a man named Felix Conces, who had already left the district.

In 1800, Dr. Water saw Mason again in New Madrid, where Mason requested treatment for a head injury and medicine for his daughter. Dr. Water sold him medicine, paid for in goods that Mason had acquired. Mason also expressed his intent to settle on Spanish land near the St. Francois River and asked Dr. Water for assistance in obtaining permission from the commandant. Dr. Water agreed to introduce Mason to the commandant, stating that he had not heard anything negative about Mason at that time and believed he would behave honorably.

Regarding Thomas Mason, Dr. Water mentioned that Thomas stayed with him for about eight to ten days while delivering important papers to the Falls of the Ohio. During his stay, Thomas conducted himself honestly.

Dr. Water concluded by requesting to know what Samuel Mason had said about him. The commandant informed Dr. Water that Mason and his son Thomas had only mentioned him regarding the recommendation he had given in 1800 and that they confirmed his statements were truthful. Dr. Water had nothing further to add and confirmed the accuracy of his declaration before signing the document.

Reinterview of Sutton

On January 25, 1803, John Sutton appeared before the commandant of New Madrid to provide further information following his previous declarations. He swore on the Holy Bible to tell the truth.

Sutton began by adding to his previous testimony concerning three saddles. He claimed that Mr. and Mrs. Mason had altered one of the saddles by adding four nails to its corners and blackening the red porte manteaux. Sutton stated that he had been present when the items were blackened, about three weeks or a month after first meeting the Masons. He reiterated that Mr. and Mrs. Mason had informed him that those items had been stolen from a flatboat on the river.

He then provided new information regarding a pair of pistols that were part of the inventory. Sutton stated that he saw John Mason remove a piece of silver from the pistols, which originally belonged to Colonel Baker, a victim of a robbery on the public road. According to Sutton, John Mason engraved the letters "W" and "N" on the pistols, which were later given to Judge Dawn's son in Nogales. The pistols had initially belonged to Sheriff N. Nickolson, providing a key detail tying the pistols to a known law enforcement officer.

When asked who had blackened the saddle and porte manteaux, Sutton said it was John and Thomas Mason. That corroborated the involvement of multiple Mason family members in altering stolen goods, as previously suggested in other testimonies.

Regarding the pursuit of individuals near Nogales, Sutton explained that he was with John and Thomas Mason on the Yazoo River when they spotted two Frenchmen in a boat. They gave the Frenchmen some whiskey and later met them again in New Orleans, providing them with a bag of meat. That claim loosely aligned with earlier testimonies from the Masons about encounters with travelers, although the Frenchmen's identity and purpose differ slightly.

Sutton identified Glass and Campbell as individuals robbed on the public road near Natchez. He denied his involvement in the robbery, stating that he was at Little Prairie on the St. Francois River at the time, in the company of Gibson, Wigger, Fulson, Patterson, and Philip. That directly contradicted the Mason family's earlier suggestions that Sutton may have been involved in the road robbery, as Sutton firmly denied both participating in the crime and giving any money to those unable to return home.

Sutton was then asked to name those sent by Mason to "kill and assassinate." He named Barrat and Brown but noted that he had never met Brown. Barrat, who sometimes called himself Taylor, was said to have been left at Philip's place at Little Prairie. That claim to the Mason family's alleged connections to violent individuals also shifts blame for violent acts away from Sutton himself.

Regarding the mention of a man named Musique, Sutton denied knowing him but stated that he was familiar with a man named Woods, who was part of the group of robbers and currently resided in Arkansas. Sutton concluded his testimony by stating he had nothing further to add. Sutton confirmed his truthfulness and signed the document.

Mason's Property

On January 26, officials inspected the Masons' possessions, finding items like saddles, pistols, and twenty pieces of human hair that seemed forcibly taken (scalps). Recall that territories and states in the United States used scalp bounties from the seventeenth through the nineteenth centuries. The total value of their belongings was around $600, with an additional $7,000 in silver and paper money, much of which was counterfeit.

Derousse's Testimony

On January 27, 1803, Francois Derousse, a citizen of New Madrid, appeared before the commandant, Dr. Henry Peyrouf de la Coudimiere, to provide a declaration regarding the prisoners detained at the post, specifically Samuel Mason. Derousse, a Catholic born in Illinois, swore on the cross to tell the truth.

Derousse recounted an encounter with Samuel Mason, that took place in 1791 while he was hunting on the river near Red Bank. During the encounter, Mason threatened him by placing a gun to his stomach and forced him to walk to Mason's house. Upon arrival, Derousse saw several people, including members of Mason's family. Mason accused him of stealing horses and selling them to Native Americans, charges which Derousse vehemently denied, stating that he had no dealings with any Native Americans. He attempted to prove his innocence by offering references from Michel Bordeleau and Fitreau Francais, both of whom were present.

Mason, however, remained angry and held Derousse in his house for the entire day, repeatedly threatening to kill him. It wasn't until the next day that Mason, appearing calmer, believed Derousse's denials and allowed him to leave. Despite that, Derousse was forced to stay with Mason's group for two months, unable to return to his family despite his attempts to do so.

During his time with Mason's band, Derousse was coerced into working for Mason, who promised to pay him with 30 yards of linen, 8 yards of calico, and two blankets. After two months, Mason delivered the promised goods, but only a few hours later, Mason, along with a man named Bradley (who currently resided in Cape Girardeaux), forcibly took the goods back, cutting them up for their own use. Derousse noted that Eustache Peltier of New Madrid was present when the goods were reclaimed by force. Derousse eventually managed to escape with his family by boat, navigating through ice during the night while Mason and his group slept.

After reading his declaration, Derousse confirmed that everything he had said was true, and he had nothing further to add or remove. Unable to sign his name, Derousse made his mark.

Peltier's Testimony

On January 27, 1803, Estache Peltier, a native of Canada and a Catholic, appeared before the commandant of New Madrid to provide testimony regarding events involving Samuel Mason and Captain Bradley. After swearing to tell the truth, Peltier was questioned about his presence in 1791 during an incident involving Francois Derousse and Mason.

Peltier confirmed that he was present when Derousse received his wages after two months of service, which were paid in merchandise. However, shortly after, Mason and Captain Bradley forcibly reclaimed the goods. They threatened Derousse, swore, cursed, and had Mason's wife cut up the merchandise. Those aggressive actions caused fear among Peltier, another man named Tetreau, and a Spaniard named Joseph. All three, along with Derousse and their families, fled the scene by boat.

Peltier added that Tetreau and Joseph abandoned their wages, fearing retaliation from Mason and Bradley. He noted that their fear was heightened by the disappearance of Laford, a European merchant who had stayed at Mason's home to collect debts. Laford had vanished along with his merchandise, and no one knew what had happened to him. Laford was a merchant from New Orleans who had obtained a passport from Dr. Pierre Foucher, the commandant of New Madrid.

Peltier also revealed that Bradley was Mason's business partner in a salting operation, intended to pay off the merchandise owed to Laford. The salted provisions had already been sold to Mr. Handley, a local magistrate, prior to Laford's disappearance.

Peltier confirmed its truthfulness, stating that he had nothing further to add or erase. Unable to sign his name, he made his mark.

Billeth's Testimony

On January 27, 1803, Pierre Billets, a resident of New Madrid and a native of France, appeared before the commandant to provide testimony against Samuel Mason and his associates. After swearing an oath on the cross to tell the truth, Billets recounted an event from 1798.

Billets stated that in August of 1798, he overheard a conversation between a Black woman who was formerly owned by Mason and a man named Riee Jones. In the presence of Billets and Sheriff James Dawn of Kaskaskia, the woman revealed that, under Mason's instruction, she had helped drag a man her master had killed to the river to steal his valise, which contained a large sum of money. The murder occurred while Mason was living on the Cumberland River.

Billets believed the man was killed with a knife and then dragged by a rope tied around his neck. When asked about the fate of the Black woman, Billets explained that she had since been sold at auction by Sheriff Dawn to a man named Maxwell, a priest in St. Genevieve.

Billets had no further information to provide. He confirmed that everything he had said was true and signed the document.

Cost of the Trial

After all witness testimonies and official statements, on January 29, 1803, the commandant ordered a detailed cost report for the trial and associated expenses, including arresting the prisoners at Little Prairie. The costs included payments for 19 militiamen who guarded the prisoners for 17 days and other expenses like shackles, totaling around 1,053 piasters, or approximately $1,000 (over $25,000 in today's dollars).

The trial revealed that the Mason family was adept at manipulating legal and social structures to their advantage. They consistently professed innocence, with Samuel Mason Sr. claiming that his family was attempting to clear their names by uncovering the true culprits of the robberies. The records also show that they kept known criminals like Sutton close to them under the guise of using them to expose the real robbers. The strategy of providing alternative narratives to criminal activities showed that Mason's time as a judge was well spent.

Travel and Tasting Notes

Missouri:

> New Madrid Historical Museum
>
> Little Prairie (Caruthersville)

Mississippi:

> Natchez Under-the-Hill
>
> King's Tavern, Natchez
>
> Natchez Trace Parkway

See the Appendices for more travel and tasting notes and the master timeline of Mason's life. Consider planning a visit to some or all of these locations. You'll be glad you did!

Investigative Team

Coates, Rothert, and Wagner were investigators who contributed to this investigation phase. For more on these team members, see the introduction—assembling the team.

10
GOOD DAYS AND BAD (1803–04)

On January 31, 1803, the trial documents, evidence, and seized money from Mason's gang were ordered to be sent to the Spanish governor general in New Orleans, the capital of Spanish Louisiana, for further proceedings. Commandant Peyroux of New Madrid sent Mason and his gang under guard to his superior, Intendant Manuel de Salcedo. The journey, spanning approximately 500 miles, took more than two weeks by boat. The trip represented Mason's final passage through the regions where he had been notorious.

The topography of Louisiana featured a mix of flat alluvial plains, swamps, and hills, significantly shaped by the Mississippi River and its tributaries. Extensive wetlands covered much of the southern parts, while the northern regions comprised higher ground. New Orleans had a mix of low-lying swampy areas and elevated ridges, shaped significantly by the Mississippi River's delta.

The journey down the Mississippi River from New Madrid likely involved a flatboat carrying the evidence seized from Mason, the Mason gang, and the soldiers guarding them. The arrival of Captain McCoy and his prisoners in New Orleans was not well documented. Still, an unpublished official letter from the Mississippi Department of Archives and History provided the following events.

Transferred to Natchez

Upon their arrival in New Orleans, the trial records from New Madrid were reviewed by the governor general of Louisiana and his secretary of war. A letter, dated March 3, 1803, from Secretary of War Vidal, approved by Governor Manuel Salcedo, was sent to Governor Claiborne of the Mississippi Territory. It explained that the case's jurisdiction was the United States, not Spain. Vidal recounted the arrest of Mason and his gang near New Madrid, highlighting that since no crimes were committed in Spanish jurisdiction, they were transferring Mason and his gang approximately 170 miles upriver to Natchez for further legal proceedings.

The decision was influenced by findings that the criminals were US citizens, had committed most of their crimes in the United States, and had primarily lived in US territory. Furthermore, at least one member of the gang had already faced punishment in the United States for related crimes. Also, the evidence necessary to prove the crimes and the testimonies needed were mainly located in Mississippi and neighboring states. Given the strong ties and good relations between the United States and Spain, transferring jurisdiction to the United States, where the crimes occurred, was deemed appropriate to ensure justice was served.[1]

Escape from Captivity

In early March 1803, Captain McCoy was tasked with transporting Mason and his gang to Natchez for trial. The journey upriver from New Orleans was arduous, hindered by spring storms and strong currents. By March 26th, they had only reached Pointe Coupee Parish, about 110 miles from New Orleans and 90 miles from Natchez.

While historical records lack detailed documentation of the event, the likely scenario involved significant challenges. Sutton played a crucial role, possibly turning against Mason and testifying about various crimes and conspiratorial activities. The boat was crowded with about seventeen people, including guards, crew, and prisoners. Sutton was likely chained visibly to prevent him from conspiring with Mason or manipulating potential confessions.

As they journeyed upriver, a damaged mast on the boat forced the group to stop for repairs. The prisoners escaped after some of the guards left the vessel to craft a new mast, leaving the remaining guards to watch over the prisoners. Taking advantage of the chaos, Mason and his gang overpowered the guards that were left behind. Amid the turmoil, McCoy confronted Mason, resulting in an exchange of gunfire. Rothert (and Smith below) claimed Mason killed McCoy during the escape.

McCoy was shot in the breast and shoulder, and Mason managed to regain control of the boat until the evening when a superior force (the guards with the mast) appeared, prompting him and his group to flee. Accounts vary on whether Mason was wounded in the leg or head during the incident. Conflicting reports also suggest that either a gang member shot McCoy or Mason himself fired the fatal shots. Coates reported that McCoy shot Mason in the head. McCoy was said by a Missouri historian to have died in 1840, neither crippled nor killed by Mason.[2]

The Mason gang's escape quickly became widely reported news. Natchez soon shared the initial report featured in *The Western Spy* on April 2, which appeared in various newspapers with less detail. Those publications included *The Tennessee Gazette* on April 27, *The Kentucky Gazette* on May 3, and *The Palladium* on May 5. Alongside the news of the escape, the reports also noted that Governor Claiborne had received official notification about the arrival of the French Prefect for the Colony of Louisiana in New Orleans.

A news article from the period detailed the escape:

CINCINNATI, May 4.

Extract of a letter from the reverend John Smith to a gentleman in this town, dated Point Coupée, March 28, 1803.

. . . in a short time they threw off their irons, seized the guns belonging to the boat and fired upon the guard. Captain McCoy hearing the alarm ran out of the cabin, old Mason instantly shot him through the breast and the shoulder; he with the determined bravery of a soldier, though scarcely able to stand shot him through the head. Mason fell and rose, fell and rose again, and although in a gore of blood, one of his party having shot a Spaniard's arm to pieces, he drove off McCoy's party and kept possession of the boat till evening, when, discovering a superior force they left the boat, the women and children with great precipitation. There is a party of Creoles after them, and it is supposed they will succeed in taking them. The commandant at this place has offered one thousand dollars for taking old Mason dead or alive. They will be pursued with the utmost diligence by a set of determined fellows.

Who Had Jurisdiction?

In Mason's time, Spain and France had significant control over parts of the American continent. Spain controlled much of the American Southwest, including present-day California, Arizona, New Mexico, and Texas. Spain also controlled much of the Mississippi River and its tributaries, which were essential routes for trade and communication between the Gulf of Mexico and the continent's interior. France controlled much of the American Midwest, including present-day Louisiana, Mississippi, and Illinois.

In the late 1700s and early 1800s, Spain and France began to lose control of their territories on the American continent due to the increasing influence and expansion of the United States, as well as internal factors such as economic decline, political instability, and revolution. As we saw in the previous chapter, Louisiana had been transferred from France to Spain in 1762, and Spain returned the property to France on September 1, 1800. In 1801, the United States discovered that Louisiana had been transferred from Spain to France, prompting President Thomas Jefferson to send Robert Livingston to France in hopes of purchasing New Orleans. When Napoleon initially refused, Jefferson dispatched James Monroe to secure the deal. However, before Monroe's arrival in Paris, Napoleon unexpectedly offered to sell not only New Orleans but the entire Louisiana territory.[3]

Napoleon sold the territory to the United States as part of the Louisiana Purchase, finalized on April 30, 1803. The Senate ratified the Louisiana Purchase Treaty on October 20, 1803. The official transfer began on November 30, 1803, when Spanish governor Salcedo and the Marqués de Casa Calvo transferred Louisiana to France's representative, Pierre Clément de Laussat, in a ceremony at the Sala Capitular in the Cabildo. Although Laussat was instructed to transfer the territory to the United States the following day, a twenty-day gap occurred during which Laussat served as governor.[4] On December 20, 1803, the French flag was lowered in New Orleans' main square, and the American flag was raised.[5] No historian that I have found mentioned the problem with Spain conducting the trial of Mason after they had transferred possession (and presumably jurisdiction) of the land west of the Mississippi River back to France in 1800.

The United States purchased a vast amount of land (530 million acres) from France, including present-day Arkansas, Missouri, Iowa, Oklahoma, Kansas, and several other states. It added approximately 828,000 square miles, doubling the nation's size for a mere $15 million. The acquisition granted the United States control over the Mississippi River and its tributaries, although the region remained contested by various Native American tribes who had long inhabited the area. In response, the US government built several military forts to protect American interests and affirm its control.

President Jefferson appointed W. C. C. Claiborne, the former Mississippi Territory governor, the new governor of lower Louisiana. General James Wilkinson supported Claiborne militarily.[6] You may recall that Wilkinson had played an often controversial role during the Revolutionary War and the years following. After the war, he became embroiled in various political and military dealings, often switching loyalties between different factions. In the postwar years, Wilkinson became involved with Spanish authorities, secretly accepting a pension from Spain in exchange for intelligence about American affairs. Despite that, he maintained his role within the US military and politics, rising to become the senior officer of the US Army and being honored with the naming of the short-lived Cantonment Wilkinson in southern Illinois.

In 1803, the United States' population was approximately 5.5 million people. The closest census years to 1803, 1800, and 1810 helped provide the estimate.[7] In 1800, the population was about 5.3 million; by 1810, it had grown to about 7.2 million, reflecting the rapid growth and expansion of the young nation following the Louisiana Purchase.

GOOD DAYS AND BAD (1803–04)   151

Figure 10.1 Mason's face on a wanted poster, with two locals looking at it. Wanted posters were not used until several decades later, but Mason would have been a good candidate for the first one. Sketched by Jekaterina Hagen, with Fiverr.

A Wanted Man

On July 26, 1803, Governor Claiborne advised then president James Madison that he (Claiborne) had offered $500 as a reward for capturing Samuel Mason and his gang.[8] According to Carr, Secretary of War Henry Dearborn contributed $400.[9] It has been said that Claiborne offered a $2,000 "dead or alive" reward or perhaps increased it after Mason escaped.[10] Roxby explained that, though it may not sound like much by today's standards, $2,000 represented nearly four years of salary for a skilled workman during the period ($100,000–200,000 today). It was designed to attract anyone brave or desperate enough to tangle with a killer like Mason and to get the attention of any potential turncoats in his gang.

It has been said that Mason's end came in a drama worthy of Hollywood.[11] James May (who may have been Isaac or Samuel May, AKA Peter Alston, who was in Red Banks in 1797) and John Sutton (who some claim was Wiley/Little Harpe and had an alias of John Taylor or Wells) were arrested in Natchez. As the story went, the two offered, if released, to bring in Sam Mason. Desperate to be rid of Mason, the authorities agreed. The two went into Louisiana territory and returned a month later with a giant ball of clay in their canoe.

The two reported finding Mason hiding near Lake Concordia in East-Central Louisiana, about 12 miles west of Natchez. Some historians claim that Mason died from wounds he suffered in the escape from McCoy, and others argue that his men killed him for the reward. The two outlaws showed up at the courthouse in Old Greenville, Mississippi (a town no longer in existence) in Jefferson County, Mississippi, with Mason's head. Old Greenville, located on Mud Island Creek, six miles northwest of present-day Fayette and 25 miles north of Natchez, was the biggest town on the Trace between Natchez and Port Gibson. Greenville was named after Major-General Nathanael Greene, a Revolutionary War hero revered by George Washington. See Appendix C for more on this and other bits of historical misinformation.

No Reward

Many people examined the head and confirmed that it was Mason. The judge prepared the death certificate and sent an affidavit to the governor to claim the reward, so the men had to wait a few days. Swaney later recalled the governor doubted the truth of the story involving Mason's death, so he invited several men familiar with Mason, including Swaney, to identify the severed head as Mason's. None recognized it as Mason's, unanimously agreeing it wasn't his.[12] Consequently, the governor had Sutton and May arrested and charged with murder. They were later tried, convicted of first-degree murder, and hanged in Greenville. Where Samuel Mason is buried and what happened to his head and corpse will probably remain a mystery. Regardless of how he died and where he was buried, Mason was "a striking example of a lawless man receiving his just reward."[13]

Maybe Mason was buried in Old Greenville cemetery.[14] Another story was that Governor Claiborne sent Mason's wife, Rosanna, to authenticate the head. She examined the head and determined the murdered man was not Samuel

GOOD DAYS AND BAD (1803–04)

Mason. That appeared to be the foundation for ordering the arrest of Sutton and May since they had killed someone who was not the person for whom a reward was offered (Mason). Some believed Sam may have escaped to Canada, where he died a peaceful death and was buried in a Canadian cemetery.[15] With all the children and subsequent descendants he had, and none of them providing corroboration for that theory, that possibility hasn't been developed. What was more likely, if the head was not Mason's, was that he died from an injury he received while escaping from McCoy and his soldiers.

When the two took the head to the courthouse in Natchez, Captain Stump from Kentucky publicly identified Sutton as Wiley Harpe. In response to Sutton's denial, Stump admitted he couldn't be sure. Many others who said they knew Harpe agreed, but only one could prove it to the court. On the day of the execution in 1804, John Bowman of Knoxville, Tenn., having just arrived in town, did a double take when he saw John Sutton. "You're Little Harpe," Bowman claimed. Sutton denied it. However, according to Swaney, an eyewitness to the events, Bowman "persisted and said if you are Harpe, you have a scar under your left nipple where I cut you in a difficulty we had at Knoxville." Bowman ripped open Sutton's shirt. The crowd gasped as they saw the scar as Bowman had described it.[16] May and Sutton were scheduled to be executed by hanging on February 8, 1804 at Old Greenville. The hangings were conducted on the outskirts of Greenville, known as "Gallows Field," an area that was still identifiable in the early 1900s.

Although the details differ in how and for what, the record is clear that both Sutton and May were tried in separate courts and represented by separate attorneys; the two were tried for robbery and were sentenced to be hung up by the neck until they were "dead, dead, dead." In traditional hangings of those days, the prisoner was seated in a wagon, bound hand and foot, and taken to the place where they would be hung. The noose at the end of a rope extending from a pole extending between two trees would be affixed around their neck, and the horses pulling the wagon made to rush forward, leaving the prisoner to dangle from the rope. A ladder was used to replace the wagon with Sutton and May. When the two were made to mount the ladders, the ladders were dropped, causing their bodies to fall until the length of the rope stopped them.[17] After the execution, their heads were cut off.[18]

Sutton's head was mounted on a pole along the Natchez Trace just north of Old Greenville to celebrate the closure of that chapter in history and as a deterrent to would-be criminals. May's head was also mounted on a pole and displayed just south of town along the Trace. Their bodies were buried in the town graveyard, causing family members of those already buried there to exhume and relocate their loved ones' remains. The two bodies remained, to be lost to history as the Trace was expanded to include the old graveyard, and their coffins and bodies inside were trampled further into the ground by the movement of commerce and travel along the trail they once made dangerous.

Delayed Closure

On February 27, 1804, Governor Claiborne wrote to Col. Cato West to celebrate the closure of the long and grueling chapter of river piracy.

> Your letter of the 15th Instant was handed to me, by Mr. Robert Williams. The Execution of Sutton and May presents a good example; it will tend to deter others from committing rapine and murder, and to give safety to those who visit the Territory either by Land or Water. The expences attending the arrest, confinement and execution of these abandoned Men, seem to me, to be a just charge against the United States; they offended not against the Territory alone, but made war on the Lives and properties of all who fell in their way, and selected for their Scene of action positions where the United States are particularly bound to extend protection to her Honest Citizens. I shall however, write fully to the Secretary of State on this subject, and will commit my Letters to Mr. Robert Williams, who can himself make such explanations as will greatly assist in the attaining our object. It gives me real satisfaction to hear that the Territory is tranquil, and I hope that a pleasant state of things may long continue.
>
> With Respect & Esteem I am D. Sir
> Your obdt . St.
> (SIGNED) WM . C. C. CLAIBORNE[19]

Claiborne followed up by notifying James Madison, the Secretary of State, a few weeks later.[20]

NEW ORLEANS, March 15, 1804

Sir,

Two Men of the names of Sutton and May were lately convicted in the Mississippi Territory of Piracy and Felony, and have since been Executed. These Men were two of Masons Party, who committed such frequent outrages on the Mississippi River, and on the Wilderness road. This Banditti had become a terror to all persons who navigated the Mississippi or travelled the Wilderness road, and a reward of four hundred dollars for apprehending them was offered by the Secretary of War, and five hundred dollars by myself, in my character as Governor of the Territory.

Sutton and May were arrested previous to my leaving Natchez, but no part of the reward, has I believe been claimed. The Jail in which these felons, were confined being very insecure, I directed (with a view to their safe keeping) a guard of Militia on constant duty; their trial was necessarily delayed for some months but they were lately convicted of and executed for, offences committed without the limits of the Territory against the Laws of the United States.

I therefore think that the expense attending their confinement and trial should be paid by the United States, and I pray you Sir to ascertain upon this Subject the opinion of accounting officers of the Treasury. This Expense will indeed be a trifling charge against the United States, but if it should devolve upon the Territory, I fear it will prove embarassing to her Treasury, against which there are already more claims, than its present resources can meet.

Accept assurances of my respect and esteem.

(SIGNED) WM. C. C. CLAIBORNE

THE REAL JOHN SUTTON

Most of the following analysis was conducted by Wagner, one of the more thorough (and contemporary) investigators. At the time of publication, internet graves and genealogy sites had no information regarding a John McDowell Sutton, John M. Sutton, or John M. Setton, and there was neither burial information nor descendants. That indicated the possibility that Sutton was hung as described here. Rothert examined the suspicion Sutton was really Wiley Harpe. He suggested nobody could be sure whether Little Harpe was part of the gang, and noted Mason would not have knowingly permitted that based on the violent reputation of the Harpe Brothers. Later researchers accepted that conclusion without reservation.

Draper found Sutton was originally from North Carolina and had met a man named Bass from Williamson County, Tennessee (20 miles southwest of Nashville), while traveling along the northern stretch of the Natchez Trace. The two got along, and Sutton accompanied Bass to his home, where he met and began courting his sister. Not long afterward, Sutton and Ms. Bass married and headed to North Carolina. When they reached Hawkins County in East Tennessee (250 miles east of Williamson County, near Kingsport and the border with North Carolina and Virginia), Sutton reported his new wife was dragged by her horse when her feet were stuck in the stirrups. He buried her, sold her saddle, and left with their two horses and other possessions shortly afterward. Her body was later exhumed when folks realized his story was suspicious, and she was found to have received several blows to the head. Sutton fled the area and enlisted at Chickasaw Bluff—Fort Pickering near present-day Memphis. He was promoted to sergeant because of his skills, and one day, he borrowed a rifle and a canoe to go hunting. While out, he connected with Mason.[21] While Sutton's reported actions could have been expected of Harpe, making the story possible while not proving he wasn't who he was suspected to be, Draper did not express suspicion at the time.

Claiborne initially indicated that he had information that Little Harpe was one of the Mason gang.[22] He later identified the two that were tried as Sutton and May.[23] In addition, at the preliminary inquiry of Mason and his gang, one of the Spanish interrogators directly asked Sutton: Are you acquainted with "the man [Wiley] Harpe?" Sutton replied he did not know Wiley Harpe but knew his brother Big Harpe on the Cumberland River.[24] That response, a strange answer if he was Wiley Harpe, seemed to satisfy the investigators, who did not ask Sutton or any of the other gang members further questions regarding Sutton's identity.

Sutton's denial that he was Little Harpe was supported by an account by Colonel James Sevier of Tennessee. Colonel Sevier, the son of General John Sevier, told Draper that the "Harpes were personally known by [him] . . . when they lived on Beaver Creek, some 8 miles from Knoxville, Tennessee."[25] In addition, his father had personally ordered Mason and "several worthless louts. . . [none of whom] were known to work" to leave East Tennessee after they "[stole items] from negro cabins on Sabbath day when their occupants were attending church."[26]

Colonel Sevier denied to Draper that Sutton was Little Harpe, stating, "It was not Little H. hung in Mississippi."[27] Instead, Sevier noted in his account that several of his family members and acquaintances identified the man in the Greeneville jail as Sutton, not Little Harpe. That included his brother, Tennessee militia captain George Washington Sevier, and an acquaintance—militia captain Gilbert C. Russell—who later became the commanding officer of the army post at Chickasaw Bluff (Memphis). Additionally, Sevier and Russell had men in their companies who lived on Beaver Creek in Tennessee, the same creek that the Harpes had once lived on. They sent the men to the jail to "see if they could identify him [Sutton] as Harpe—they all said he was not Harpe." Other men from Williamson County, Tennessee identified Sutton as the "man who had married Miss Bass [from their county], under another name" rather than as Wiley Harpe. Finally, on the gallows, at a time when it could no longer do him any good to deny his identity if he indeed was Little Harpe, Sutton once again "unequivocally denied being Harpe, said he knew nothing of him, that his name was John McDowell Sutton."[28]

Nearly two years after his letter to the secretary of state, Governor Claiborne still believed Sutton was one of the two hung in 1804, as indicated by his correspondence to Edwd. Turner Esqr. Natchez:

New Orleans 16: Jany. 1806.

... The Proclamation, offering a Reward for apprehending Samuel Mason & his associates, being issued in my character as Governor of the Mississippi Territory, I am of Opinion, that Mr. Caston should make his application to my Successor in Office. There can be little doubt, but that John Sutton & James May, were associates of Samuel Mason, and if they were apprehended by Mr. Caston, he unquestionably ought to receive the Reward which was offered. I have written upon this subject to Governor Williams who will I am persuaded on your application, do that which his Powers may admit & Justice shall require.

I AM SIR,
VERY RESPECTFULLY
YOUR HBLE. SERVT.
W. C. C. CLAIBORNE

In the letter, Governor Claiborne identified the two gang members as Sutton and May, instead of Harpe and May or any of the other names bantered about by historians since that time. It stands to reason that if Claiborne's investigation was sufficient to convince him of their identities, it should be sufficient to convince us of their identities.

The Masons, After Sam Sr.

Most of Mason's children ultimately lived respectable lives. I was unable to find any information about Thomas, the oldest son. Much of the following was gathered by Coker and Bell:

Mason's daughter Elizabeth married Philip Briscoe, who lived from 1758 to 32. They lived in Bayou Pierre, Mississippi, in 1803.[29] Bell determined she died in 1815. Children included Rosannah (Briscoe), Elizabeth (Clark) 1809–98, Thomas, Margaret (Grissom), and John M, who lived in Mississippi.

Mason's son, John Mason, married Margaret Douglas in Fayette County, Pennsylvania. Margaret (Margaruite) was with her husband when the Masons were captured near New Madrid in 1803. They may have moved to Canada afterward, according to Bell's notes.

Mason's son Isaac Mason married and had eight children (source DAR record). Isaac and brother Dorsey lived in Ohio. Bell added that Isaac may have died in Champaign County in 1838, leaving children: William, Sebastian, John, Isaac, Rachel, Ann, Sarah, and Elizabeth.

Mason's son Dorsey Mason married his cousin Hannah Meason (born 1782) in Fayette County, Pennsylvania, in 1799. She was the daughter of John Meason—Sam's brother I (1739–03). They moved to Fairfield County, Ohio, in the early 1800s. Dorsey died in 1814. They had seven children. Coker descends from their youngest child, Magness (or Magnus) (1813–84).[30] Bell noted Hannah died August 3, 1859 near Montpelier, Indiana. The two had children named Samuel 1800-, John 1802–19, Rosannah (Howe) 1804–66, Harriett 1806–39, Thomas 1808–83, Dorsey 1811–80, and Magnus 1813–83.

Mason's youngest daughter Mary, may have been the one who married a Kuykendall in Kentucky. No additional information was found.

Mason's son Samuel Mason (Jr.) apparently followed the judge's advice to avoid trouble in 1803 while he was in custody in New Madrid, Spanish Territory. He went on to lead a successful and lawful life, with no known record of misconduct. He married Mary (Polly) Searcy, became a wealthy planter, and lived in Warren County, Mississippi, for many years. He moved to Fort Bend, Texas in the 1840s, and died in Fort Bend County, Texas, in 1863. Children included Dorsey, Roseanna (Kenchelow), Elizabeth (Nolan), Susan (Briscoe), and Thomas. Samuel Jr.'s daughter, Susan, married James Montgomery Briscoe, whose brother Andrew played a notable role in Texas's fight for independence in 1835–36. Harrisburg (now part of Houston) and Harris County were named after Andrew's father-in-law. Additionally, former Texas Governor Dolph Briscoe, Jr., was a direct descendant of Samuel Mason through his mother, Georgie Briscoe.

Mason's son Magness (or Magnus) was with his father and brothers Thomas, John, and Samuel (Jr.) when they were on trial in New Madrid in 1803. No other information was found about him.

As we wrap up the story with his family, we must still address the original question–where is Sam? In the next chapter, we will spend some time getting to know Sam, his thought process, and his inspiration. We will then look at some possibilities that may explain why he was the way he was. While we have tracked Sam to the end of his life, we have yet to actually find him. Don't assume that the hunt is over just because his life ended. There's a lot more to learn about this fellow and the times he lived in, so get ready!

Travel and Tasting Notes

Louisiana:

Jackson Square, New Orleans

The Cabildo, New Orleans

Christ Church, New Orleans

The Presbytère, New Orleans
Madame John's Legacy, New Orleans
Lafitte's Blacksmith Shop, New Orleans
The Little House, Algiers (New Orleans)

See the Appendices for more travel and tasting notes and the master timeline of Mason's life. Consider planning a visit to some or all of these locations.

Investigative Team

Bell, Coates, Coker, Lach, Nicodemus, Rothert, Roxby, and Wagner were among the investigators who contributed to this investigation phase. For more on these team members, see the introduction—assembling the team.

11
SAM MASON

The Making of an American River Pirate

By now, nothing you read about Sam Mason would likely surprise you. So, how can we reconcile the obvious conflict? Sam was a captain in the militia, raised a family, served as a judge and leader in the community, and *then* became a river pirate and land pirate. He seemed to have had a normal childhood, joined the military, and started a career shortly after. And then he repeatedly committed crimes—as an adult, and a mature one at that. For the many people I have talked to about Sam, that's where the questions start. He was said to be a juvenile delinquent, likely carrying his propensity for criminal behavior into his young adult life. One would think that his time in military service would have given him the discipline and skill sets necessary for an admirable and honest career. So why did he, a Revolutionary War Captain in his thirties and an appointed Justice of the Peace and Associate Judge in his early forties, turn to and stick with a life of crime from approximately age forty-five until he died in his early sixties? Does a midlife crisis explain that?

The years after the Revolutionary War were brutal for a lot of Americans, including veterans, many of whom struggled to find jobs and support themselves. Some veterans may have turned to criminal activity, including river piracy, to earn a living. Mason served his country during wartime and had little to show for it. He had more life experience as a wartime citizen than most US residents in the twentieth or twenty-first centuries. He may have been disillusioned with the new government that he had fought to create. He may have felt that the government was not doing enough to help him or to address the economic problems that were facing the country. He may have been drawn to river piracy because he had already experienced the dangers of war. He may have turned to river piracy to get revenge on people he believed had wronged him, or river piracy may have been a way to strike back at the government.

Ward noted the effect of the Revolutionary War on the citizens of that time. The successful, prolonged revolt against their mother country (England) brought with it a vicious predation of neighbors against neighbors, and while the violence such a war encouraged spread from the military campaigns to the marauding opportunistic criminal gangs, neither British nor American military held the gangs accountable.[1] Does that explain such a drastic character shift?

Let's Ask Sam

On January 17, 1803, Captain McCoy and his unit arrested Mason and his gang in Little Prairie. Mason and his gang were transported to New Madrid, where they were interviewed, as detailed earlier. I'll pause so we can quickly recap how we got to this point.

Mason managed his river pirate gang from about 1797 to 1803 along the Ohio and Mississippi Rivers. His gang members were known to rob and kill many a river traveler. In 1800, Mason moved his pirate operations to Wolf Island, between Kentucky and Missouri (the United States and Spain). In addition to river piracy, Mason's gang terrorized boatmen and travelers returning from Natchez and New Orleans, ambushing them along the Natchez Trace. In the spring of 1801, Colonel Baker headed to New Orleans, sold livestock and produce, and, in early August, headed home on the Trace. When he and his group arrived at Twelve Mile Creek, Mason and his gang robbed Baker of his horses and $2,300 in cash. In early 1802, Baker headed back down the river from Kentucky to the market. When his flatboat passed Walnut Hills, he was again robbed by Mason and his gang. In response, Governor Claiborne alerted many government troops and associated individuals to be on the lookout for the gang. Later in 1802, the gang moved their headquarters to Little Prairie, where Captain McCoy and his unit found them.

All caught up? Now let's sit in on just Sam's interview. Perhaps we can get a firsthand perspective and learn why he did all this. The full interview is part of the trial transcripts, but this summary should give you some good insights.

Interview with Sam Mason

Q: Please state your name, place of origin, and religious beliefs.
A: My name is Samuel Mason. I am a native of Pennsylvania and a Protestant.
Q: Where is your ordinary residence?

A: I live in the Natchez district, specifically at Bayou Pierre, near the crossing and the grindstone.

Q: Do you own any real estate?

A: No, I sold my land before coming here, specifically to Mr. Bryan, who owns land nearby.

Q: Do you have property anywhere else?

A: I have claims in the Monongahela area, inherited from my late brother who had no children.[2]

Q: Do you possess any passports from where you came?

A: Only the passport issued to me in early 1800.

Q: Why didn't you use the passport to establish yourself as promised?

A: I was occupied with personal matters, gathering my family who had been separated, and managing my affairs.

Q: How did you supported yourself during that period?

A: I survived on income from my plantation, cattle, my children's work, and occasional labor from hired workers.

Q: Do you have any papers besides those found in your baggage at Little Prairie?

A: No, those are all the documents I have.

Q: Who is Philip Briscot?

A: He is my son-in-law and he resides in Natchez.

Q: Public opinion accuses you of crimes. Will you make a confession if any wrongdoing is involved?

A: I am prepared to tell the truth. I have committed no crimes on the Spanish side and am innocent of the crimes attributed to me in America.

Q: What were your intentions upon arriving at Little Prairie?

A: We arrived there by mistake due to bad weather. Our goal was to reach New Madrid to request land for a settlement.

Q: Did you mention the possibility of settling at Little Prairie?

A: Yes, we said we would consider it if the land was suitable.

Q: Are you expecting anyone else to join you?

A: Yes, two of my sons from Monongahela, along with my son-in-law and daughter from Natchez. I also mentioned to Mr. Le Sieur that friends might join if they learned of my location.

Q: Why didn't you use the permission granted to establish yourself in the past three years?

A: I was delayed by circumstances. However, I believe my sister, a widow now married to a Mr. Thompson at Cape Girardeau, could vouch for me, along with Mr. Ramsey, General Harrison, and Mr. Bradley, who also reside at Cape Girardeau.

Q: What do you plan to do upon reaching New Madrid?
A: I intend to ask the commandant for permission to take some land.
Q: Do you have business with Harrison, Water, and Reagan?
A: I don't know Reagan and have no business with the others, but I would visit Harrison and Water as acquaintances.
Q: Can Mr. Water vouch for you?
A: I'm unsure, but I would ask him.
Q: Why don't you have reputable associates or any papers or correspondence to prove your background?
A: I have always conducted my business independently.
Q: Why did Mr. Water recommend you?
A: I have no dealings with him and only know him indirectly from America.
Q: What do you know about a robbery involving the purchase of carbines and a flatboat?
A: I heard that my son-in-law, Philip, bought the carbines. Later, I learned of the robbery from my sons, who had been informed by two men at their camp.
Q: Were you present during that robbery?
A: No, I was not there.
Q: Did you know the robbers involved?
A: My sons learned of the robbery from Wigger, Gibson, and a third man. The stolen goods were divided among Philip, Fulson, and others, and later traded for horses.
Q: Do you know a man named Taylor?
A: I've never seen him, but I heard he bought stolen goods and had samples checked to verify they were stolen.
Q: Are you aware of other robberies?
A: I have knowledge of some and can name people involved. I'm willing to disclose this for a pardon.
Q: Who committed the robbery near St. Francois?
A: Sutton, Wigger, and another man robbed a traveler named Glass, taking money, horses, and a pistol. The robbers helped the wounded Glass afterward, giving him money for his care.
Q: Do you recall the robbery's aftermath?
A: Yes, they left a message on a tree declaring themselves robbers and headed to Little Prairie, where they divided the spoils.
Q: Was Patterson aware of their actions?
A: Yes, he knew of their activities, and his family wore some of the stolen goods.
Q: What happened with Basset, who joined your group?

A: Basset joined after stealing horses from the Arcs and kept watch for any pursuits.
Q: What was the involvement of soldiers Sutton and Wigger?
A: They deserted from American forces and later joined with Basset and my sons. They had stolen goods, some of which they sold to us.
Q: Did you know about the stolen banknotes found in your possession?
A: I accidentally acquired some banknotes while among travelers. I didn't attempt to exchange them.
Q: What about the banknotes found with your daughter-in-law?
A: I was unaware of any banknotes hidden among her belongings.
Q: Who gave you those banknotes?
A: A man named Phules gave me some, but I can't recall the others' names—they were travelers from Monongahela.
Q: Do you have anything more to add?
A: No, my statement is complete.

What Made Him Tick?

Coates suggested that Mason weakened when he chose the life of crime and then showed a bunch of hypocrisy.[3] He spoke out publicly against tyranny and persecution but became a welcher (someone who tricks you by not repaying a debt or wage) and double-crosser once arrested. In Mason's trials, he proclaimed his innocence in a way that made some think he believed it. Coates noted that Mason's last remark before his trial, after drinking his share of whiskey, was that he was one of the boldest soldiers in the Revolutionary War who became a great robber and kidnapper.

Rothert identified Mason as a black sheep while noting how patriotic and influential his brothers were. To explain the contradiction, Rothert pointed out that the Mason brothers were a product of their environment, each in a different way. He noted that after fighting for the freedom of his country, Sam began a wild and free career that was unrestrained by either human or divine law.

Roxby found American Wild West historian Paul Wellman called Mason the first real genius of outlawry on the frontier. John James Audubon wrote of Mason in 1815:

> The name of Mason is still familiar to many of the lower Ohio and Mississippi navigators. By dint of industry in bad deeds, he became a notorious horse stealer, forming a line of worthless associates from the eastern part of Virginia (a state celebrated for its fine breed of horses) to New Orleans.[4]

Roxby explained that if the modern reader cannot conceive of just how dangerous a menace Mason was during his lifetime, perhaps a comparison to more modern criminals would help put it into perspective.[5] Even his New York Mafia contemporaries considered Al Capone a mad-dog killer. That's quite a testimony coming from the folks who ran an organization called "Murder Inc." Capone's score of eight victims killed in the St. Valentine's Day Massacre still stands as a modern record. With the Mason gang's murders of entire families and boat crews, Roxby thought Mason's victims must have numbered well over 100, and no outlaw of the American Wild West approached those numbers.[6] The country has never produced another criminal of Mason's stature, and no past or present-era outlaw ever came close to running such a bloody tally.[7]

Mason and Capone offer two contrasting but insightful examples of criminal leadership in American history. Both men led violent criminal organizations, though they operated in very different eras, with different societal and legal structures, impacting their communities and commerce in significant ways. The majority of Mason's criminal career spanned from the 1790s until his capture and death in 1803. During most of that time, he was in his fifties, having begun his activities relatively late in life compared to modern criminals. Mason led a gang of river pirates that preyed upon travelers and merchants along the Ohio and Mississippi Rivers. His crimes included robbery, smuggling, and murder. Operating during the early years of the United States, Mason exploited the lack of organized law enforcement in the frontier regions, terrorizing a sparse and vulnerable population. His gang's actions had a direct and significant impact on interstate commerce, as they targeted riverboats and trade routes that were vital for moving goods through the interior of the country. The disruption caused by Mason's gang threatened the growth of the new nation's economy, particularly in the Mississippi River Valley, which was a critical commercial artery for westward expansion.

In contrast, Capone's reign lasted from the early 1920s until his imprisonment in 1931. Capone, much younger than Mason when he rose to prominence, was only in his mid-twenties when he took over the Chicago Outfit, leading a vast criminal enterprise built on illegal alcohol distribution during Prohibition. Capone's crimes ranged from bootlegging to gambling, prostitution, bribery, and murder. Like Mason, Capone used violence strategically, eliminating rivals and enforcing his control over the illegal liquor trade. However, Capone operated in a far more structured and industrialized society, where the consequences of his actions reverberated throughout the city of Chicago and beyond. His control over the illegal alcohol market had a significant impact on interstate commerce, as he monopolized the supply chain for bootleg liquor, affecting businesses across state lines and undermining legal commerce.

Both men led their gangs during periods of rapid change in the United States, but their impacts were felt in different ways. Mason's gang primarily terrorized rural, frontier communities, where the loss of goods or life had an outsized impact due to the fragility of settlement economies. His activities directly affected the early infrastructure of the United States, disrupting the movement of goods and people along critical trade routes. Capone's operations, on the other hand, disrupted urban centers and had a much larger national impact, particularly in terms of interstate commerce and law enforcement. His bootlegging network extended across state lines, corrupting officials and destabilizing the legal market for alcohol. The violence Capone brought to Chicago, epitomized by events like the St. Valentine's Day Massacre, further undermined public confidence in law enforcement and governance.

While both Mason and Capone operated for roughly a decade at the height of their powers, the scale of their influence reflected the United States' growth. Mason's crimes were localized but significant in the context of a fledgling country still establishing its commercial and legal framework. Capone, operating in a more industrialized and interconnected America, had a much broader reach, influencing not only Chicago but also national markets and even federal law enforcement policy. Each man, in his time, disrupted the flow of commerce, terrorized his community, and challenged the capacity of the state to control organized crime. However, the intensity of their influence must be viewed within the context of the society in which they operated: Mason as a pioneer of frontier lawlessness and Capone as the symbol of organized crime in an urbanized, modern America.

Finding Sam Mason

Let's face it: Samuel Mason wasn't exactly born with a pirate's hat on his head, but something led him down that notorious path. He started life as the son of law-abiding English citizens in an established colony that England proudly claimed as its own. Mason grew up in Virginia, a place well-known for its historical significance, but as with many things in Sam's life, even the details of his birthplace are up for debate. But here's the real question, the one that makes historians and Mason's descendants alike scratch their heads:

How did Sam Mason, who grew up in a family full of law-abiding folks, end up as a river pirate?

Modern researchers would likely throw a bunch of theories at the wall to see what sticks—each one trying to explain his behavior through the lenses of history, law, and socio-economic realities. Today, we'd probably call piracy organized crime, a term that conjures images of violent, illegal activities stretching across borders. And pirates like Sam? Well, they were a real threat to the growing trade along the rivers, where merchants risked not only their goods but sometimes their lives.

But back to the big question: What was it about Sam's life that led him astray, especially when the rest of his family stayed on the straight and narrow? There are a few select theories we should consider, each offering a different perspective on how a Revolutionary War captain became a notorious river pirate.

One theory is Social Disorganization Theory, which blames weak social institutions and a lack of community cohesion for the rise of crime. Out on the Ohio and Mississippi Rivers, settlements were tiny and isolated, and law enforcement was practically non-existent. So, it's no wonder that river pirates could operate without much fear of being caught. In a place where there's no one to stop you, why wouldn't crime take root?

Then there's Cultural Deviance, which basically says that people like Sam get mixed up in criminal behavior because they're in an environment where crime is the norm. On the frontier, where the rules were a little more . . . let's say, flexible, Sam might have found himself in a subculture where violence and theft weren't just acceptable—they were survival strategies. Life out there was hard, and for someone like Mason, crime could have seemed like a logical, even reasonable, way to get by. After all, why struggle through back-breaking labor when you could make a quick buck robbing boats and travelers?

And there's Life Course Theory, which takes a longer look at things—asking how key moments in a person's life shape their choices. For Mason, his time fighting in the French and Indian War and the American Revolution likely exposed him to violence and hardship in ways that would forever alter his view of the world. Once the wars were over, the wild frontier offered little in the way of opportunity for a man like him, and so his descent into crime seemed almost inevitable. With each passing year, as the frontier got wilder and opportunities fewer, Sam's criminal behavior escalated.

But here's the twist in Sam's tale: while he embraced a life of piracy, the rest of his family did not. His brothers, Thomas and Joseph, fought alongside Colonel Clark in the Illinois campaign of 1778, trying to secure the territory from the British. Sam's sister married a Methodist preacher, John Fell, while his brother Isaac made a fortune in the iron industry and rubbed shoulders with Pennsylvania's wealthiest families, working with Ben Franklin on the Supreme Executive Council of Pennsylvania. Quite a contrast, right? So, why did Sam's path veer so wildly from theirs?

Life Course Theory tells us that life is full of turning points—moments that can change the trajectory of someone's future. But for Sam, the frontier didn't offer many positive turning points. Instead, it offered more hardship, more lawlessness, and fewer chances for redemption. As the years went by, Sam's criminal activities only intensified, reflecting not just his personal choices but also the increasingly violent world he inhabited.

At the end of the day, understanding Sam Mason means accepting that no single theory can fully explain why he chose the life he did. Sure, criminological theories offer some pretty good insights, but let's not pretend we can tie it all up with a neat little bow. People are complex—Sam was no exception. His story reminds us that human behavior is anything but simple, and maybe that's the point. Trying to explain Sam Mason with a single theory? Well, that would be oversimplifying things, and Sam never seemed like the kind of guy you could explain away easily.

Sam Mason was the first Military-Trained Gang Member (MTGM) identified in the United States. MTGMs, quite simply, are gang members with military training.[8] Just after the Second World War, members of several outlaw motorcycle gangs demonstrated the similarity of attraction for the military and a criminal organization built on solid and trustworthy friendships and common criminal goals. Although it would not be difficult to contrast contemporary policing and government leadership with those in the eighteenth century, that exercise is unnecessary. Many contemporary government leaders, including police, have been shocked when organized crime leaders with military connections or experience are identified. Said another way, "regular" MTGMs surprise people today when they are identified, so why would it have been difficult in Mason's time to convince folks he was a typical, law-abiding citizen?

But what could make such a man turn to a full-time life of crime as he reached middle age? One of my reviewers suggested consideration of the phrase: "One man's pirate is another man's entrepreneur." That expressed the philosophical fact that Sam Mason may have felt that fighting for America and "Its" interests and fighting for himself and "his" interests were morally identical. Or at least, in his world of the frontier, there was little difference. We know that many of the *Founding Fathers* accumulated land and other personal wealth while building the new country. Many received land grants for their service in the military or purchased large tracts of land in western territories. They often relied on enslaved labor to make those lands productive, especially in the South, where large plantations were common. How is that different from the way Mason made a living? Mason wasn't just a pirate; he was a product of a country still figuring out its own identity.

Wherever we went on our investigative travels, whether to historic sites or places of interest nearby, almost everyone we talked to expressed a genuine interest in the book. It was funny how folks felt they instantly knew what I was writing about when I told them the book was about a Revolutionary War captain who became a river pirate. But when I expounded on the geography in which he operated or the age he was when he started the full-time crime spree, it felt like they kept being shocked and amazed, as I was and have been while learning more about this rather intriguing man. Sam Mason, a criminal mastermind, was someone who, despite his dark inclinations, possessed a complexity of character that was not easily understood.

Maybe it was my passion for research and investigation or my vivid imagination. He was, after all, a criminal. In all these activities, I learned a lot about Mason, his environment, and his society. But I never found *him*. Despite all the investigative hours spent, passionate research, and coordination, I failed at what I set out to do: *Find Sam Mason*.

Let's Look Deeper

Could Sam represent more than the simplicity of a man who lived in a specific time? Is it possible that he represented the evil in the world and was tapping into the power ascribed to that supernatural force? Perhaps, but I (again) have a different theory, and not one that is academic.

In many religious contexts, sin is seen as a moral failing or a deliberate transgression of divine law, creating a separation between individuals and God. That separation prevents individuals from thoroughly enjoying God's favor and blessings. Similarly, self-sabotage, the behaviors and thought patterns that undermine one's success and well-being, can prevent individuals from achieving their full potential and experiencing personal fulfillment if they don't have an understanding from a religious or faith perspective. But stay with me. This is critical.

When we sin, we often act against our own best interests and the values we hold dear. Sin can lead to feelings of guilt, shame, and unworthiness, as it creates an emotional and spiritual barrier between us and God. That barrier can be likened to self-sabotage, where negative actions and thoughts interfere with our goals and happiness. Both sin and self-sabotage involve a departure from a path that leads to fulfillment and favor, whether divine or personal.

Consider how self-sabotage works: an individual might procrastinate, engage in negative self-talk, or avoid opportunities out of fear of failure or a belief that they are undeserving of success. Underlying insecurities and unresolved emotional issues often drive these actions. Similarly, sin can stem from deeper spiritual and moral conflicts, leading to actions that distance us from God's favor. In both cases, the result is a cycle of negative behavior that perpetuates a sense of failure and separation.

Individuals must first recognize the behaviors and patterns holding them back to break free from self-sabotage. That involves self-reflection, seeking guidance, and consciously trying to change. In a religious context, overcoming sin requires repentance, seeking forgiveness, and striving to align one's actions with divine will. Both processes require a commitment to personal growth and a desire to restore a positive relationship with oneself and God in the case of sin.

Addressing the root causes of sin and self-sabotage allows individuals to begin healing and moving forward. The healing process opens the door to experiencing God's favor and personal success. It involves nurturing positive habits, building self-esteem, and developing a sense of worthiness. In spiritual terms, it means embracing God's love and grace, which are always available but often obscured by our actions and attitudes.

Sin and self-sabotage keep us from enjoying favor and success by creating barriers rooted in negative behaviors and thoughts. Overcoming these obstacles requires self-awareness, a willingness to change, and a commitment to personal and spiritual growth. Doing so can restore our connection to God's favor and unlock our potential for success and fulfillment. And this is why it is important to consider all of this.

What if Sam represents each of us at some level? What if finding Sam meant seeing the paradoxical potential we each have to live a respectable and detestable life simultaneously? A sort of "there but for the grace of God, go I" revelation is what I am suggesting. Humans can have a wide spectrum of unexplainable behaviors. How often have you been genuinely shocked by the behavior of our fellow humans? Could we each possess something that would push us over the edge if the circumstances, environment, and timing were right?

What should we call it? How could we identify it? How would we contain it? Is there any hope in making sure we don't take some and pass it on? I think we each make that sort of decision, often daily. All of us have the potential to lead honorable lives in service to our country and community. We can also decide that laws and moral codes don't apply to us in certain situations, especially when the folks tasked with enforcing the law are absent or not paying attention.

As I learned more about Sam's life, applying my imagination generously, I found several instances where I felt it wouldn't be too difficult to live as Sam did. There were many times when, like leaders and members of organized crime groups today, Sam demonstrated humanity, leadership, and many other honorable qualities despite his bad deeds. I think we are all a bit like that.

He told folks he wasn't beyond stealing but didn't kill anyone just for the sake of killing. That told me he had a moral compass or at least knew he should have one. Perhaps he was trying to avoid having a bad reputation, or maybe he was trying to justify his bad behavior. Does anyone you know do that?

Do we know what it takes to avoid going down the wrong path? Do we know what it takes to lead others, including family members, in such a way that they become productive members of a civilized society? Perhaps, but to what extent do the actions of dishonorable people influence us, maybe even our peers, neighbors, or government leaders?

We need to learn from others' mistakes, lift each other up, and strive daily to be the best we can be for others, ourselves, and the God we serve. Do you believe in a higher power but are confused about which religion or God to follow? Ask them all to speak to you about what is on your heart. Follow the one who answers you!

I think many of us will have questions for God (or whomever we see the second our life ends).[9] That's the problem I have with the process, though. We need to make decisions now that will determine where we go next after this life ends, and our destination will answer many of those questions.[10] Decisions about our destiny are more impactful than where to send our kids to kindergarten, whether to move for a career, or what organization to join. They are about where we will spend the rest of eternity, which promises to be a lot longer than the relative handful of decades we spend on Earth. If I am right, it's not something we can wait to discuss until after the bell rings, the whistle blows, or the trumpet sounds.[11]

Said another way, living in a manner that benefits others and leaves a legacy for future generations involves a balance of personal integrity, service, and foresight. We must start by living purposefully and aligning our actions with admirable values like compassion, honesty, and responsibility, no matter what others do. We must prioritize helping people through acts of kindness, mentorship, or community service, focusing on how our skills and resources can improve the lives of those around us. We should contribute to causes that matter, aiming to create positive change that outlasts our lifetime. If we invest time in building solid relationships and uplifting others, those connections can form the foundation of a legacy. By striving to make a positive difference, we create a ripple effect, inspiring future generations to continue our work and remember our impact.

I think we found Sam Mason. He is the opposite of all that. He failed the greatest test of his life and left a legacy of sin, self-sabotage, and worship of the world.

Don't be Sam Mason.

APPENDIX A

INVESTIGATIVE TEAM TRAVELING AND TASTING NOTES

Map with locations from Virginia to Louisiana. Sketched by Rotna, with Fiverr.

Cities included:
Winchester, Virginia; Pittsburgh, Pennsylvania; Wheeling, West Virginia; Marietta, Ohio; Kingsport, Tennessee; Knoxville, Tennessee; Henderson, Kentucky; Russellville, Kentucky; Wolf Island, Kentucky; Cave-In-Rock, Illinois; Metropolis, Illinois; Cairo, Illinois; Cape Girardeau, Missouri; New Madrid, Missouri; Caruthersville, Missouri; Memphis, Tennessee; Vicksburg, Mississippi; Natchez, Mississippi; New Orleans, Louisiana; Nashville, Tennessee

Writing the Book

I launched *From Patriot to Pirate* while writing another Rowman & Littlefield (Bloomsbury) book, *Gangs and the Military: Gangsters, Bikers, and Terrorists with Military Training*. Mason was identified as the first military-trained gang member from a referenced book by Asbury written over 100 years prior. Many historical references addressed Mason as one of many River Pirates, Outlaws, Banditti, or Highwaymen. However, none had focused exclusively on this intriguing historical character. The interest I had in the topic and the relatively limited coverage was overwhelming.

Mason's trial in New Madrid was well documented, with over 100 handwritten pages of transcripts containing interviews, inventories, and observations. Until recently, the transcripts were difficult for contemporary researchers to access due to the fragility of the paper on which both the original transcripts (in French) and the English translation were recorded. We located a decades-old photocopy of the translation and digitally converted it to a typed (and searchable) manuscript. I made many site visits to Mason's haunts and documented what I found to provide current perspectives on his past criminal activities. Many of the period's architecture, weapons, tools, and other materials have been and will continue to be identified and photographed.

I used artificial intelligence (AI) as an assistant in a few areas. I believe AI is best used as an assistant rather than a partner, much like a very capable graduate student or apprentice able to create something for the artist or author to work with and start from (like an outline), so the artist or author starts at a higher level than if they were creating something from nothing. That was done in some segments of the book (give me talking points on the geography of eastern Missouri or the population of the colonies in a certain year). It was invaluable in piecing together the broken and misspelled words from the transcripts and lightly contemporizing the interview language so we could all understand what was said. It was helpful for sampling the layout of the maps and a couple of the more intricate sketches. In all those instances, the finished work was fully that of the credited artist or author.

On-site Research

I had written a few books before and found having experience with the topic area helpful. While I had been studying Sam Mason and his activities for quite a while, I felt something was missing. Although I had located many references and read countless articles, I did not have the confidence that hands-on experience brings. I realized that on-site research would be helpful, and I began planning many of the visits detailed here. I added the travel and tasting notes so there would be another level of interest for those who, like me, weren't simply drawn to history because it was history. That way, you could invite a friend to your contemporary river pirate adventure, whether they have read the book or not (none of mine had until after I finished writing it).

We stayed in Airbnbs or BnBs when feasible. We planned locations to visit in advance, most related to the period in some way, using various travel sites, maps, and applications. We often sought out local wineries and restaurants with decent wine lists for our evening adventures. We did that because, well, we enjoy drinking wine, especially red wine, and I have found that restaurants that serve wine tend to focus more on quality food. We also did it because wine has a much broader history in America than most folks know, as you will see later in this file.

Travel Table

This travel table shows the main locations we visited, roughly in the order of the book. You can easily bunch them up by city or state for a one- to three-day trip or map out a region for a week or so. Between the map, the timeline, and the tasting notes, you should be able to plan multiple trips—both long and short. Imagine organizing a bus tour, caravan, or motorcycle ride to each of the places here. I know we plan to visit the places we hadn't gotten to by the time the book was printed and visit many of these places again. Contact us on social media to share your photos as we have ours. We would love to see where you have been and what you see that we were unable to. Bonus points if you do it wearing some variation of pirate garb (see the photo of the pillory)!

Check off the locations on the map as you visit, and post pics on social media (especially Instagram, Facebook, TikTok, and X). Tag us and use #piratesammason and #huntingsam. You'll find more info at www.piratesammason.com.

State	City	Visited	Notes
New York	Fort Niagara	2024	Viewed from across river
Pennsylvania	Pittsburgh	2024	Fort Pitt, Museums, View of River
West Virginia	Wheeling	2024	Fort Henry, library, sites
West Virginia	Fairmont	2024	Pricketts Fort
Virginia	Wytheville	2024	1776 Restaurant
Tennessee	Elizabethton	2024	Rocky Mount and Sycamore Shoals
Tennessee	Kingsport	2024	Netherland Inn
Tennessee	Knoxville	2018	James White Fort
Tennessee	Castalian Springs	2024	Cragfont
Tennessee	Castalian Springs	2024	Bledsoe's Fort
Tennessee	Russellville	2024	Bibb House
Kentucky	Russellville	2024	Logan County Courthouse
Kentucky	Henderson	2017	Park, River, Downtown
Illinois	Cave-In-Rock	2017	Cave-In-Rock, View of River
Illinois	Metropolis	2017, 2023	Downtown and Fort Massac
Kentucky	Paducah	2017, 2023	View of River and Fort Massac
Illinois	Cairo	2023	Fort Defiance
Missouri	Cape Girardeau	2023	Museums, Parks, View of River
Missouri	New Madrid	2023	Museum
Kentucky	Wolf Island	2023	Unable to access
Missouri	Caruthersville	2023	Cemetery, View of River
Tennessee	Mud Island	2023	Unable to access
Tennessee	Duck River	2024	Gordon House/Duck River Ferry
Mississippi	Natchez	2018	Start of Trace, Kings Tavern
Louisiana	New Orleans	2018, 2024	Jackson Square, Cabildo, others

If you are interested in having your own adventures by visiting the spots that we (and Mason) visited, here are extended travel notes to get you started. We tried to see all the significant locations and have fun in the process. I recruited my *favorite*

APPENDIX A

friends and family members to serve on the investigative team. The site-visit team included, in alphabetical order, Donna, Joe, Kim, Liam, Lucian, Paul, and Sharmyn. We enjoyed walking through history and visiting current sites with a unique, conversation-worthy backstory, followed by some (usually) excellent food and drink.

Additional Travel and Tasting Notes (by Location)

Niagara, Ontario

Fort Niagara, New York

Fort Niagara, where the peace treaty that stabilized the region was agreed upon in July 1764, was initially built by the French in 1678 as "Le Magazin Royal," a small trading post that was later expanded into a fort. The fort, on Lake Ontario where it meets the Niagara River, was intended to protect French interests in the New World. In 1759, during the French and Indian War, the fort fell into British hands after a nineteen-day siege. The British held control over Fort Niagara throughout the American Revolutionary War. Today, Old Fort Niagara is open to the public.[1] A Coast Guard Station is also located there. There is a beautiful view of the fort from Niagara-on-the-Lake, in Ontario, Canada.

Prince of Wales Restaurant, Niagara-on-the-Lake

The Prince of Wales Noble Restaurant offers a downtown dining experience with intricate brickwork, antique furnishings, and crystal chandeliers. The menu blends classic British and contemporary cuisine, using locally sourced ingredients. Dining there is an experience enriched by impeccable service from staff in period attire, a serene atmosphere with live piano music, and an ambiance that evokes a sense of regal sophistication. We thoroughly enjoyed the service, ambiance, food, and wine list, and found an excellent wine from the Organized Crime Winery to fit the trip's theme.

Organized Crime Winery, Beamsville Bench

The Organized Crime Winery, not far from Lake Ontario, derived its unique name from a quirky piece of local history. In the early 1900s, a feud between two Mennonite churches led to a dramatic, covert relocation of a pipe organ—hence the moniker "*Organ*ized Crime." The narrative lends the winery a distinctive character that sets it apart from others in the region. The winery produces small-batch, high-quality wines that reflect the unique terroir of the Niagara

Escarpment. At the Noble Restaurant, we were introduced to *Pipe Down*, an excellent Bordeaux-style blend, but we learned about *Download*, a higher-end blend, when we visited the winery.

Pennsylvania

Fort Pitt Museum, Pittsburgh

The Fort Pitt Museum is a two-floor museum where Fort Pitt once stood. The museum also has detailed models of Fort Pitt and Fort Duquesne, the earlier French fort it replaced. The museum thoroughly explores western Pennsylvania's role in the French and Indian War and the American Revolution. We learned about the construction and history of Fort Pitt and the strategic importance of the fort and the region in colonial North American campaigns.

Fort Pitt Blockhouse, Pittsburgh

The Fort Pitt Blockhouse, built in 1764, is the oldest architectural landmark in Pittsburgh and the only remaining part of Fort Pitt. Originally constructed as a defensive redoubt (a fortified base for a few soldiers), the Blockhouse was used as a defensive position to protect the fort from attacks by Indian tribes and French forces. Over the centuries, it has served various roles, from a military fortification to a private residence and later as a trading post.

Heinz History Center, Pittsburgh

The Heinz History Center featured exhibits that delve into various aspects of American history, including the Revolutionary War. We saw the exhibit "Pittsburgh's Role in the American Revolution," which included various artifacts, interactive displays, and detailed narratives. Additionally, the exhibit provided insights into the daily lives of those living in and around Pittsburgh during the late eighteenth century, including European settlers and Indian tribes. There was a lot about the frontier conflicts of the period, as well as more current topics of interest.

West Virginia

Fort Henry Marker, Wheeling

The Fort Henry marker is near the intersection of 11th and Main Streets downtown, close to the Ohio River. It marks the site of Fort Henry, which played a significant role in the American frontier during the late eighteenth century.

APPENDIX A

The Betty Zane Monument, Wheeling

The Betty Zane Monument commemorates Elizabeth "Betty" Zane's heroic actions. It is situated near the site of the original Fort Henry and serves as a tribute to Zane's bravery and determination. Her story has become a symbol of courage and resilience in American folklore.

Zane's Blockhouse, Wheeling

Zane's Blockhouse, also known as the Fort Henry Blockhouse, was part of Fort Henry, initially built in the 1760s by Ebenezer Zane. Today, the site of Zane's Blockhouse is marked and remembered as part of the area's rich colonial and revolutionary heritage.

Zane's Log Cabin, Wheeling

Generally considered the first building in Wheeling, the cabin was thought to be built in 1769 by Ebenezer Zane. The cabin, previously located on Market Alley, between Main and Market Streets, was demolished on July 14, 1908. The property owner stored away the logs and many relics when the workmen excavated the foundations.[2]

Zane's Island, Wheeling

Zane's Island, commonly known today as Wheeling Island, is surrounded by the Ohio River and within the city limits of Wheeling, West Virginia. The island holds significant historical importance and is named after the Zane family, including brothers Ebenezer, Silas, and Jonathan, as well as their sister Elizabeth, who were instrumental in the establishment of Wheeling. Today, Wheeling Island hosts the Wheeling Island Hotel-Casino-Racetrack.

The island also has a large residential community with various housing options, including the historic (though not colonial era) house we stayed in, overlooking the river and downtown Wheeling (and the former site of Fort Henry) from the west. Being an island, it is susceptible to flooding, which has historically impacted its development and the lifestyle of its residents. It was also susceptible to a thick fog, like that described as a de facto defensive strategy for Fort Henry, and we were able to enjoy that connection to history, as well, during our springtime visit.

McCulloch's Leap Marker, Wheeling

The McCulloch's Leap marker commemorates the daring escape by Major Samuel McCulloch during the American Revolutionary War. The marker was the only indication of the historic event but take the time to read more about it above.

Madonna of the Trail, Wheeling

The Madonna of the Trail is a series of twelve identical monuments dedicated to the spirit and courage of pioneer women in the United States. The statues span twelve states on the National Old Trails Road, commemorating the historic route taken by settlers moving west. The monuments depict a pioneer woman clasping a baby with one hand while gripping a rifle with the other, a vivid symbol of tenderness and strength.

Ohio County Public Library, Wheeling

The Ohio County Public Library has a comprehensive collection of books and other resources, including an online database, demonstrating its commitment to preserving local history. The library has significant archives that contain documents, photographs, and other materials related to the history of Wheeling and the surrounding areas. The collections are invaluable for historians, genealogists, and anyone interested in the region's heritage, and the staff was extremely helpful.

Good Mansion Wines, Wheeling

Good Mansion Wines is set in a beautifully restored mansion. It is a unique spot for those looking to enhance their gourmet/culinary horizons or just for a rare bottle of wine, artisanal bread, or high-quality olive oils. We enjoyed their excellent selection of new and old-world wines and their variety of olive oil and balsamic vinegar.

Figaretti's Restaurant, Wheeling

Figaretti's Restaurant is known for its traditional Italian cuisine. The atmosphere was warm and inviting, and the menu was well complemented by the beverage menu, including the wine list. We ate there the first night we were in Wheeling and had a great meal.

Elle & Jack's, Wheeling

Elle & Jack's is a contemporary American restaurant with a menu emphasizing fresh, locally sourced ingredients and sophisticated flavors. The restaurant is known for its inventive desserts, phenomenal wine list, and selection of craft cocktails. The ambiance is stylish yet comfortable, and the service is attentive and professional. We enjoyed a nice dinner.

APPENDIX A

Generations Pub, Wheeling

Generations Pub is a popular local restaurant and bar on the National Road in Wheeling. We visited for lunch after scouting where Mason's Tavern had been located a few feet away. The pub had many choices on its lunch menu and wonderful service. No one who worked at the pub was aware of the location's historical connection to Mason's Tavern.

Later Alligator, Wheeling

Later Alligator is a restaurant and bistro in the historic Centre Market district. The interior has an array of alligator-themed art and a cozy, inviting ambiance. We enjoyed dinner outside (in springtime). We had a wonderful conversation with the bartender after ordering a delicious (and price-conscious) wine called Illusion, which was half price the night we visited. Unlike many restaurants we have been to, they have a cellar where they keep their wine at—brace yourself—cellar temperature. For the uninformed, that's the temperature at which wine should be stored and served. *Not room temperature!*

Pricketts Fort State Park, Fairmont

Pricketts Fort State Park is south of Wheeling, near the confluence of Prickett's Creek and the Monongahela River. Today's Prickett's Fort, built initially when Fort Henry was built in 1774, is not a replica of the original structure but is based on typical frontier fort designs from that era. It includes over a dozen log structures, including a blacksmith shop, a meeting house, and several cabins that house various artisans demonstrating traditional crafts. We browsed the library, looked around the fort, and acquired several historical manuscripts that you will find in the notes at the end of the book. We particularly enjoyed seeing a sectioned-off vegetable and herb garden just outside the fort's walls.

Virginia

Washington's Office Museum, Frederick County (Including Winchester)

Washington's Office Museum offers visitors a unique glimpse into the early military career of George Washington, long before he became the first president of the United States. Situated in the heart of Winchester, the stone building served as Washington's military headquarters from 1755 to 1756, during the French and Indian War. Visitors can explore a collection of artifacts, including maps, weapons, and personal items. One of the highlights of the museum is a carefully preserved map of the region, annotated by Washington himself, which reveals his detailed knowledge of the rugged frontier terrain.

Abram's Delight, Frederick County (Including Winchester)

Abram's Delight is the oldest house in the area and a treasured symbol of the region's early settlement history. In 1728, Abraham Hollingsworth, a Quaker, acquired 582 acres where the house now stands, and his family became one of the most prominent in the region. The name "Abram's Delight" is a testament to the satisfaction Hollingsworth found in the fertile land along the Opequon Creek. Built in 1754 from local limestone, the home was designed to withstand the challenges of frontier life while providing a comfortable living space when the Shenandoah Valley was on the edge of the American frontier.

The Log House 1776 Restaurant, Wytheville

The Log House 1776 Restaurant offers a unique historical dining experience. The restaurant is in a log house built in 1776 and focuses on dishes found on the tables of early American settlers. Dining there was an experience that combined history with the pleasure of good food. We stopped there on our way from West Virginia to East Tennessee.

The Bolling Wilson Hotel, Wytheville

The Bolling Wilson Hotel is a boutique hotel that uniquely blends historic charm and modern luxury. Named after Edith Bolling Wilson, the second wife of President Woodrow Wilson, each floor features a theme related to different aspects of Edith Bolling Wilson's life, including her time in the White House, her love for orchids, and her Appalachian heritage.[3] We enjoyed the affordable upscale accommodations, fine dining at the on-site restaurant, the wonderfully friendly bar just off the lobby, and a visit, despite the rain, to the otherwise unoccupied rooftop terrace with stunning views of the surrounding mountains and downtown Wytheville. We stayed there overnight on our way from West Virginia to East Tennessee.

Tennessee

Sycamore Shoals State Historic Park, Elizabethton

Sycamore Shoals had a role in two major historical events: the Transylvania Purchase and the gathering of the Overmountain Men before the Battle of Kings

Mountain during the American Revolutionary War. The Transylvania Purchase (1775) was the largest private real estate transaction on the American continent, where Judge Richard Henderson of the Transylvania Company negotiated with Cherokee leaders to purchase over 20 million acres of land that now constitutes parts of Kentucky and Tennessee (more on him in chapter 6). The land deal was crucial in the westward expansion of the American frontier. Sycamore Shoals was also the muster ground for the Overmountain Men before the Battle of Kings Mountain. A replica of Fort Watauga offers a glimpse into eighteenth-century frontier life.

The Carter Mansion, Elizabethton

The Carter Mansion is one of the oldest houses in the state. Dating back to the 1770s, the mansion was constructed by John Carter and his son Landon Carter, prominent figures in early Tennessee history. Its unique architectural style was quite elaborate compared to the more common frontier log cabins of its time, with fine woodwork, detailed interior design, and a level of craftsmanship that indicated the wealth and status of the Carter family. Visiting the Carter Mansion, even when it wasn't open, provided a glimpse into the early history of Tennessee and the American frontier.

Rocky Mount State Historic Site & Museum, Piney Flats

Rocky Mount was known as the first territorial capital of the Southwest Territory before Tennessee became a state. Rocky Mount was the home of William Cobb, who hosted the territorial governor, William Blount, from 1790 to 1792. The site offers insights into the political and daily life of the settlers, highlighting the challenges and responsibilities of early American governance on the frontier.

Netherland Inn, Kingsport

The Netherland Inn originally served as both a boatyard and an inn during the early nineteenth century. Built around 1802, the Netherland Inn was the only place where a stage line, a boatyard, and an inn converged along the early frontier, making it a vital hub for travelers and commerce. The inn was strategically located on the Holston River, facilitating the transportation of salt and other goods. It became a stopping point for people traveling westward through the wilderness of Tennessee, offering a place for rest and replenishment. The inn's boatyard significantly contributed to the regional economy, mainly by building and launching flatboats loaded with produce and iron that would float downriver to Knoxville and sometimes even as far as New Orleans. Along the river below the inn was a full-size model of a flatboat. Those vessels were used to transport large quantities of salt, iron ingots, animal skins, herbs such as ginseng, Plaster of Paris, and other items to Knoxville, Huntsville, St. Louis, Natchez, and New Orleans.

Knoxville

The investigative team traveled to Knoxville. We saw quite a few sites present during the period in which Mason operated, including the Tennessee River, one of the major waterways in the southeastern United States. The Tennessee originates near Knoxville, travels across eastern Tennessee, cuts south into northern Alabama, then reenters Tennessee to the west. It heads northwest, forming the boundary between Tennessee and Kentucky, and empties into the Ohio River at Paducah, Kentucky, over 300 miles northwest by the current roadway (not the river) from Knoxville.

James White Fort, Knoxville

James White moved to Tennessee in 1783 from North Carolina. Having served as a Captain in the Revolutionary War, he was given a land grant of 1,000 acres, and he built his two-story log house and the fort in 1786. Like other frontier forts, the fort initially functioned as a home and a defensive structure. The fort soon led to the establishment of a surrounding settlement, which rapidly grew into the town of Knoxville, named after Henry Knox, President Washington's War Secretary. White's leadership and the fort's strategic location played crucial roles in developing Knoxville as an essential regional trading and political center.[4]

Ramsey House, Knoxville

The Ramsey House was built in 1797 for Colonel Francis A. Ramsey. The Ramsey House is an example of early American architecture in the Georgian style. Built from pink Tennessee marble and blue limestone, the structure is elegant and robust, contrasting with the more utilitarian styles typical of frontier homes of that period. The house's estate includes several gardens and outbuildings, showcasing the economic activities vital to the survival and prosperity of such estates, including agriculture and animal husbandry.[5]

Memphis

Memphis was first known as Fort Assumption, a French fortification constructed in 1739 on the fourth Chickasaw Bluff on the Mississippi River by Jean-Baptiste

Le Moyne, Sieur de Bienville's French army. The area sits along the east bank of the Mississippi River, and the fort was used as a base against the Chickasaw in the abortive campaign of 1739. On April 3, 1790, a town at Chickasaw Bluffs was promoted with leases offered by John Rice, Esq. for purchases to families that arrived at the landing near the mouth of the Big Hatcha River. In 1796, the site that would become Memphis became the westernmost point of the newly admitted "state" of Tennessee in the newly independent United States. However, West Tennessee was then occupied and historically controlled by the Chickasaw tribe.

Mud Island, Memphis

While in town, we attempted to visit the Mississippi River Museum at Mud Island. The museum offered a wax sculpture of Mike Fink and David (Davy) Crockett, featured with Mason in the 1956 Walt Disney film *Davey Crockett and the River Pirates*. We noted the two were an unlikely historical pairing with Mason. Crockett was born on August 17, 1786, in East Tennessee. From 1798 (age twelve) to 1802 (age sixteen), Crockett worked or lived in Morristown, Tennessee, and Gerrardstown, West Virginia, with a couple of cattle drives into Virginia. As he was slightly older than Crockett, Mike Fink was more likely to have been a contemporary of or interacted with Mason, though that was still unlikely. Fink was born between 1770 and 1780 at Fort Pitt and served as an Indian scout in his teenage years at Fort Pitt. When the Indian wars of the region ended in the mid-1790s, Fink, like many other scouts, spurned a sedentary life as a farmer. Instead, he drifted into the Ohio and Mississippi Rivers transport business and earned a reputation as an excellent boatman. Crockett and Fink were well-known to be associates. Neither of the two men likely encountered Mason, who had left the Fort Pitt/Fort Henry area by 1785, and their interaction in the movie was fictional.

Flight Restaurant and Wine Bar, Memphis

We had dinner at Flight Restaurant and Wine Bar in Memphis, Tennessee. The restaurant featured American cuisine, focusing on local and seasonal ingredients. The menu was based on the "flight" concept—grouping-related dishes, wines, or spirits served in smaller portions. The atmosphere of Flight was upscale yet comfortable, and the interior was elegantly decorated. We thoroughly enjoyed our meal, the wine, and the hospitality from everyone who worked there.

Residence Inn Downtown Memphis

The Residence Inn was constructed in 1930, initially known as the William Len Hotel. The hotel retained many original Art Deco features, including ornate detailing and a distinctive façade. Its downtown location near Beale Street, the National Civil Rights Museum, the Mississippi River, and Flight Restaurant made it a convenient choice. The rooms were quiet, comfortable, and spacious.

Kentucky

Bibb House, Russellville

The Bibb House is an example of Federal-style architecture, popular in the United States from roughly 1780 to 1830. The style is characterized by its symmetry, classicizing ornament, and use of brick, reflecting the lifestyle and status of wealthy landowners in the early nineteenth century. Revolutionary War Major Richard Bibb, born in Virginia in 1752, came to Lexington, Kentucky, in 1798 and moved to Logan County the following year. Major Bibb's actions in freeing his slaves and providing for their welfare with his will were ahead of his time.[6]

Logan County Courthouse, Russellville

The Logan County Courthouse, built in the early 1900s, is an example of Classical Revival architecture, featuring grand columns, a prominent clock tower, and detailed ornamentation. The structure features grand architectural details such as a prominent dome, large columns, and symmetrical design elements. The building is constructed primarily from brick and stone, and its dome is visible from various points in the town, symbolizing the courthouse's central role in Logan County's history and governance.

Henderson

The investigative team traveled to Red Banks (Henderson), Kentucky. Early on, Henderson leveraged its riverfront location to flourish in trade and agriculture. Today, Henderson's economy has broadened to encompass manufacturing, healthcare, and various service industries. We visited an area on the Ohio River and explored the town. Not much was identified historically.

John James Audubon Museum, Henderson

The museum is dedicated to the life and work of John James Audubon, one of America's most renowned naturalists and wildlife artists. Audubon (1785–1851) was a French-American ornithologist, naturalist, and painter known for his extensive studies documenting all types of American birds and detailed illustrations depicting them in their natural habitats. The museum was established to honor Audubon's legacy and to preserve and showcase his work and life. It is housed in a building designed to reflect the period in which Audubon lived.

Farmer and Frenchman Winery, Henderson

The winery combines traditional farming and French winemaking elements, creating a unique destination that blends local agriculture and European flair. The winery features an on-site restaurant that offers a farm-to-table dining experience. The menu often includes locally sourced ingredients and French-inspired cuisine, complementing the wines produced at the vineyard.[7]

Paducah

Paducah is situated at the confluence of the Ohio and Tennessee Rivers and is very close to the Cumberland and Mississippi Rivers. Because of the central location and the number of towing and barge companies based here, Paducah is considered the *hub of the inland waterways*.[8]

Purple Toad Winery, Paducah

The founders started their venture into winemaking with a few experimental batches, earning a loyal following. The staff shares insights into the winemaking process and the stories behind each wine. One team member chose the parking lot to change clothes for our dinner engagement, adding to the memories of that trip.

Freight House Restaurant, Paducah

Housed in a renovated railroad freight depot, the restaurant was designed to merge historical charm with modern culinary innovation. Its menu respects traditional roots while embracing contemporary twists. The space has a warm, inviting atmosphere complemented by exposed brick walls and rustic decor that reflect the building's historic past. We enjoyed a lovely meal with excellent wine at a decent price. The restaurant provided a view of the Ohio River, though not from where we sat.

Wolf Island

No evidence of Mason was found in the area. Still, with a bit of imagination and a legitimate survey of the land, it was easy to imagine why he chose the location for a headquarters. We observed that the river flowed on both sides of the island, but the water levels were unusually low at the time, exposing significant portions of the river bottom. The Mississippi River experienced critically low levels in 2022 and remained low in 2023, even after periods of rainfall.[9]

Illinois

Cave-In-Rock

The investigative team visited Cave-In-Rock, Illinois, approaching it by water and land to gain a comprehensive perspective. Today, the area is part of Cave-In-Rock State Park, which spans about 204 acres. Known for its scenic views of the Ohio River, the park is popular for outdoor activities, including hiking, picnicking, fishing, and boating. We walked over, around, and through the cave, imagining the activities that took place many years before our arrival.

The team rented a pontoon boat from Golconda Marina for the water approach and traveled eastward toward the park. That route allowed us to experience the park as historic river travelers might have, encapsulating the anticipation and relief felt by weary voyagers as they navigated the river's bends and were greeted by the imposing but welcoming sight of the cave's opening. The dramatic entrance, set against the river backdrop, provided a vivid understanding of the historical and geographical significance of the location.

San Damiano Retreat

While in the area, we stayed at the San Damiano Retreat, not far from Golconda, Illinois. The cabins were roomy and clean, and the secluded natural surroundings created a peaceful atmosphere. A bonus was the beautiful overlook of the Ohio River, which showed the pronounced cliffs on the north side of the river with fireworks shortly after a beautiful view of the sunset.

Garden of the Gods

Garden of the Gods displayed natural sandstone sculptures that seem to defy gravity. The rocks have been shaped by centuries of wind and water, forming unique structures. A quarter-mile looping trail offers easy access and provides panoramic views of the forest and the wilderness beyond. As the sun rises and sets, the colors shift dramatically, highlighting the intricate details of the rock faces. The surrounding forest offers more rugged trails to explore further into the wilderness.

Golconda Restaurant

Though the restaurant's name escapes me, we stopped to eat in Golconda. At a nice little restaurant downtown near the square, as we were being seated, I saw an interesting sight that let me know I was in the right place. On the wall, I saw a painting of a pirate. Although it was a painting of a more traditional pirate, complete with a three-corner hat and eye patch, I was enthralled. I soon learned that most, if not every, school or community sports team in the county was called the Pirates. I would like to know if the students are taught why that is the case.

Metropolis

The Superman Statue is a proud symbol of the small city's claim to fame as the "Hometown of Superman." The impressive bronze statue of Superman, posed heroically with his hands on his hips and his cape flowing behind him, stands about 15 feet tall in the center of Superman Square. Nearby, the Super Museum offers an extensive collection of Superman memorabilia and history, adding depth to the visitor experience in Metropolis. We found no indication that Mason and the Man of Steel ever interacted, but there's no sense in visiting the Paducah area without seeing Superman. Had the two met, this book would likely never have been written.

Fort Massac, Metropolis

The investigative team explored Fort Massac, which commands a strategic position and an impressive view of the Ohio River. The site has a beautiful park atmosphere with many opportunities to learn and experience the historic surroundings. Additionally, the view of the Ohio River and the city of Paducah, Kentucky, across the river was impressive. In addition to the living quarters and community spaces, we saw a sectioned-off vegetable and herb garden outside the walls. Strangely, some seeds from very tasty tomatoes were found among our belongings after the trip. They were safely stored in our seed collection until they were planted the following spring.

Fort Defiance, Cairo

We traveled to Fort Defiance State Park, the southernmost tip of Illinois, bounded on either side by the Ohio (coming from the northeast) and the Mississippi (coming from the northwest) rivers. While researching the location, we learned the currents of the two rivers stay separate for about a mile down from where they meet. Bridges near the fort lead east to Kentucky over the Ohio River and west to Missouri over the Mississippi River, though the latter was closed for repairs.

Wagner advised that the Mississippi and Ohio converge farther south today than in 1800, and all the land where the Fort Defiance overlook was located was created by eroded soil washing down the Ohio and Mississippi Rivers. The original convergence and the actual Fort Defiance were located farther north near the southern end of Cairo (personal communication, M. Wagner, October 20, 2023).

Missouri

Cape Girardeau

The investigative team traveled to Cape Girardeau. Mason's daughter Elizabeth had moved there from northern Kentucky, near Red Banks and Diamond Island, presumably before Mason and the rest of the family moved to Cave-In-Rock. During his trial, Mason reported to the Spanish authorities that he believed his sister, Rachel, was also at Cape Girardeau. He described her as a "widow at first from a man by the name of Worthington and presently married to a man by the name of Thompson."[10] Cape Girardeau was named after Ensign Sieur Jean Baptiste de Girardot, who had been stationed at Kaskaskia in the Illinois Country of New France since the early eighteenth century. Cape Girardeau, chosen for its strategic position overlooking the Mississippi River, was originally a trading post founded in 1733 and attracted many trappers and river travelers. The settlement evolved as frontiersman Louis Lorimier arrived in 1793, under the commission of the Spanish governor general, to establish a military post to facilitate trade and relations with the local Native American populations. Lorimier, from his base at the "Red House," became the region's first goodwill ambassador. His welcoming nature was marked by encounters with notable figures such as Meriwether Lewis and William Clark in 1803 and Davy Crockett in 1834, who were seeking recruits for frontier service.

Red House Interpretive Center, Cape Girardeau

We visited the Red House Interpretive Center, which overlooked the banks of the Mississippi River, and saw an example of a trapper's outfit from the early 1800s. The Red House Interpretive Center demonstrated the early 1800s settlers' lifestyle in the area; a virtual copy of an actual trading post and the gardens on the north side of the house reproduce what gardens might have looked like a couple of hundred years ago. The man who was hosting the tour of the Red House was very interested in the period and very helpful during our visit. They had an impressive collection of herbs and vegetables during our fall visit.

Cape River Heritage Museum, Cape Girardeau

We visited the Cape River Heritage Museum, learned about the city's history since the 1800s, and saw a model of the typical frontiersman clothing. Housed in a historic firehouse dating back to 1908, the museum has various exhibits and artifacts that span the city's history from its founding to the present day. The museum's collections include items related to the maritime history of the river, the evolution of public safety, and various aspects of daily life that define the region's history.

Trail of Tears State Park, Cape Girardeau

Our exploration took us to the area around Trail of Tears State Park, located north of downtown Cape Girardeau, where Green's Ferry was believed to have operated in the late 1790s. Joseph Waller, who passed away in 1821, initiated the ferry service between 1797 and 1799 while Cape Girardeau was under Spanish control. Erosion along the Missouri shore and sediment buildup along the Illinois shore gradually moved the river away from the ferry's original location, eventually rendering it inoperable as it became landlocked. Despite those historical details, a report by the National Parks Service does not mention Green's Ferry's operation in the eighteenth century. The exact historical presence and operations of Green's Ferry, while rooted in documented licenses and operations, lack specific national historical recognition.[11]

Cape Rock Park, Cape Girardeau

Located in the northeast part of the City on North Cape Rock Drive, the park is 21.3 acres and offers a breathtaking view of the Mississippi River. It was the original trading post established by Ensign Girardot. The park is mainly undeveloped to promote the natural area on the property's west side.

36 Restaurant & Bar, Cape Girardeau

The 36 Restaurant & Bar provided an upscale atmosphere and a classic and contemporary American cuisine menu. The ambiance was elegant and refined, and the team members tried Bumbu Rum there for a pirate-themed toast. The label had a traditional pirate theme, with a *tarnished metal* X on the front label and a *map of the Caribbean on the* back.[12] Some of us detected a hint of bananas foster. There was a solid wine list, from which we sampled several excellent choices while we wandered around the spacious two-story building. They have a wonderful second-floor deck with a fabulous view of the Mississippi, which backlights well with the sunset (the restaurant is west of the river, so west is behind, toward the front door).

River Ridge Winery, Scott City

River Ridge Winery, located in a century-old farmhouse, offers a picturesque setting in the hills above the Mississippi River, off the beaten path in the woods, providing a tranquil and scenic escape. The setting and proximity to the Mississippi River made it a delightful destination where we enjoyed a nice casual lunch and a wine tasting afterward.

New Madrid Historical Museum

The New Madrid Historical Museum featured a variety of exhibits that explored the region's early history, including its Native American heritage, early European exploration and settlement, and the pivotal role of the Mississippi River in the town's development. Special attention was given to the earthquakes of 1811 and 1812, among the most powerful in US history. The museum hosted a collection of artifacts, including tools, clothing, and personal items from the colonial days when New Madrid was a Spanish possession, a French trading post, and into its American frontier period.

Little Prairie (Caruthersville)

The investigative team traveled to the Little Prairie section of the cemetery on Cemetery Road in Caruthersville, Missouri. Nothing related to Mason was identified, and there appeared to be little chance of that as the town was demolished by the same earthquakes that devastated New Madrid. The City of Caruthersville was incorporated on May 18, 1874. We were able to experience an uninhibited view of the Mississippi River from the park as a storm came down the river from the north.

Mississippi

Historic Linden Bed and Breakfast, Natchez

The Linden Bed and Breakfast is an antebellum home from the 1790s. The property spans seven acres and features beautiful gardens and majestic oak trees. The house is furnished with Federal-style antiques, and the front door was famously replicated in the design of Scarlett O'Hara's home, Tara, in the film *Gone with the Wind*. Linden is a sixth-generation family-owned home that offers a unique blend of historical authenticity and modern amenities. We stayed in one of the six renovated rooms.

Natchez Under the Hill

Natchez Under-the-Hill, located along the Mississippi River in Natchez, Mississippi, was known for its rowdy atmosphere, particularly during the eighteenth and nineteenth centuries. Despite its lawless reputation, it played a crucial role in the regional economy, facilitating the transport of critical commodities like cotton and timber. Today, it offers scenic riverfront walks and a glimpse into its colorful history, reflecting a mix of danger and opportunity that characterized American frontier life.

King's Tavern, Natchez

King's Tavern is a restaurant and bar renowned for its wood-fired pizzas and craft cocktails. The building has rustic wooden beams, original brickwork, and fireplaces that offer a cozy, inviting atmosphere. As we sat enjoying a meal, it was easy to imagine the hustle and bustle of the eighteenth-century tavern, the plotting river pirates, the secretive meetings, and the weary travelers grateful for a moment of rest in Natchez at the base of the overland Natchez Trace route. The bartender pointed out that the Natchez Trace began at the back door.

Natchez Trace Parkway

When we left King's Tavern, we traveled up the Natchez Trace. While it was not the precise route traveled in Mason's day, the Trace gives a perspective unavailable in other locations. The National Park Service maintains the Parkway and offers a scenic, recreational drive for road trips, cycling, and hiking, with numerous pull-offs, exhibits, and trails. The places worth stopping to explore include:

- Mount Locust Inn and Plantation Milepost 15.5: One of the oldest structures along the trace, Mount Locust dates to the late 1700s. It served as an inn for travelers and is a well-preserved example of early American frontier life.
- Sunken Trace Milepost 41.5: The deeply eroded section of the old trail vividly reminded us of the thousands of travelers returning north from selling goods in Natchez who once walked this path.
- Rocky Springs Milepost 54.8: Once a thriving town, Rocky Springs now offers a glimpse into the past with its remnants of a church, cemetery, and nature trails that tell the story of its rise and fall due to yellow fever and the Civil War.

French Camp Historic Village Milepost 180.7: The living history village includes a museum, log cabins, and a blacksmith shop, illustrating life in the early 1800s.

Colbert Ferry at milepost 327.3. An additional 20-minute stroll will take you along the Old Trace to the bluff overlook and back.[13]

Meriwether Lewis Death and Burial Site Milepost 385.9: The explorer of the Lewis and Clark Expedition died under mysterious circumstances in 1809 at an inn on the Natchez Trace. His grave and monument mark the spot where he died.

Gordon House and Duck River Ferry Site is on the Natchez Trace Parkway at milepost 407.7. Gordon's ferry crossed the Duck River for over 90 years until a bridge was opened in 1896.[14]

Louisiana

Jackson Square, New Orleans

Jackson Square, located in the heart of New Orleans' French Quarter, is a historic park that has been a central gathering place since the city's founding. Originally designed in 1721 as the Place d'Armes ("Place of Arms" in English) by French military engineer Adrien de Pauger, the square served as a parade ground and an open-air market. The square's name was changed to Jackson Square in 1856 to honor Andrew Jackson. In the nineteenth century, Jackson Square was the site of public executions and military drills, but it also served as a venue for celebrations and public gatherings. The square's lush gardens, well-manicured paths, and historical statues create a picturesque setting. Today it's filled with artists displaying their creations and musicians playing.

The Cabildo, New Orleans

The Cabildo, where Mason would have been tried, is on Jackson Square in the heart of the French Quarter. Constructed between 1795 and 1799, the architecture reflects the Spanish colonial style, with its elegant façade, thick walls, arched windows, and a central courtyard to accommodate the local climate. The Cabildo was also the site of the Louisiana Purchase transfer ceremonies.[15]

Christ Church, New Orleans

Christ Church, officially known as Christ Church Cathedral, is a testament to the city's rich historical and spiritual heritage. Founded in 1803 to establish a place of worship amid the predominantly Catholic French and Spanish colonial influences, it is the oldest Protestant Episcopal church in the territory. The first permanent church building was completed in 1816.

The Presbytère, New Orleans

The Presbytère, initially intended to house clergy, was designed by the same architect as the Cabildo and built from 1791 to 1813. Despite its initial purpose, the Presbytère never housed clergy but served various functions, including commercial space and a courthouse.

Madame John's Legacy, New Orleans

Madame John's Legacy, located in the historic French Quarter of New Orleans, was built in 1788 in the French colonial style with influences from the Caribbean and Mediterranean. The name comes from an 1874 short story in which the residence was referred to as the home of a character named Madame John. The house's history is even more intriguing, though, as it was built for Don Manuel de Lanzos, a Spanish military officer, on the site of an earlier French colonial home that burned down in the Great New Orleans Fire of 1788.

Lafitte's Blacksmith Shop, New Orleans

Lafitte's Blacksmith Shop, on the corner of Bourbon Street and St. Philip Street in the French Quarter of New Orleans, was constructed sometime between 1722 and 1732 and is reputed to be one of the oldest surviving structures in New Orleans and among the oldest buildings in the United States used as a bar. Lafitte's Blacksmith Shop's story was based on the notorious pirate and privateer Jean Lafitte, who operated primarily in the Gulf of Mexico not long after Mason. According to local legend, the bar was a front for Lafitte's smuggling operations.[16]

The Little House, Algiers (New Orleans)

The Little House in Algiers, New Orleans, is a historic cottage-style home in the Algiers Point neighborhood, a five-minute ferry ride across the Mississippi River from the busyness that is the French Quarter. Built in the late nineteenth century, the Creole cottage-style building is a wine bar and restaurant with a wonderful selection and knowledgeable staff. Algiers itself is one of New Orleans' oldest neighborhoods, known for its peaceful, village-like atmosphere and stunning views of the city skyline.

Alabama

La Fête Wine Bar, Birmingham

La Fête Wine Bar is a cozy, stylish wine bar and restaurant with an excellent selection of boutique wines. With a warm, intimate atmosphere, it was a wonderful place for our last supper before returning home. The staff was exceedingly helpful and welcoming, and the food was the best part of the trip.

Wine in America

Though we do not know if Mason or his associates drank wine, we do know that members of the investigative team did. And several of the founders of the United States were known to have a particular affection for wine. Notably:

1. Thomas Jefferson: Jefferson was perhaps the most famous wine connoisseur among the Founders. He developed a deep appreciation for wine during his time as the American minister to France. Jefferson's extensive wine cellar at Monticello included varieties from France, Italy, Spain, and Portugal. He was a firm believer in the virtues of wine and even attempted to cultivate European grapevines at his estate.
2. Benjamin Franklin: Franklin enjoyed wine and advocated for its moderate consumption. He is known for his humorous writings on the benefits of wine over other alcoholic beverages. Franklin also praised the health benefits of wine and included it in his famous list of thirteen virtues, emphasizing temperance.
3. George Washington: Washington was also an appreciator of wine. While not as deeply involved in the wine culture as Jefferson, he regularly enjoyed Madeira wine (more later) and other varieties. His estate at Mount Vernon had a wine cellar, and he frequently served wine to guests.
4. John Adams: Adams enjoyed wine, particularly Madeira, and included it in his daily routine, believing in its beneficial effects.

The first commercial winery in the United States was established in 1799 by Kentucky State Statute. "First Vineyard" operated until 1809. The founder, a Swiss immigrant by the name of John James Dufour, received monetary backing from stockholders (then called subscribers), including US Congressman and later Secretary of State Henry Clay, US secretary of the treasury George Bibb,

APPENDIX A

Kentucky governor Garrard, both US Senators John Brown and John Edwards, and the editor of the Lexington Gazette. Daniel Boone surveyed the property in Nicholasville, Kentucky, just 12 miles south of Lexington.

Today, wine is produced in all fifty states in the United States. While California is the most famous for its wine production, other states, such as Oregon, Washington, and New York, have also gained significant recognition for producing high-quality wines. These states are known for their unique climates and conditions that favor different grape varieties, contributing to their wine industry reputations. Tennessee, Virginia, and Missouri have also worked hard to attract loyal followings.

Madeira Wine

In the 1700s, Madeira wine (fortified Portuguese wine, somewhat like port) was popular because of its international origins (European goods were in high demand then). The unique creation process of Madeira allowed it to survive transatlantic trips easily and remain unspoiled for long periods after purchase. Madeira wine was diluted with "neutral grape spirits" and then packed at the bottom of ships. Transatlantic travel's "sweltering conditions" were integral to the Madeira creation process, as it required an oxidization process in high heat.

At the end of the 1700s, Madeira became more than just a symbol of transatlantic trade; it became a symbol of the American Revolution. Jefferson was introduced to it during his time in Europe and favored it for its durability and complex flavor. At his Virginia estate, Monticello, he stocked Madeira in his well-curated wine cellar and frequently served it at dinners and social events. As President, Jefferson also served Madeira at official functions, helping to popularize it among the American elite.

Madeira was one of the products that British authorities attempted to collect expensive import taxes on in 1768. When customs officials seized a ship packed with the wine, its owner, John Hancock, refused to pay. Colonists later burned the ship in an act of defiance. That incident, and several other events related to taxation, contributed to the sociopolitical upheaval in Boston surrounding the Stamp Act of 1765. The episode played a significant role in defining the twenty-seven colonial grievances clearly stated within the text of the Indictment of George III section of the United States Declaration of Independence, enabling the organized colonial resistance that led to the American Revolution in 1775.[17]

Revolutionary Herbs and Vegetables

The kitchen garden in Mason's time was a mix of practical and experimental cultivation. Herbs and vegetables were grown for sustenance and their ability to improve the flavor of the somewhat monotonous diet of the time. Culinary herbs like parsley, dill, and basil enhanced the taste of soups, stews, and roasts.

Vegetables were often preserved for winter through drying, pickling, and fermentation. Cabbage was commonly fermented into sauerkraut, while beans and peas were dried for long-term storage. That ensured a steady food supply even when fresh produce was not available. Thomas Jefferson, a prominent figure of the era, was an avid gardener who documented his extensive efforts to cultivate a wide range of vegetables at Monticello, his Virginia estate. His gardens included over 330 varieties of vegetables and herbs, highlighting the diversity and experimentation that characterized early American gardening.[18] In June 1777, General Orders for the army included this observation:

> As there is a plenty of common and French sorrel; lamb's quarters, and water cresses, growing about camp; and as these vegetables are very conducive to health, and tend to prevent the scurvy and all putrid disorders—The General recommends to the soldiers the constant use of them, as they make an agreeable sallad, and have the most salutary effect. The regimental officer of the day to send to gather them every morning, and have them distributed among the men.[19]

Colonial Recipes

If you are interested in more than just an imaginary tasting experience, we compiled several recipes used circa 1800 in the United States and before then in the colonies, many of which the Mason gang may have prepared and consumed. As you experiment, please share your results with us on social media. Photos and tips are appreciated! These recipes reflect the simplicity and resourcefulness of early American cooking, utilizing locally available ingredients and straightforward preparation methods. You will notice that none of the instructions include the words "preheat the oven to 350 degrees," or "melt the butter in the microwave."

Roasted Squash with Rosemary

Ingredients

One medium squash
A couple of spoonfuls of butter
A few sprigs of rosemary (dry or fresh can be used)
Salt to taste
Pepper, if you have it

Instructions

Preparation

Take your squash and peel it, then cut it into chunks.
Remove the seeds and the stringy parts.

Seasoning

Place the squash in a large bowl.
Melt the butter and pour it over the squash.
Strip the rosemary leaves from their stems and chop them finely. Add to the bowl.
Sprinkle with salt (and pepper, if you have it).
Toss the squash well so it is covered in butter and rosemary.

Cooking

Heat a large iron skillet over the hearth.
Once hot, place the squash in the skillet.
Cook the squash, turning occasionally, until tender and nicely browned. This should take about thirty to forty minutes.

Serving

Once the squash is done, remove it from the skillet and let it cool slightly.
Serve warm as a side dish.

Vegetable Soup

Ingredients

One quart of water
Two large carrots, sliced

Two parsnips, sliced
Two turnips, diced
One large onion, chopped
Two stalks of celery, chopped
One small cabbage, chopped
Two potatoes, diced
One tablespoon of butter
One teaspoon of salt
Half teaspoon of pepper
One teaspoon of thyme (dry or fresh can be used)
One teaspoon of parsley (dry or fresh can be used)
One bay leaf
Half teaspoon of marjoram (dry or fresh can be used)

Instructions

In a large pot, melt the butter over medium heat.
Add the chopped onion and cook until it becomes translucent.
Pour in the quart of water and bring it to a boil.
Add the carrots, parsnips, turnips, celery, cabbage, and potatoes to the pot.
Stir in the salt, pepper, thyme, parsley, bay leaf, and marjoram.
Reduce the heat to a simmer and cook for about thirty to forty minutes, or until the vegetables are tender.
Remove the bay leaf before serving.
Serve hot, accompanied by a loaf of bread if desired.

To Make Bread

Ingredients

One quart of fine wheat flour
One pint of warm water
Two large spoonfuls of molasses
One large spoonful of barm (yeast)
A pinch of salt

Method

Sift the flour into a large bowl. Warm the water until it is neither hot nor cold but in a temperate state.

APPENDIX A

Add the molasses to the water, stirring until well mixed. Then, stir in the barm until it is fully dissolved.

Make a well in the center of the flour and pour in the liquid mixture. Add a pinch of salt.

With a wooden spoon, draw the flour gradually into the liquid, working it into a smooth dough. Knead it well upon a floured board until it is elastic and smooth to the touch.

Cover the dough with a clean linen cloth and set it in a warm place to rise until it has doubled in size, which may take an hour or more.

Once risen, punch down the dough and knead it lightly again. Shape it into a loaf and place it in a greased baking tin or on a hearthstone.

Cover and let it rise once more until it has again doubled in size.

Bake the loaf in a moderate oven for nearly one hour, or until the crust is golden brown and the loaf sounds hollow when tapped on the bottom.

Remove from the oven and let cool on a rack before slicing.

To Make a Bramble Pie

Ingredients

One quart of brambles, be they blackberries or raspberries, freshly gathered.
Three-quarters of a pound of fine sugar.
Half a pint of water.
Pastry crust sufficient for a pie, both for the bottom and a lid.
A spoonful of flour.

Method

1. Prepare Ye Berries:

   Take thy brambles and place them in a colander, rinsing them well with cool water. Once cleansed, set them aside to drain fully.

2. Sweeten Ye Berries:

   In a large pan, place the sugar and water together and stir well. Bring the mixture to a gentle boil, ensuring the sugar is wholly dissolved. Add the brambles to the boiling syrup and let them cook for five minutes or until the berries are softened but not broken. Remove from the heat and allow to cool.

3. Prepare Ye Pastry:

   Roll out half of thy pastry dough and line a pie dish with it. Ensure the pastry is evenly spread and pressed into the dish, leaving no air pockets.

4. Assemble Ye Pie:

Once the berries have cooled, sprinkle a spoonful of flour over the pastry-lined dish to prevent sogginess. Then, pour the berry mixture into the dish, spreading it evenly. Roll out the remaining pastry dough and cover the top of the pie, crimping the edges together to seal.

5. Bake Ye Pie:

Preheat thy oven to a moderate heat. Place the pie within and bake for about forty-five minutes or until the crust is golden brown and the filling is bubbling.

6. Serve Ye Pie:

Allow the pie to cool slightly before serving. This pie is best enjoyed warm, with a dollop of fresh cream or a spoonful of rich custard.

To Choose and Dress a Fowl (Caution, Details Are Appropriately Graphic)

To Choose a Chicken: Take heed to select a young and tender fowl. Ye shall know it by its smooth legs, tender skin, and pliable breastbone. Avoid those with rough, scaly legs and hard breastbone, for they are old and tough.

To Slay the Chicken: When ye have chosen your chicken, take it by the feet and wings, and with a swift motion, wring its neck. Let it bleed well by hanging it with the head downward.

To Scald and Pluck: Heat a kettle of water until it doth almost boils. Immerse the fowl therein for but a moment, then pluck away the feathers with speed so that the skin is not torn.

To Singe and Dress: Hold the fowl over the flame to remove any remaining down. Cut off the head and feet. Slit the skin down the middle of the belly and draw forth the entrails. Be sure to remove the craw and lungs. Rinse the fowl well with cold water, both inside and out.

To Truss the Fowl: Truss the legs and wings neatly to the body. This may be done with a bit of string or a skewer.

To Roast the Fowl: Spit the chicken on a long iron skewer. Place it before a brisk fire, turning it often. Baste it with butter, and season it with salt and pepper. Roast till the skin is crisp and golden, and the juices run clear when pierced.

To Make Sauce for the Fowl: In a pan, take the giblets and boil them with a cup of water, a bit of parsley, and a spoonful of vinegar. When tender, strain the liquid and add a knob of butter, a pinch of salt, and a dash of pepper. Serve the sauce hot over the chicken.

APPENDIX A

To Make Sweet Cider

Take of the ripest apples, and having well cleansed them, grind them in a mill until they be well crushed.
Place the crushed apples into a press, and extract the juice into a clean vessel.
Let the Juice stand and settle for a day or two, then draw off the clear liquor into another clean cask or Barrel.
To preserve the sweetness, keep the cask well stopped and cool.

To Make Hard Cider

Take of the ripest apples, and having well cleansed them, grind them in a mill until they be well crushed.
Place the crushed apples into a press and extract the juice into a clean vessel.
Let the Juice stand and settle for a day or two, then draw off the clear liquor into another clean cask or barrel.
Place the barrel in a cool cellar and allow it to ferment. That will require some weeks, during which the cider will clarify.
Once fermentation hath ceased, the cider may be racked off into another barrel, or bottled for use.

To Make Pippin (Apple) Cider

Take the best Pippins, and having well cleansed them, grind them in a mill, and press forth the juice.
Let the juice stand for a day, then draw off the clear liquor into a barrel.
To that, add a pint of fine honey, and a pint of brandy. Let it stand in a cool cellar, and ferment until it becomes clear.
This cider is of excellent taste and strength.

Johnnycakes (Journey Cakes)

Ingredients

One cup cornmeal
One teaspoon salt
One tablespoon sugar (optional)
One cup boiling water
Butter or oil for frying

Instructions

Mix the cornmeal, salt, and sugar in a bowl.
Gradually stir in the boiling water until the mixture forms a thick batter.
Heat a griddle or frying pan over medium heat and grease it with butter or oil.
Drop spoonfuls of batter onto the hot griddle and flatten slightly.
Cook until golden brown on each side, about four to five minutes per side.
Serve hot with butter, honey, or maple syrup.

Hasty Pudding

Hasty pudding is a simple and hearty dish made from cornmeal and milk, popular in Colonial America for its ease of preparation and nourishing qualities.

Ingredients

Four cups milk
One cup cornmeal
Half teaspoon salt
Two tablespoons molasses or maple syrup (optional)

Instructions

Heat the milk in a large pot over medium heat until it begins to simmer.
Gradually whisk in the cornmeal and salt, stirring continuously to prevent lumps.
Reduce the heat to low and cook, stirring frequently, until the mixture thickens, about twenty to thirty minutes.
Stir in the molasses or maple syrup, if using.
Serve hot, optionally with a drizzle of cream or a pat of butter.

Indian (Native American) pudding

Indian pudding is a traditional New England dessert made with cornmeal, molasses, and spices. It has a long baking time but is worth the wait.

Ingredients

Four cups milk
Half cup cornmeal
Half cup molasses
Quarter cup brown sugar

APPENDIX A

Two tablespoons butter
One teaspoon ground cinnamon
Half teaspoon ground ginger
Quarter teaspoon ground nutmeg
Half teaspoon salt
Two large eggs, beaten

Instructions

Grease a 2-quart baking dish.
Heat the milk in a large saucepan over medium heat until it begins to simmer.
Gradually whisk in the cornmeal and cook, stirring constantly, until thickened, about ten to fifteen minutes.
Remove from heat and stir in the molasses, brown sugar, butter, spices, and salt.
Gradually whisk in the beaten eggs.
Pour the mixture into the prepared baking dish and bake at a moderate heat for about two hours, or until set and the top is browned.
Serve warm with vanilla ice cream or whipped cream.

Period Clothing

For a seriously authentic experience, you could add some clothing to your wardrobe! Another invaluable contributor to the endeavor was Chris Utley, who helped ensure the sketches were as close to historical reality as they could be. Take a few minutes to peruse his business, South Union Mills, for reproduction clothing, textiles, straw hats, knit goods, and other living history accessories, especially from the eighteenth and nineteenth centuries—http://www.southunionmills.com/

APPENDIX B

TIMELINE OF SAMUEL MASON'S LIFE

The timeline, as recorded herein, was informed by Bell and Coker's work:[1]

Date(s)	Age	Activity
1739, November 8	0	Born in Virginia
1754	15	Living in father's home near Charles Town, WV, Jefferson Co, earlier Frederick Co and Berkeley Co
1758	19	Served in the French & Indian War in Frederick County, VA
1760	21	Stole horses in Frederick County, VA
1762, September 5	22	Incurred 4 pound 4 shilling debt to John Bozworth
1767	28	Married to Rosanna Dorsey
1767, July 18 or 19	28	Daughter, Elizabeth born
1769, October 24	29	Son, Thomas born
1771, April 29	31	Son, John born
1773	34	Moved to Ohio County, VA (now Wheeling Creek, WV), bought two claims from Paul Stull, one from James Clarke
1774, Mar 31	34	Son, Isaac born
1774, May	34	Arrested for killing an Indian at Fort Pitt, PA
1776, August 11 or 12	6	Son, Dorsey, born

(Continued)

APPENDIX B

Date(s)	Age	Activity
1777, January 7	37	Named Captain of Militia in Wheeling, WV (Fort Henry)
1777, January 28	37	Attended council at Catfish, now Washington, PA
1777, January–March	37	Established road connecting Fort Henry to Shepherds Fort, at the first forks of Wheeling Creek via Mason's Bottom
1777, May–September	37	Pursued Indians after attack
1777, June 8	37	Wrote letter to Genl Hand (see Crumrine)
1777, July 17	37	Wrote letter to Genl Hand about Grave Creek
1777, August 12	37	At Fort Henry, wrote to Genl Hand
1777, August 22	37	Patrolled from Fort Henry to Grave Creek
1777, September 1	37	Wounded in Indian ambush
1777, October 8	37	Took oath of allegiance
1777, October 13	37	Paid for a drum
1778	38	On Ohio Co tax list (surety and appraiser several times)
1778	38	Moved 30 miles east, to Washington County, PA
1778, March 1	38	Witness of will of Thomas Worthington
1778, April 7	38	Administrator of Rodgers McBride estate
1778, June 2	38	Stole supplies from Fort Henry, sued by James Caldwell
1778, July	38	Accompanied General Clark on Illinois Campaign
1778, August 4	38	Hugh Sidwell a witness for Mason Sued by Joseph Tumbleston, paid fee to David McClure
1778, November 2	38	Ohio Co juror.
1779, March 3	39	Bought farm, moved from Wheeling Creek to Buffalo Creek
1779, March 14	39	Received 5 shillings ($50–100 today) from father's estate
1779, May 3	39	Witness for Samuel Williamson

(*Continued*)

Date(s)	Age	Activity
1779, August–September	39	On Brodhead campaign
1779, November 1	39	Jury foreman
1779, November 2	39	Road overseer—road from forks to Williams Hawkins'
1779, December 11	40	Accompanied neighbors applying for certificates of ownership, land in Washington County
1780, January 6	40	To Coxe's fort on Ohio for more Virginia certificates
1780, March 6 and June 5	40	Juror Ohio Co
1780, November 7	40	Militia court-martial, Ohio Co
1781, February 3	40	Daughter, Mary born
1781, May 17	41	Militia court-martial, Ohio Co
1781, May	41	Retained captaincy in the militia until then
1781, July 15	41	Elected Justice of the Peace in Donegal Twp, newly formed Washington Co—formerly Ohio County
1781, August 24	41	Named Associate Judge for Washington County
1782	41	Indians stole some of his slaves
1782–84	42	Taxed in Donegal Township
1782–83	42	Stole from Sevier's slaves in Holston River area (East TN)
1784, December 3	45	Son, Samuel, born in PA
1784	44	Sold phony land titles in Marietta, OH
1784, March	44	Sued by Thomas Waller, Samuel Johnson, John McWilliams
1784, June	44	Sued by Jacob Pyatt, Magness Tate—Joseph Beeler, bail
1784, likely Fall	44	Moved to Western KY, near Russellville
1784, December	45	Sued in PA by David Duncan—Brice Virgin, Hugh Sidwell
1785, March	45	Sued in PA by John Henderson, Christopher Hays—James also sued by David Shepherd, Andrew Zane, Clemens

(*Continued*)

APPENDIX B

Date(s)	Age	Activity
1785, June	45	Sued in PA by Peter Houghman, Abraham Johnston, Jr.
1785, June 3	45	Sam in KY deeded farm in PA to son, Thomas
1785, June 18	45	High Sidwell in PA said he saw Mason sign deed
1785, July 2	45	Sheriff levied Mason farm to pay debts
1785, September	45	In PA Mason by attorney Ross sued Charles Cracraft "for use of Thomas Mason"
1785, November 22	46	Sheriff sold Mason farm to Daniel Leet
1786, March 19	46	Son Magnus born in KY
1786, March 31	46	Final report to court by sheriff
1789, February 23	49	PA attempted to collect taxes by sending David Bradford to KY.
1789, April	49	Jeremiah Clemens, visited Mason near Russellville
1790	50	Samuel and Thomas signed petition to establish Logan County, KY
1791	51	Mason met Dr. Water at Red Banks/Henderson
1791	51	Held Derousse hostage at Red Banks
1792	51	Mason family counted in census at Red Banks
1792	52	Mason got medicine for wife from Dr. Water
1794	54	Moved to Red Banks/Henderson
1794, April	54	Abraham Clemens, brother of Jeremiah, heading down Ohio for New Orleans. Got passport in New Madrid May 5.
1794, June	54	John Dodd killed returning from New Orleans
1794, July 9	54	Benjamin Van Cleve in journal tells of visit to Mason near Henderson
1795	55	Mason and his gang attacked Constable Dunn
1797	57	Member of Mason gang killed Constable Dunn
1797	57	Moved to Diamond Island
1797	57	Moved to Cave-In-Rock, IL

(*Continued*)

Date(s)	Age	Activity
Summer 1799	59	Relocated to Wolf Island, KY
1800, March 29	60	Got passport at New Madrid, MO
1801	61	Expanded activities to Natchez Trace
1801, August 14	61	Robbed Colonel Joshua Baker on the Trace
1802, April	62	Robbed Colonel Baker on the Mississippi
1802	62	Owsley robbery on Spanish side
1802	62	Moved to Little Prairie (now Caruthersville, MO)
1802, Fall	62	In accident, according to son Thomas.
1803 January	63	Living in Little Prairie, MO
1803, January 17	63	Captain McCoy arrested Mason and his gang
1803, January 17	63	Trial at New Madrid, MO
1803, January 31	63	Trial Transferred to New Orleans, LA
1803, March—early	63	Trial Transferred to Natchez, MS
1803, March 26	63	Overpowered guards and escaped on the way
1803	63	Reward offered for Mason's head
1803, April–September	63	Mason killed and beheaded in Natchez, MS
1804, February 8	NA	John Sutton and James May hanged in Old Greenville, MS

APPENDIX C
INCIDENTS OF HISTORICAL MISINFORMATION

The term *historical misinformation* refers to the dissemination of inaccurate or misleading information about past events. This phenomenon can stem from various sources and has been prevalent throughout history due to political agendas, limited access to information, and the biases of those recording history. One significant reason for historical misinformation is the influence of political power. Those in authority have often manipulated historical narratives to strengthen control or justify their actions.

Another cause of historical misinformation is the lack of reliable sources and difficulty verifying facts. Before the widespread availability of print media and the internet, information was often spread through word of mouth, manuscripts, and limited print runs. That made it easy for inaccuracies to be perpetuated, intentionally or unintentionally. The biases of historians and chroniclers also played a significant role in shaping historical narratives. Historians often recorded events from their perspectives, which could be influenced by their personal beliefs, cultural background, or the prevailing attitudes of their time.

Historical misinformation has profoundly impacted societies by shaping collective memory and influencing contemporary attitudes and policies. Understanding its prevalence and reasons is crucial for critically assessing historical narratives and striving for a more accurate understanding of the past. In providing the list, I do not intend to proclaim one rendition of historical truth over another. As I said before, we do not have a time machine. However, we hope to present what we learned during the investigation and challenge you to decide, much like a jury traversing time and space as the investigative team did.

Here is how our research brings into question some of what has been put forth in Mason's History. While expounding here is not the proper forum, we recommend you evaluate each for accuracy.

Mason's Lineage

Mason's lineage has been traced to a long line of colonists. His great-grandfather, Lieutenant Francis Mason, born in 1594, arrived in Jamestown in 1613. Colonel Lemuel Mason, Francis' son, died in 1702. Lemuel had ten children, including George Mason, born in 1655, who served as a Justice in Norfolk and a Captain of the Militia. George died in 1710. Mason's father, Thomas Mason, born in 1707, also spelled Meason or Measor, was thought to have married Mary Newton. The family was then thought to have moved from Norfolk to Frederick County, Virginia, around 1754. What appeared to have happened was that Sam's father, Thomas Mason, had lived in the Frederick County, Virginia, area long before 1754, the soonest many Mason historians had placed the family in the area. He was not from Norfolk and was married to Elizabeth, not Mary. Mason's father's name was Thomas. There were two to choose from, living in very different parts of Virginia.

Mason's Birthdate

Sam Mason was born on November 8, 1739. Rothert and Lach mistakenly thought he was born in 1750. Nothing was found to support that notion or to explain the mistake.

Mason's Inheritance

When Mason was interviewed, he claimed rights to land on the Monongahela River, stating his brother had died without children. We suspect the statement was mistranslated. Many historians cite a version of the statement as "he has some pretensions on lands on the Monongela [sic] as heir from his brother, who died without children." This comes from the English translation of the transcripts, but there is no evidence Mason or his brother owned land on the Monongahela River. Records show that Joseph Mason (Meason), Sam's brother, had contested land in Kentucky. Joseph left the land to his nephew, Joseph Worthington, through a nuncupative (oral) will. Joseph was believed to have died in Fayette County, Pennsylvania, in the early 1780s. That area was part of the disputed territory near the Monongahela River, and while his death occurred in Pennsylvania, the contested land Joseph referenced in his nuncupative will was in Kentucky. There is no evidence he had property near the Monongahela River, though his family had connections to both Pennsylvania and Kentucky during that period. Kentucky, for most of that time, was part of the Commonwealth of Virginia and was admitted to the Union on June 1, 1792.

First Siege on Fort Henry

Simon Girty's involvement in the siege was questioned by Nicodemus, who suggested that Girty was serving in the Pennsylvania Militia at Fort Pitt at the time. General Hand was no fan of Girty and may have had him set up. Girty left the Fort Pitt area for Fort Detroit in the late spring of 1778, where he went to work for the British. Read more on Nicodemus' account.[1]

McCulloch's Identity

The debate about which McCulloch brother made the famed leap involves Major Samuel McCulloch and his younger brother, Major John McCulloch. Initially, some argued it was John, but the timeline of their promotions clarifies the matter. Samuel was commissioned as a major in 1775 and was known as a terror to the Native Americans. John, however, was not promoted to major until 1795, long after Samuel died in 1782. The famed leap was in 1777. Samuel was killed during a scouting mission with John on July 30, 1782. Samuel was shot, and John's horse was also shot. John escaped with a slight wound after securing Samuel's horse. The Native Americans disemboweled Samuel and ate his heart, believing it would grant them his bravery. There were two McCulloch brothers. Only one of them made the leap.

Betty Zane Legend

During an attack on Fort Henry in 1782, the fort's gunpowder ran low, requiring someone to dash to the Zanes' cabin for more. A woman volunteered, deeming herself more expendable. She reached the cabin during a lull in the shooting, but on her return with the gunpowder, attackers opened fire. Despite this, she returned safely, allowing the settlers to defend the fort until reinforcements arrived.

Traditionally, this act of bravery is credited to Elizabeth (Betty) Zane, Colonel Zane's sister. However, in 1849, Lydia Cruger claimed Molly Scott retrieved the ammunition from the Zane residence, suggesting a possible historical inaccuracy. Unless there were two or more events, only one woman made the run.

DeHass noted that other witnesses supported Mrs. Cruger in her claims and suggested it was barely possible that there were two instances when a female was used to procure gunpowder for the fort.[2] DeHass also noted that Colonel Zane was married to Elizabeth McCulloch, sister of Major Samuel, Major John, and Abraham McCulloch (the oldest). For more on that dispute (and a bit of drama), see Nicodemus' analysis in *the Mostly True Story of Betsy Zane*.[3] He observed Molly Scott's daughter stated her mother often told the story of Betsy Zane's gunpowder run and how it had saved the fort. Also, Betsy's (Nicodemus referred to Elizabeth by this nickname) own daughter said that her mom didn't say much about it other than that the musket balls kicked up dust, which blew into her eyes, making it difficult to see where she was going.[4]

Sterner reported that Cruger suggested that Elizabeth Zane was not in town in 1782 and that Scott had never been in danger because the Indians had withdrawn well outside the range of their muskets and rifles. He noted that Cruger was eighty-three years old and there was only one living witness to the event who could contradict her. As a result of the claim, historian William Hintzen investigated the matter and found that the descendants of Molly Scott had always proclaimed that Elizabeth Zane made the dash in 1782. Hintzen concluded that Cruger likely confused the events of three different attacks on Fort Henry in 1777, 1781, and 1782.[5]

Origin of Wilson's Bar

At Cave-In-Rock, Mason converted the cave into a tavern with a liquor supply. Above the entrance was a prominent sign reading "Wilson's Liquor Vault and House of Entertainment" to help the pirate gang lure river travelers to stop. Some investigators suggest Mason went by the name Bully or James (Jim) Wilson, though it's debated whether Mason and Wilson were the same person. Others believe James Ford used the moniker for a bar at the cave. Ford, operating a ferry across the Ohio River in the late 1790s, was secretly a river pirate and leader of the "Ford's Ferry Gang," hijacking flatboats like Mason's gang. Business records don't go back that far. Mason ran the establishment during his time at Cave-In-Rock. The question is whether the name was attached to the establishment, and if so, when? It is possible that more than one group operated the bar, with or

APPENDIX C

without the name, as none were there more than a few years, and the cave was there long before and will be there long after.

Identity of Colonel Fluger

Colonel Fluger, also known as Plug, carved out a notorious legacy eerily similar to Mason's. Born in Rockingham County, New Hampshire, Fluger rose in the local militia but fell into disgrace due to debts and imprisonment. After his release, he moved west, near Fort Massac, and formed a fearsome gang with his girlfriend Pluggy and an associate nicknamed "Nine Eyes." The gang's tactic involved secretly boarding docked flatboats at night, tampering with them to cause delayed sinking, and then posing as rescuers to steal the cargo. Despite colorful tales of his exploits, there is little historical evidence of his military service or existence, suggesting he might be an embellished or fictional counterpart to Mason. Whether fact or fiction, Colonel Plug's legend remains a vivid chapter in America's riverfront outlaw folklore.

Identity of James Sutton

John Sutton, suspected by some to be Wiley/Little Harpe, also used the aliases John Taylor and Wells. Captain Stump from Kentucky publicly identified Sutton as Wiley Harpe but later admitted uncertainty. Others who claimed to know Harpe agreed but lacked proof, except for John Bowman of Knoxville. On the day of Sutton's execution in 1804, Bowman recognized him and insisted Sutton was Little Harpe, pointing out a specific scar. When Sutton's shirt was ripped open, revealing the scar, the crowd was convinced. Rothert and later researchers concluded Sutton was indeed Wiley Harpe.

John Sevier of Tennessee was just as adamant that Sutton was not Wiley Harpe. Although Spanish governor Claiborne of New Orleans initially identified Harpe as part of the Mason gang, the inquest in 1803 revealed Sutton claimed to know Big Harpe, AKA Micajah, not Wiley, which seemed to satisfy investigators. Despite those claims, the legend and confusion around Sutton's identity persisted. Grave and genealogy sites provided no information on a John McDowell Sutton or similar names. Sutton and his associate May were hanged on February 8, 1804, at "Gallows Field" near Old Greenville. Sutton's head was mounted on a pole as a deterrent to other criminals. Ultimately, because of the doubt surrounding the identification of the head Sutton and May alleged was Mason, the two were tried for murder, indicating the judge did not believe it was

Mason's head, and was that of someone else who did not have a reward offered for their capture. The graves of both were thought to have been lost to history.

Identity of James May

James May, possibly also known as Isaac or Samuel May, and Peter Alston, operated around the Red Banks and Diamond Island area after the Masons left. After stealing some horses, May and a woman he identified as his sister fled toward Vincennes, Indiana, 60 miles north across the Ohio River. Governor Claiborne spoke of May as one of the two who turned in what they alleged to be Mason's head for the reward. May and Sutton were hanged on February 8, 1804, at "Gallows Field" near Old Greenville.

Mason's Death

May and Sutton were arrested in Natchez. The two allegedly offered, if released, to bring in Sam Mason. They went into Louisiana territory and returned a month later with a giant ball of clay in their canoe. The two reported finding Mason, killing him, and beheading him. Some historians claim that Mason died from wounds he suffered in the escape from McCoy. Either way, a head was produced that Sutton and May said was Mason's.

Numerous people examined the head and confirmed that it was Mason. The Governor invited several men familiar with Mason to identify the severed head as Mason's. None recognized it as Mason's. Sutton and May were arrested and charged with murder. That's a twist you might not have seen coming. One instance of historical misinformation is whether Mason died from injuries in the escape. A second is whether the head was his. And potentially, a third was whether Sutton and May should have been tried for murder, as the reason for their trial appeared to be that the head was not Mason's. As with the others, we will never know.

Misinformation Example

A contemporary example of how historical misinformation was created would be the following. Using your imagination, come along with me on our trip to Pittsburgh. We were there to visit Fort Pitt, see where the Monongahela River started the Ohio River, and get a feel for the history of the area during the latter

APPENDIX C

half of the eighteenth century. We knew that Sam Mason, the Revolutionary War Captain who became a river pirate, was at Fort Pitt before he was at Fort Henry. And we know that he likely had traveled every mile of the Ohio River, which began in Pittsburgh. While in downtown Pittsburgh, we noticed PNC Park, the home of the Pittsburgh Pirates, a mile from the Heinz Museum and less than a mile and a half from the Fort Pitt Museum. Are you thinking what I am thinking?

I wondered if the Pittsburgh Pirates got their name from the activities of the River Pirate Sam Mason!?! It wasn't too much of a stretch since the Golconda sports teams near Cave-In-Rock were called the Pirates. Search as I might, all I could come up with was the history of the team shared on their public-facing internet documents but find no historical documentation (not saying there isn't any, just that I didn't find any).

So, what's a plausible way to connect those dots? In 2024 when I was writing this, I turned to a relatively new artificial intelligence tool called ChatGPT. Specifically, I asked it if the name chosen for the team had anything to do with river pirates being near there after the Revolutionary War. I learned that

> The naming of the Pittsburgh Pirates baseball team did not directly relate to historical pirates operating near Pittsburgh after the Revolutionary War. The team originally began as the Pittsburgh Alleghenys in 1882, named after the Allegheny River. The name "Pirates" came into use in the 1890s after the team was accused of "pirating" a player, Louis Bierbauer, from the Philadelphia Athletics. The term "pirates" stuck, and the team officially adopted the name in 1891.

That was the same story I found on their webpages.

The summary continued, "While the Ohio River, which flows through Pittsburgh, did see some river piracy and banditry in the late 18th and early 19th centuries, these historical events did not influence the naming of the baseball team. The team's name more directly reflects a colorful episode in baseball history rather than any direct connection to historical pirates."

So I asked if it *was* named because of river pirates, how would you tell the story to make it believable? And I got this: "To craft a plausible and engaging story linking the naming of the Pittsburgh Pirates to actual river pirates near Pittsburgh after the Revolutionary War, you would need to blend historical facts with a narrative that feels authentic. Here's how you might tell the story."

The Origins of the Pittsburgh Pirates

The Pittsburgh Pirates, a storied Major League Baseball team, have a name that evokes the daring and lawlessness of river pirates. But is this just a clever moniker, or does it trace back to a deeper, more turbulent history along the rivers of Pittsburgh?

In the years following the Revolutionary War, the Ohio River, which flows past Pittsburgh, became a crucial artery for commerce and travel. Flatboats, keelboats, and rafts crowded the waters, transporting goods and settlers to the western frontier. However, these waters were not always safe. Bands of river pirates, led by notorious figures like Samuel Mason, prowled the rivers, preying on unsuspecting travelers and merchants.

Samuel Mason, a former militia captain turned outlaw, was infamous for his ruthless raids. His gang terrorized the Ohio and Mississippi Rivers, committing robberies and murders. The local lore is rich with tales of Mason and his men attacking flatboats, looting their cargo, and leaving no witnesses. The pirates were a scourge on the early American frontier, and their exploits left an indelible mark on the collective memory of the region.

Fast forward to the late nineteenth century, when Pittsburgh's burgeoning baseball team sought a new identity. Initially known as the Pittsburgh Alleghenys, the team's management wanted a name that would resonate with the city's robust spirit and storied past. During this period, a controversy arose when the team signed star player Louis Bierbauer, who had seemingly been "pirated" from another team. The press and public seized upon this term, calling the team the "Pirates" in jest.

The name stuck, but deeper reflection reveals it was more than just a playful jab. It was a nod to the region's history, to the days when the rivers around Pittsburgh were the domain of real pirates. The new name evoked a sense of adventure and daring, qualities that resonated with the gritty, hardworking spirit of Pittsburghers.

Thus, the Pittsburgh Pirates were born—a name rooted not only in a baseball dispute but also in the echoes of the river pirates who once haunted the waters near the city. It is a name that connects the past with the present, reminding fans of the colorful and sometimes dark history that helped shape the region.

So, when you cheer for the Pirates at PNC Park, remember that you are not just supporting a baseball team. You are celebrating a legacy that harks back to the wild, untamed rivers of post-Revolutionary America, where the spirit of the pirate—bold, adventurous, and unyielding—still lives on.

This narrative ties the team's name to historical events, adding a layer of depth and authenticity while remaining engaging and believable. That's pretty concerning, though. I found it interesting that Sam J. Mason was listed as a relief pitcher for the Pirates at some point.[6] I wonder if he knew?

APPENDIX D

THOMAS MASON TIMELINE AND REFERENCE DOCUMENTATION

Compiled by Marc Coker, May 2024

Thomas Meason in Virginia

1738–43. Frederick County formed from Orange County and Augusta County. "Thomas Mason (b. 1706 c.) 'lived on the east side of Opechon Creek about 1736 or 1737,' and for several years afterword near present day Middleway, West Virginia. 'Andrew Hampton attempted to sell him a tract of land, but they could not agree on the price.'"

Source: Page 209, *Pioneers of Old Fredrick Co., Virginia*, Cecil O'dell, published 1995. Note: O'Dell cites Hite/Fairfax Lawsuit, British Copy, Hunter McKay Extracted Copy, p. 1613.

November 22, 1740. Nathaniel Thomas of Opeckon in Orange County, Mason, to John Harden of Shenandoah of said county, planter. Lease and release; for £42 current money. 3890 acres in Opeckon known by the name of the Meason's Meadow.

Source: Pages 182–6, Orange County, Virginia, Deed Book 1741–3.

April 2, 1745. Isaac Pennington versus James McKee. In case on slander. This day came the parties by their attorneys and a jury, to wit, John Hardin, William Mitchell, Robert Wilson, Samuel Walker, Robert Worthington, Isaac Vanmetre, Jeremiah Smith, Owen Thomas, Joseph Williams, Peter Hedges, Thomas Mason, Job Curtis, who . . . find for plaintiff five pounds . . . damages . . . and thereupon considered by court that said plaintiff recover against said defendant said sum . . . together with costs

Source: Page 321, Frederick County, Virginia, Order Book 1.

November 18, 1752. S-327: John Smith, assignee of Patrick Vance, assignee of Barnaby Hogan, assignee of William Holdbruck 142 acres S(18 November 1752) in Frederick county where Holdbruck formerly lived, adjacent Thomas Mason on Opeckon. November 24, 1787.
   Source: Page 61, Virginia Northern Neck Land Grants, compiled by Gertrude F. Gray, Baltimore, 1983.

March 27, 1753. John Neavill, assignee (1770) of Cuthbert/Colbird (his signature) Anderson or heirs of Thomas Lewis, assignees of Thomas Mason; 27 March 1753–27 March 1754; 85 acres on Mill Creek, branch of Opeckon; adjacent Robert Cunningham, Patrick Riley, John Hampton, James Anderson. CC-Thomas Goalding and Thomas Mason. Surveyor William Baylis.
   Source: Frederick County, Virginia, HN W. Survey, Joyner.

September 27, 1754. The old court house, adjoining the new one in Winchester, Virginia, records a deed therein Thomas Mason acquired, on September 27, 1754, from Thomas Low, both of the County of Frederick, Colony of Virginia, 370 acres of land in the aforesaid county and colony, which has been patented to Thomas Low, bearing date June 1, 1754, lying on Mill Creek, whereon he lives . . . bounded . . . line . . . 150 poles . . . granted to the said Thomas Mason.
   Source: Pages 340–8, Robert H. Torrence, *Torrence and Allied Families*, published by Wickersham Press, Philadelphia c. 1937, West Kentucky Wilson Library 929.2 T6353.

September 2, 1756. At a court-martial held for Frederick County on Friday, the second day of September 1756, recorded in the County Clerk's Office, Winchester, Virginia.
Present: The right honorable Thomas Lord Fairfax, County Lieutenant. George William Fairfax, Colonel; Thomas Bryan Martin, Lieutenant Colonel; Meredith Helm, Major. Richard Morgan, John Fund, Junior, Jeremiah Smith, Samuel O'Dell, Jacob Funk, William Bethel, Isaac Perkins, Edward Rodgers, John Hardin, John Linsey, Cornelius Ruddell, William Vance, Lewis Stephens, John Denton, Captains. Robert Rutherford was appointed clerk of the court-martial.
   (Extracted): John Linsey, captain of a troop, returned his list of delinquents— William Joliff, Junior; Henry Bowen; Jeremiah Archer; Thomas Green; John Ridgway; Morriss Reece, Junior; Thomas Mason; John Marpool; Daniel Marshall; George Tollis; Morriss Reece, Senior; Richard Reece.
   Source: Officers and Men of the Frederick County Militia in the Year 1756, by Flora I. Ward, San Diego Chapter, D.A.R.

December 5, 1759. There is also a deed wherein Thomas Mason and his wife Elizabeth, both of Frederick County, Colony of Virginia, convey this same described property (see September 27, 1754 above), to George Fallis, of the

APPENDIX D

aforesaid county and colony, the indenture bearing date December 5, 1759. The signatures to this deed were Thomas Meason and Elizabeth Meason. The spelling throughout the document was Mason and it was indexed as Mason.

Source: Pages 340–8, Robert H. Torrence, *Torrence and Allied Families*, published by Wickersham Press, Philadelphia c. 1937, West Kentucky Wilson Library 929.2 T6353.

May 1, 1760. K-119: William Merchant of Frederick County 81 acres on Mill Creek Branch of Opeckon in said County. Survey William Paylis. Adjacent Thomas Golding, Thomas Mason. May 1, 1760.

Source: Page 117, Virginia Northern Neck Land Grants, compiled by Gertrude F. Gray, Baltimore, 1983.

August 3, 1760. Another deed, found in Winchester, Virginia, is of special interest, because of mentioning of the names of Thomas Mason, and others who later, intermarried with the children of this (now) Thomas Meason.

This indenture between Joseph Thompson, of the County of Frederick, Colony of Virginia, of the first part, and Thomas Mason, of the second apart, conveys a tract of land on a branch of the Shenandoah River called Everett Run, being a part of a tract of 300 acres granted to Robert Worthington, by patent October 3, 1734, and being part of 3000acres, which were laid off for Robert Worthington by Andrew Campbell. Lewis Neil, David Vance, John Smith, and John McCormick, by virtue of orders and decrees made in the County of Orange, Virginia, for the division of the said 3000 acres, dated August 3, 1760 and signed by Joseph Thompson.

Source: Pages 340–8, Robert H. Torrence, *Torrence and Allied Families*, published by Wickersham Press, Philadelphia c. 1937, West Kentucky Wilson Library 929.2 T6353.

August 14, 1762. M-17: Thomas Mason of Frederick County 180 acres in Hampshire county. Survey Mr. Guy Broadwater. Fork of Indian Run. .

Source: Page 143, Virginia Northern Neck Land Grants, compiled by Gertrude F. Gray, Baltimore, 1983.

August 20, 1765. M-444: Thomas Mason of Frederick County 400 acres between Opeckon and Worthington's Marsh in said County. Survey Thomas Rutherford. Adjacent Moses Walton, Mr. Washington, Worthington, Isaiah Pemberton.

Source: Page 166, Virginia Northern Neck Land Grants, compiled by Gertrude F. Gray, Baltimore, 1983.

October 25, 1768. O-198: Thomas Mason of Frederick County 100 acres on Rock Gap Branch in said County. Survey Guy Broadwater.

Source: Page 199, Virginia Northern Neck Land Grants, compiled by Gertrude F. Gray, Baltimore, 1983.

October 26, 1768. O-199: Thomas Mason of Frederick County 400 acres on Indian Run in said County. Survey Guy Broadwater.

Source: Page 199, Virginia Northern Neck Land Grants, compiled by Gertrude F. Gray, Baltimore, 1983.

November 2, 1768. O-205: William Merchant of Frederick County 115 acres on Opeckon in said county. Survey Thomas Rutherford. Adjacent his own land, Richard Fowler, David Lewis, James Anderson, by Mill Creek, George Cunningham, Thomas Mason.

Source: Page 199, *Virginia Northern Neck Land Grants*, compiled by Gertrude F. Gray, Baltimore, 1983.

November 3, 1769. O-240: Bryan Bruin of Frederick County 405 acres on Rock Gap Run in Hampshire County. Survey Richard Rigg. Adjacent Thomas Mason, Warm Spring Ridge, Great Cacapehon Mountain.

Source: Page 201, *Virginia Northern Neck Land Grants*, compiled by Gertrude F. Gray, Baltimore, 1983.

August 1, 1777. "At Martinsburg, Berkeley County, Virginia, now West Virginia, there is a deed, dated 1st, 2nd, August 1777, Book 4, page 222, by which Thomas Mason conveys to George Cole Briscoe, two tracts of land adjoining 255 and 300 acres respectively, at Charlestown, Jefferson County, West Virginia."

Source: Pages 340–8, Robert H. Torrence, *Torrence and Allied Families*, published by Wickersham Press, Philadelphia c. 1937, West Kentucky Wilson Library 929.2 T6353.

August 1, 1777. Another reference to this land transaction of Thomas, Mason (Meason), is found, wherein Thomas Mason made a deed, dated August 1, 1777, recorded August 19, 1777, conveying two tracts, one of 255 acres, the other of 300 acres, to George Cole Briscoe, both grantor and grantee being of the County of Berkeley, Colony of Virginia. This land lying on Everett Run, a branch of the Shenandoah River, is now in Jefferson County, West Virginia. In this deed, the spelling is Mason, but in the index, it is Meason.

In a deed previously quoted, it was shown that Thomas Mason, while living in Frederick County, Virginia, acquired the tract called "Everett Run" from Joseph Thompson, August 3, 1760, and sold it to George Cole Briscoe in 1777. Berkeley County was formerly a part of Frederick. It should be noted that Thomas Meason

APPENDIX D

in selling this land to George Cole Briscoe, was not joined in the sale by his wife Elizabeth. It may therefore be assumed that her death was prior thereto.

Source: Pages 340–8, Robert H. Torrence, *Torrence and Allied Families*, published by Wickersham Press, Philadelphia c. 1937, West Kentucky Wilson Library 929.2 T6353.

Thomas Meason in Pennsylvania

March 15, 1779. Will of Thomas Meason. In the name of God, Amen, I, Thomas Meason this fourteenth day of March one Thousand seven hundred and seventy nine, of the county of Westmoreland, in the State of the Commonwealth of Pennsylvania being aged and weak of body but of perfect mind and memory, thanks be to Almighty God for the same, and calling to mind the uncertainty of this transitory life, and that all flesh must die, when it may please Almighty God to call, do make and ordain and publish this my last will and testament, in manner and form following, to wit: Imprimis, and first of all, I give and recommend my soul to God, who first gave it to me, and my body to, be decently buried in the earth in a decent Christian like manner making no doubt of receiving the same again at the General Resurrection by the mighty power of God, and as to what transitory estate the Lord has been pleased to bestow upon me in this life, I do give and bestow and bequeath as follows.

Item, my will and desire is that all my just and funeral expenses be first paid out of my personal estate by my executors hereafter named.

Item, I give and bequeath to my son Thomas Mason, one certain tract of land lying and being in the County of Westmoreland, in the State of Pennsylvania, the right of the said Land and Improvement, I have lately purchased of and from one John Minter, which said Land and premises I do give my son Thomas Meason and his heirs and assigns forever.

Item, I do give and bequeath to my son Joseph Meason one certain tract of Land lying in the County of Westmorland in the State of Pennsylvania, called "Green Lick," which said Land and improvements I have lately purchased of and from one James Blackstone, which land and improvement I give and bequeath to my son Joseph Mason and his heirs and assigns forever.

Item, I give unto my son Samuel Meason the sum of five shillings current money to be paid him by my Executors hereinafter named.

Item, I give unto my son Isaac Meason the sum of five shillings current money to be paid him aforesaid, he having already received his portion.

Item, I give unto my son George Meason, the sum of fifty pounds current money to be paid him as aforesaid.

Item, I give unto my daughter Hannah Meason the sum of fifty pounds, current money as aforesaid.

Item, I give to my daughter Rachel Worthington, wife of Robert Worthington, Junior, the sum of five shillings to be paid to her as aforesaid, she having received her portion already.

Item, I give unto my son John Meason the sum of fifty pounds current money aforesaid.

Item, I give unto my daughter Sarah Briscoe, wife of George Cole Briscoe the sum of five shillings current money, to be paid to her, she having received her portion already.

Item, I give to my daughter Ann Meason, the value of one of my Negroes in ready money, to be paid to her by my Executors hereinafter named.

Item, I give to my daughter Mary Meason, my Negro Solomon to her and her heirs and assigns forever.

Item, I give and bequeath to son Joseph Meason the best horse belonging to me at the time of my death.

Item, my will and desire is that my son Joseph Meason should possess my two Negroes two years after my decease.

Item, my will and desire is that my three youngest daughters, namely Ann, Mary, and Elizabeth, shall have my three featherbeds and furniture and my pewter, equally divided among them.

Item, my will and desire is that the residue of my estate be equally divided between my three sons, John, Thomas, and Joseph, and I do hereby nominate, ordain and appoint my three before mentioned sons, John Meason, Thomas Meason and Joseph Meason, Executors of this my last will and testament, revoking, disallowing and making void, all other wills and Testaments by me made, and this only, to be my last will.

In witness whereof, I have hereunto set my hand and Seal, the day and year aforementioned.

Thomas Meason

Signed and Sealed and Published in Presence of us;

Samuel Wells

James Blackstone

Samuel Wells, Junior

Edward Rice.

State of Pennsylvania, Westmoreland County.

I, Edward A. Cramer, Register of Wills in and for said County, hereby do certify the foregoing to be a true and correct copy of the original Last

APPENDIX D

Will and Testament of Thomas Meason, late of Westmoreland County, Pennsylvania, deceased, as the same remains on file and is of record, at Greensburg, Pennsylvania, in Will Book, No. 1, page 17. Will proved 15 March 1779.

Source: Page 17, Westmoreland County, Pennsylvania, Will book No. 1.

February 1, 1790. Report by John Mason, Thomas Mason, and Joseph Mason, executors of Thomas Mason, showing a balance on the estate. Ordered to be distributed to Samuel Mason, Rachel Worthington, Sarah Briscoe, Isaac Mason, John Mason and Ann Mason.
Source: Partition Records, Westmoreland County, Virginia, Docket 3.

September 11, 1789. U-368: Thomas Mason 400 acres (14 August 1775) in Frederick and Hampshire Counties adjacent his purchase of Thomas Low in Indian Run. 11 September 1789 (Grant canceled and granted James Wilson March 15, 1800, Book Y folio 409.)

Source: Page 112, Volume III, *Virginia Northern Neck Land Grants*, compiled by Gertrude F. Gray, Baltimore, 1983.

March 20, 1807.

There is another deed, 20 March, 1807, Book 4, page 215, by which John M. Briscoe and Marie, his wife; Cuthbert and Elizabeth his wife; George Cole Briscoe, by John Briscoe, his attorney-in-fact; Philip Briscoe, Samuel Briscoe, Harrison Briscoe, and Edward Briscoe, all of Jefferson County, West Virginia, convey to William Cameron, of Lancaster, Pennsylvania, the two tracts of land devised by George Cole Briscoe, he having bought the land from Thomas Mason, one tract being next to Richard McSherry's. The land conveyed by George Cole Briscoe to his seven sons, was purchased from Thomas Mason.

Source: Pages 340–8, Robert H. Torrence, *Torrence and Allied Families*, published by Wickersham Press, Philadelphia c. 1937, West Kentucky Wilson Library 929.2 T6353.

APPENDIX E

ADDITIONAL READING, WATCHING, AND LISTENING

Books

Baldwin, Leland D. *The Keelboat Age on Western Waters*. Pittsburgh, PA: University of Pittsburgh Press, 1980.

Claiborne, William C. C. *Official Correspondence Regarding the Governance of the Mississippi Territory, 1801–1805*. Jackson, MS: Mississippi Department of Archives and History.

Davis, William C. *A Way through the Wilderness: The Natchez Trace and the Civilization of the Southern Frontier*. New York, New York: Harper Collins, 1995.

Kastor, Peter J. *The Nation's Crucible: The Louisiana Purchase and the Creation of America*. New Haven, CT: Yale University Press, 2004. https://www.jstor.org/stable/j.ctt1nq6h3

Wagner, Mark J. *The Wreck of the "America" in Southern Illinois: A Flatboat on the Ohio River*. Carbondale, IL: Southern Illinois University Press, 2015.

Weber, David J. *The Spanish Frontier in North America*. New Haven, CT: Yale University Press, 1992.

Wellman, Paul I. *Spawn of Evil: The Invisible Empire of Soulless Men Which for a Generation Held the Nation in a Spell of Terror*. New York, New York: Doubleday, 1964.

Podcasts.

American Revolution Podcast. A Chronological (weekly) Journey through the Revolutionary War. Also has a blog. https://blog.amrevpodcast.com

Ben Franklin's World. Episodes on law and crime in early America. https://www.benfranklinsworld.com

Dispatches – Podcast of the Journal of the American Revolution. Interviews highlighting the latest in scholarship, news, and opinions regarding the American Revolutionary Era. https://jardispatches.podbean.com/page/2/

Emerging Revolutionary War. A public history platform that explores all aspects of the Revolutionary War with up-and-coming historians and connects this history to the places where it occurred. https://emergingrevolutionarywar.org

The American Legal history Podcast. Episodes on law in early Colonial America. https://alhtji.libsyn.com/

YouTube Channels

American Battlefield Trust. Devoted to the preservation of our nation's endangered Civil War, Revolutionary War, and War of 1812 battlefields. https://www.youtube.com/americanbattlefieldtrust

Colonial Williamsburg. Williamsburg was the thriving capital of Virginia when the dream of American freedom and independence was taking shape and Colonial Williamsburg has the largest US history museum in the world. https://www.youtube.com/@ColonialWilliamsburg

Dispatches—Podcast of the Journal of the American Revolution. Interviews highlighting the latest in scholarship, news, and opinions regarding the American Revolutionary Era. https://www.youtube.com/@JournaloftheAmericanRevolution/videos

Early American. Follow the lives of Ron and Justine as they meander through 1820s Missouri. https://www.youtube.com/@EarlyAmerican

History Channel. The premier destination for historical storytelling. https://www.youtube.com/@HISTORY

The History Guy. History that deserves to be remembered. https://www.youtube.com/@TheHistoryGuyChannel

Townsends. Exploring the 18th Century lifestyle. https://www.youtube.com/@townsends

National Museum of American History. Frontier Life and Justice in the Early United States. https://www.youtube.com/watch?v=zblVDyZ_I_8

NOTES

Preface

1 Mississippi Department of Archives and History (MDAH), Mason (Samuel) Trial Records. Call number Z/0273.000, MDAH, Archival Reading Room, Manuscript Collection. Jackson, MS, 1803, http://opac2.mdah.state.ms.us/phpmanuscripts/z0273.php
2 Record of Samuel Mason's trial for robbery by the military authorities of New Madrid, January 11–31, 1803, https://search.worldcat.org/title/5232376

Chapter 1

1 Raymond M. Bell, *Samuel Mason 1739-1803: Captain in Virginia, Judge in Pennsylvania, River Pirate in Kentucky, Desperado in Mississippi*. Washington, Pennsylvania (1985), https://wvancestry.com/Files/Samuel_Mason_1739-1803.pdf
2 Winchester, Virginia. George Washington's Mount Vernon, https://www.mountvernon.org/library/digitalhistory/digital-encyclopedia/article/winchester-virginia
3 WikiTree – Francis Mason, https://www.wikitree.com/wiki/Mason-1718
4 WikiTree – Lemuel Mason, https://www.wikitree.com/wiki/Mason-2737
5 WikiTree – George Mason, https://www.wikitree.com/wiki/Mason-2734#_note-5
6 C. M. L. Wiseman, *Pioneer Period and Pioneer People of Fairfield County, Ohio* (Columbus, OH: F.J. Heer Printing Co., 1901), https://ancestors.familysearch.org/en/M76T-WT9/thomas-meason-or-measor-1707-1779
7 Family Search – Thomas Meason or Measor, https://ancestors.familysearch.org/en/M76T-WT9/thomas-meason-or-measor-1707-1779
8 WikiTree – Mary Mason, https://www.wikitree.com/wiki/Newton-2875
9 WikiTree – Elizabeth Meason, https://www.wikitree.com/wiki/Meason-18
10 Beth Uiterwyk reported in 2002 that Thomas Mason of Norfolk probably died sometime between May 27, 1737 and November 3, 1740, based on a November 3, 1740 land transaction. Mary Mason—"a widow"—sold land in Norfolk she had

inherited from her father Nathaniel Newton. Uiterwyk cited Norfolk County Wills & Deeds, I, 1736–53, pp. 106–7.
11 *Pioneers of Old Frederick County*, Virginia, p. 209. Note: O'Dell cites the Hite/Fairfax Lawsuit, British Copy, Hunter McKay Extracted Copy, p. 1613 (as provided by Coker).
12 Samuel Ross Mason. Wikitree, https://www.wikitree.com/wiki/Mason-2736
13 Thomas Meason (1707–79). Wikitree, https://www.wikitree.com/wiki/Meason-8
14 Frederick County, Virginia, Order Book 1, Page 321.
15 Virginia Northern Neck Land Grants, compiled by Gertrude F. Gray, Baltimore, 1983. Page 61.
16 Frederick County, Virginia, HN W. Survey, Joyner.
17 Robert H. Torrence, *Torrence and Allied Families* (Philadelphia, PA: Wickersham Press, 1938), https://archive.org/details/torrencealliedfa00torr/page/n9/mode/2up
18 Tasting Table, "Here's What Our Founding Fathers Drank at George Washington's Farewell Party," https://www.tastingtable.com/1632124/george-washington-bar-tab-party/
19 Tasting Table, "Here's What Our Founding Fathers Drank."
20 Fort Henry, Ohio County Library, https://www.ohiocountylibrary.org/history/3698
21 Greensleeves. musopen.org. Archived from the original on May 13, 2014. Public domain music recording, https://web.archive.org/web/20140513012231/https://musopen.org/music/2096/anonymous/greensleeves/
22 LyricsTranslate, *Early One Morning: English Folk Lyrics* (n.d.), https://lyricstranslate.com/en/english-folk-early-one-morning-lyrics.html
23 O. Rothert, *The Outlaws of Cave-in-Rock: Historical Accounts of the Famous Highwaymen and River Pirates Who Operated in Pioneer Days Upon the Ohio and Mississippi Rivers and Over the Old Natchez Trace* (Cleveland, OH: Arthur H. Clark, 1924), p. 158, https://archive.org/details/outlawsofcaveinr00roth/page/n9/mode/2up
24 Rothert, *The Outlaws of Cave-in-Rock*, p. 158.

Chapter 2

1 These population estimates are often derived from colonial records, taxation lists, and other historical documents from the mid-eighteenth century.
2 M. E. Nogay, *Every Home a Fort, Every Man a Warrior: Stories of the Forts and Men in the Upper Ohio Valley during the American Revolutionary War* (Steubenville, OH: Tri-State Publishing Co., 2009).
3 David Preston, "When Young George Washington Started a War," *Smithsonian Magazine*, 2019, https://www.smithsonianmag.com/history/when-young-george-washington-started-war-180973076/

4. Winchester, Virginia. Washington's Mount Vernon, https://www.mountvernon.org/library/digitalhistory/digital-encyclopedia/article/winchester-virginia/
5. F. I. Ward, "Officers and Men of the Frederick County Militia in the Year 1756," San Diego Chapter, D.A.R., https://www.familysearch.org/library/books/viewer/221509/
6. Capt. John Stevenson's Roll (p. 143) and Frederick County roster (p. 211), https://books.google.com/books?id=0RpcjJQBm6AC&q=samuel+mason#v=
7. L. D. Bockstruck, Virginia's Colonial Soldiers, 1988, pp. 349–50. This was confirmed with a review of the Frederick County, Virginia Militia payroll in 1758, http://files.usgwarchives.net/va/frederick/military/frenchindian/fiw_frederick.txt It was further verified with the list of French and Indian War militia and provisioners to the (Frederick County, Virginia) militia in March 1758—http://files.usgwarchives.net/va/frederick/military/frenchindian/fiw_frederick.txt. Schedule of Payments to Militia & to Inhabitants for Provisions (Frederick County, Virginia Militia), September 1758, vagenweb.org/hening/vol07-11.htm also supported this theory.
8. Johannes Hite. Wikitree, https://www.wikitree.com/wiki/Hite-18
9. Rothert, *The Outlaws of Cave-in-Rock*, p. 157.
10. Edward L. Lach, Jr., "Mason, Samuel (1750–July 1803), 1999," https://doi.org/10.1093/anb/9780198606697.article.2000644
11. Samuel Mason and Jonathan Clark's debt to John Bozworth. September 5, 1762. Historic Pittsburgh, https://historicpittsburgh.org/islandora/object/pitt%3A31735061276352
12. E. A. Fenn, "Biological Warfare in Eighteenth-Century North America: Beyond Jeffery Amherst," *The Journal of American History* 86, no. 4 (2000): 1552–80, https://doi.org/10.2307/2567577
13. Fort Niagara State Park, https://parks.ny.gov/parks/fortniagara
14. Wills De Hass, *History of the Early Settlement and Indian Wars of West Virginia: An Account of the Various Expeditions in the West, Previous to 1795* (Philadelphia, PA: King & Baird, 1851), https://archive.org/details/historyofearlyse00deha/page/n7/mode/2up
15. Marriage License Information. Winchester, Virginia, www.winfredclerk.com/marriage1.htm
16. Allan W. Eckert, *That Dark and Bloody River* (New York: Bantam Books, 1995).
17. Eckert, *That Dark and Bloody River*.
18. Ohio County Public Library—Fort Henry, Wheeling, W. VA., https://www.ohiocountylibrary.org/history/3698
19. De Hass, *History of the Early Settlement and Indian Wars*.
20. De Hass, *History of the Early Settlement and Indian Wars*.
21. De Hass, *History of the Early Settlement and Indian Wars*.
22. Eckert, *That Dark and Bloody River*.
23. *The Virginia Magazine of History and Biography* (Richmond, VA: Historical Society, 1893), https://archive.org/details/virginiamagazin02socigoog/

NOTES

24 S. S. Cohen, "Captain Robert Niles and the Connecticut State Navy," *The New England Quarterly* 89, no. 1 (2016): 84–108.

25 Naval History and Heritage Command, *The American Revolution 1775-1783: The Navy's Role in the Revolutionary War* (US Navy, n.d.), https://www.history.navy.mil/browse-by-topic/wars-conflicts-and-operations/american-revolution.html

26 C. Schurr, "The History of the US Postal Service—And That Time Someone Sent Their Kid Through the Mail," HistoryNet, 1997, https://www.historynet.com/history-us-postal-service/

Chapter 3

1 Population in the Colonial and Continental periods. Census procedure in Colonial and Continental periods—population prior to 1790—recent estimates of early population—population of cities—changes in urban population 1710–1900, https://www.census.gov/history/pdf/colonialbostonpops.pdf

2 Annals of the Carnegie Museum. Historic Pittsburgh, p. 10, https://historicpittsburgh.org/islandora/object/pitt%3A31735038275974/viewer#page/12/mode/2up

3 Annals of the Carnegie Museum, p. 11.

4 De Hass, *History of the Early Settlement and Indian Wars*.

5 Nogay, *Every Home a Fort, Every Man a Warrior*.

6 De Hass, *History of the Early Settlement and Indian Wars*.

7 De Hass, *History of the Early Settlement and Indian Wars*.

8 De Hass, *History of the Early Settlement and Indian Wars*.

9 De Hass, *History of the Early Settlement and Indian Wars*.

10 De Hass, *History of the Early Settlement and Indian Wars*.

11 E. Nicodemus, "The Mostly True Story of Simon Girty: The Renegade of the Ohio Frontier," *Weelunk*, September 23, 2000, https://weelunk.com/mostly-true-story-simon-girty/

12 De Hass, *History of the Early Settlement and Indian Wars*.

13 De Hass, *History of the Early Settlement and Indian Wars*.

14 American Battlefield Trust, "Revolutionary War – Battle of Brandywine," https://www.battlefields.org/learn/revolutionary-war/battles/brandywine

15 American Battlefield Trust, "Revolutionary War – Battle of Paoli," https://www.battlefields.org/learn/revolutionary-war/battles/paoli

16 American Battlefield Trust, "Revolutionary War – Battle of Paoli."

17 American Battlefield Trust, "Revolutionary War Saratoga," https://www.battlefields.org/learn/revolutionary-war/battles/saratoga

18 M. Flint, "Bacheller vs. Wilkinson: The Quest to Understand Benedict Arnold at Saratoga," *Journal of the American Revolution* (2024), https://allthingsliberty.com/2024/09/bacheller-vs-wilkinson-the-quest-to-understand-benedict-arnold-at-saratoga/

19 American Battlefield Trust, "Revolutionary War – Saratoga."
20 American Battlefield Trust, "Revolutionary War – Siege of Fort Mifflin," https://www.battlefields.org/learn/revolutionary-war/battles/siege-fort-mifflin
21 American Battlefield Trust, "Revolutionary War – Siege of Fort Mifflin."
22 J. K. Swisher, "Lord Dunmore's War: The Battle of Point Pleasant," Shawnee Indians and Virginians waged a thunderous and bloody battle at Point Pleasant during the conflict now known as Lord Dunmore's War, 2003. https://warfarehistorynetwork.com/article/lord-dunmores-war-the-battle-of-point-pleasant/
23 Swisher, "Lord Dunmore's War."
24 Annals of the Carnegie Museum, p. 31.
25 Annals of the Carnegie Museum, p. 31.
26 Annals of the Carnegie Museum, p. 25.

Chapter 4

1 Nogay, *Every Home a Fort, Every Man a Warrior*.
2 Gemma Ware, "Indigenous Peoples Day Offers a Reminder of Native American History – Including the Scalping They Endured at the Hands of Colonists," 2023, https://theconversation.com/indigenous-peoples-day-offers-a-reminder-of-native-american-history-including-the-scalping-they-endured-at-the-hands-of-colonists-214433
3 "Upstander Project," Phips Bounty Proclamation, https://upstanderproject.org/learn/guides-and-resources/first-light/phips-bounty-proclamation#:~:text=In%2017552C%20Spencer%20Phips%2C%20lieutenant,pursuing%2C%20captivating%2C%20killing%2C%20and
4 "Upstander Project," Phips Bounty Proclamation.
5 *The Papers of Thomas Jefferson, vol. 2, 1777–18 June 1779*, ed. Julian P. Boyd (Princeton, NJ: Princeton University Press, 1950), pp. 132–3.
6 "Virginia Places – How Colonists Acquired Title to Land in Virginia," http://www.virginiaplaces.org/settleland/headright.html
7 "Revolutionary War Allotments," Kentucky State Website – KY.gov, https://www.sos.ky.gov/land/military/revwar/Pages/Revolutionary-War-Allotments.aspx
8 "Virginia Places – How Colonists Acquired Title."
9 "Virginia Places – How Colonists Acquired Title."
10 W. H. Glasson and D. Kinley, *Federal Military Pensions in the United States* (New York: Oxford University Press, 1918), https://archive.org/details/federalmilitaryp00glasuoft/page/n5/mode/2up?q=1778
11 Glasson and Kinley, *Federal Military Pensions in the United States*.
12 L. Daen, "Revolutionary War Invalid Pensions and the Bureaucratic Language of Disability in the Early Republic," *Early American Literature* 52, no. 1 (2017): 141–67, https://www.jstor.org/stable/90009795

13 Heinz History Center, "Fort Pitt During the Revolutionary War: General Brodhead's Expedition," https://www.heinzhistorycenter.org/blog/fort-pitt-museum-fort-pitt-during-the-revolutionary-war-general-brodheads-expedition/
14 Joe Roxby, "Sam Mason: Wheeling's Deadliest Outlaw," 2002/2015, https://weelunk.com/sam-mason-7032/
15 Annals of the Carnegie Museum, p. 51.
16 Annals of the Carnegie Museum, p. 55.
17 Benedict Arnold Commits Treason, "This Day in History," History.com, September 21, 1780, https://www.history.com/this-day-in-history/benedict-arnold-commits-treason
18 Benedict Arnold Commits Treason, "This Day in History."
19 D. Head and T. Hemmis, *A Republic of Scoundrels: The Schemers, Intriguers, and Adventurers Who Created a New American Nation* (New York: Simon & Schuster, 2024).
20 Kings Mountain Battle, *Encyclopedia of North Carolina*, ed. William S. Powell (University of North Carolina Press, 2006), https://www.ncpedia.org/kings-mountain-battle
21 Kings Mountain Battle, *Encyclopedia of North Carolina*.
22 Kings Mountain Battle, *Encyclopedia of North Carolina*.
23 Kings Mountain Battle, *Encyclopedia of North Carolina*.
24 Many identified Brodhead as a General at this time. He was promoted thusly upon retirement, not while in command of Fort Pitt. Colonel Daniel Brodhead, Sr. The State Society of the Cincinnati of Pennsylvania, https://pasocietyofthecincinnati.org/gallery_post/col-daniel-brodhead-sr/
25 Nogay, *Every Home a Fort, Every Man a Warrior*.

Chapter 5

1 De Hass, *History of the Early Settlement and Indian Wars*.
2 De Hass, *History of the Early Settlement and Indian Wars*.
3 The core message of the gospel is simply that God created humans to be in a relationship with Him, but sin separates us from God. Jesus Christ, God's Son, lived a sinless life, died on the cross to take the punishment for sin, and rose from the dead, offering eternal life to those who believe in Him.
4 E. Nicodemus, "Geo-history: The Gnadenhutten Massacre," *Weelunk,* May 6, 2020, https://weelunk.com/geo-history-gnadenhutten-massacre/
5 Nogay, *Every Home a Fort, Every Man a Warrior*.
6 De Hass, *History of the Early Settlement and Indian Wars*.
7 De Hass, *History of the Early Settlement and Indian Wars*.
8 De Hass, *History of the Early Settlement and Indian Wars*.

9   De Hass, *History of the Early Settlement and Indian Wars.*
10 De Hass, *History of the Early Settlement and Indian Wars.*
11 Fort Henry, Ohio County Library, https://www.ohiocountylibrary.org/history/3698
12 Nogay, *Every Home a Fort, Every Man a Warrior.*
13 Nogay, *Every Home a Fort, Every Man a Warrior.*
14 Lochte and Markgraf, "Samuel Mason: The Cave-In-Rock Pirate Who Prowled the Region's Waterways," *WKMS,* June 18, 2015, https://www.wkms.org/arts-culture/2015-06-18/samuel-mason-the-cave-in-rock-pirate-who-prowled-the-regions-waterways/

Chapter 6

1   Bell, Samuel Mason 1739–1803.
2   Bell, Samuel Mason 1739–1803.
3   "The History of Debt in America – Colonial Times to the Present Day." https://rianjs.net/media/2008/A%20history%20of%20debt%20in%20America.pdf
4   "The History of Debt in America."
5   Logan County Courthouse http://www.courthouses.co/us-states/h-l/kentucky/logan-county/ The description of Logan County as "Rogue's Harbor" is based on a combination of historical narratives, local histories, and early records that depict the area as a haven for outlaws. While the exact phrase may not be traced to a single original document, it is a well-established part of the region's lore and historical characterizations.
6   Public Broadcasting System (PBS), "Technology Timeline (1752–1990)." https://www.pbs.org/wgbh/americanexperience/features/telephone-technology-timeline/
7   Bell, Samuel Mason 1739–1803.
8   T. Carr, *Cave-in-Rock Pirates and Outlaws* (Charleston, SC: The History Press, 2019).
9   "History of the US Mint," United States Mint, https://www.usmint.gov/learn/history.
10 New England Historical Society, "How a Slave and a Counterfeiter Made the Fugio Cent, the 1st U.S. Money," https://newenglandhistoricalsociety.com/fugio-cent-1st-u-s-money-made-slave-counterfeiter/
11 David A. Martin, "The Suspicion of Corruption in Early American Coinage," *The Numismatist* 94, no. 7 (July 1981): 1119–24.
12 New England Historical Society, "How a Slave and a Counterfeiter."
13 R. G. Doty, *America's Money, America's Story: A Chronicle of American Numismatics* (Iola, WI: Krause Publications, 1998).
14 J. Daniels, "The Devil's Backbone: The Story of the Natchez Trace," p. 124. https://archive.org/details/devilsbackbonest0000dani/page/n5/mode/2up

NOTES

15 The 1792 Census of Henderson County, Kentucky (formerly known as Red Banks/Charleston) https://occgs.com/projects/rescue/locations/kentucky/HENDERSON%20County-VITAL%20RECORDS.pdf
16 Rothert, *The Outlaws of Cave-In-Rock*.
17 Rothert, *The Outlaws of Cave-In-Rock*.
18 Rothert, *The Outlaws of Cave-In-Rock*.
19 Rothert, *The Outlaws of Cave-In-Rock*.
20 Rothert, *The Outlaws of Cave-In-Rock*.
21 A. C. Finley, *The History of Russellville and Logan County, KY*. Reprint (Russellville, KY: A. B. Willhite, 1876, Reprint c. 2000), p. 42 (page number from reprint).

Chapter 7

1 Rothert, *The Outlaws of Cave-In-Rock*.
2 Rothert, *The Outlaws of Cave-In-Rock*.
3 Rothert, *The Outlaws of Cave-In-Rock*.
4 "Hurricane Island." Anyplace America, https://www.anyplaceamerica.com/directory/ky/crittenden-county-21055/islands/hurricane-island-512871/
5 Episode 491 (9-23-19): "Samuel Mason," by Andrew and Noah VanNorstrand, Recalls a Notorious, Virginia-born River Pirate. http://www.virginiawaterradio.org/2019/09/episode-491-9-23-19-samuel-mason-by.html
6 A. Graf, "Where and Why Do Modern Pirate Attacks Happen?," *The Globe Post*, September 24, 2019, https://theglobepost.com/2019/09/24/modern-piracy-explained/; R. Smith, "Cargo Theft on the Rise – Report," *Insurance Business*, January 16, 2023, https://www.insurancebusinessmag.com/us/news/marine/cargo-theft-on-the-rise--report-432971.aspx
7 ABC News, "Armed Mexican Pirates Terrorize Texas Lake," *ABC News*, May 25, 2010, https://abcnews.go.com/International/Media/armed-mexican-pirates-terrorize-texas-lake/story?id=10729
8 An example of privateering can be seen in the actions of Sir Francis Drake, an English privateer in the sixteenth century. Commissioned by Queen Elizabeth I, Drake attacked Spanish ships and settlements in the Caribbean, capturing vast amounts of treasure with England's tacit approval and seriously disrupting Spanish maritime activities, thereby contributing to England's naval dominance.
9 WikiTree – Joshua (Harper) Harp. https://www.wikitree.com/wiki/Harper-6545
10 WikiTree – William (Harper) Harp. https://www.wikitree.com/wiki/Harper-6542
11 Josephus C. Guild, "Old Times in Tennessee, with Historical, Personal, and Political Scraps and Sketches," 1878. https://archive.org/details/oldtimesintennes00guil_0
12 Guild, "Old Times in Tennessee."
13 C. F. Smith, *Gangs and the Military: Gangsters, Bikers, and Terrorists with Military Training* (Lanham, MD: Rowman & Littlefield, 2017, 2019).

14 J. Musgrave, "The Boat-Wreckers—Or Banditti of the West," *Jon's Southern Illinois History Page*, 1999, http://www.illinoishistory.com/plug.html
15 Flint, Col. Plug, in Springhouse 9, 1, 92. http://springhousemagazine.com/frontpage.htm

Chapter 8

1 U.S. Census Bureau, *Annual Estimates of the Resident Population for States and Counties: April 1, 2020 to July 1, 2023* (2023), https://www.census.gov/data/tables/time-series/demo/popest/2020s-counties-total.html
2 See also "Samuel Mason" song from All the Good Summers by Andrew & Noah VanNorstrand, https://andrewandnoah.bandcamp.com/track/samuel-mason; Rothert, *The Outlaws of Cave-In-Rock*.
3 Margot Ford McMillen, *Paris, Tightwad and Peculiar: Missouri Place Names* (Columbia, MO: University of Missouri Press, 1994), p. 2.
4 Island No. 5 (Wolf Island)/Belmont, Missouri/Columbus, Kentucky Mississippi River Walk. https://www.hmdb.org/m.asp?m=114730
5 Rothert, *The Outlaws of Cave-In-Rock*.
6 Guild, "Old Times in Tennessee."
7 Guild, "Old times in Tennessee."
8 Highwaymen were common in Europe from the sixteenth to the nineteenth centuries, particularly in England during the eighteenth century.
9 Rothert, *The Outlaws of Cave-In-Rock*.
10 Rothert, *The Outlaws of Cave-In-Rock*.
11 Rothert, *The Outlaws of Cave-In-Rock*.
12 Rothert, *The Outlaws of Cave-In-Rock*.
13 Rothert, *The Outlaws of Cave-In-Rock*.
14 Robert M. Coates, *The Outlaw Years; the History of the Land Pirates of the Natchez Trace* (New York: Macaulay Company, 1930). https://archive.org/details/outlawyearshisto0000unse
15 Coates, *The Outlaw Years*.
16 The tradition influenced colonial and early American legal systems, where authorities aimed to deliver a painful punishment that was, theoretically, one lash short of fatal. Thirty-nine lashes were severe enough to inflict lasting pain and scars but were chosen to avoid crossing the line into excessive cruelty or risk of death, reflecting early nineteenth-century legal standards on corporal punishment limits. The number thirty-nine had specific roots in Judeo-Christian traditions, particularly from the New Testament, where Paul the Apostle mentions receiving "forty lashes minus one" as a common punishment (2 Cor. 11:24).
17 Rothert, *The Outlaws of Cave-In-Rock*.

Chapter 9

1. D. Rowland, "Mississippi: Comprising Sketches of Counties, Towns, Events, Institutions, and Persons, Arranged in Cyclopedic Form" (Atlanta, Georgia: Southern Historical Publishing Association, 1907).
2. Mason (Samuel) Trial Records, 22,34,42,49.
3. W. C. C. Claiborne, *Official Letter Books of W.C.C. Claiborne, 1801–1816* (Jackson, MS: State Department of Archives and History, 1917). https://archive.org/details/officialletterb00rowlgoog/
4. Claiborne, *Official Letter Books of W.C.C. Claiborne, 1801–1816.*
5. Stanley Nelson, "Bad Men Cornered at Old Greenville." *Concordia Sentinel* (West Monroe, LA: Hanna Newspapers), June 17, 2020.
6. Claiborne, *Official Letter Books of W.C.C. Claiborne, 1801–1816.*
7. The Slave Trade. National Archives. https://www.archives.gov/education/lessons/slave-trade.html
8. Rothert, *The Outlaws of Cave-In-Rock.*
9. Little Prairie Pemiscot County, Missouri. Roots Web. https://sites.rootsweb.com/~mopemisc/pc-towns/LittlePrairie.htm
10. Rothert, *The Outlaws of Cave-In-Rock.*
11. Coates, *The Outlaw Years.*
12. Coates, *The Outlaw Years.*
13. Guild, "Old Times in Tennessee."
14. Guild, "Old Times in Tennessee."
15. Guild, "Old Times in Tennessee."
16. Colbert Ferry Natchez Trace, https://www.natcheztracetravel.com/natchez-trace-alabama/florence-tennessee-river/124-colbert-ferry.html
17. Guild, "Old Times in Tennessee."
18. Guild, "Old Times in Tennessee."
19. Guild, "Old Times in Tennessee."
20. Dan L. Flores, "Biography of Anthony Glass, (unknown–1819)," Texas State Historical Association, https://www.tshaonline.org/handbook/entries/glass-anthony
21. Coates, *The Outlaw Years.*
22. "Glass (Anthony) Papers Unspecified — Box: 2E559 Dolph Briscoe Center for American History," Natchez Trace Small Manuscript Collections, https://collections.briscoecenter.org/repositories/2/archival_objects/42969
23. L. Walser, "King's Tavern in Natchez, Mississippi. More: Historic Bars," National Trust for Historic Preservation, 2017, https://savingplaces.org/stories/kings-tavern-in-natchez-mississippi
24. Original Transcripts, https://archive.org/details/complete-trial-transcript-original-samuel-mason

25 Most historians recite some variation of Mason's statement as "he has some pretensions on some lands on the Monogela [sic] as heir from his brother died without any children," which was pulled from the English translation of the transcripts. This interview reflects the alternate translation. The French transcripts may hold the key to clarifying this, but we suspect a translation issue, regardless. There is no record of Mason or his brother having property on the Monongahela River, though there is record of land in Kentucky, the ownership of which was contested because Mason's brother Joseph Mason (Meason) died after giving a nuncupative (oral) will to two witnesses, one of whom was his sister Rachael Thompson. In the oral will, Joseph left his land (in Kentucky) to his nephew Joseph Worthington, Rachael Thompson's son from her first marriage.

26 When asked in the trial if someone else could vouch for him, Mason identified General Harrison, whose sister was married to his brother, the one who had charge of the furnace on the Youghiogheny (River). General Harrison was Benjamin Harrison. His sister, Catherine Harrison, was married to Isaac Mason, Sam's brother. Benjamin was very influential in the establishment of Kentucky, and he also had land interests and lived on the Spanish side of the river in and around New Madrid in the early 1800s.

Chapter 10

1 See Milestones in the History of US Foreign Relations, https://history.state.gov/milestones/1801-1829

2 Houck's, "History of Missouri from the Earliest Explorations," 1908, Volume 2, p. 140. According to Conrad's "Encyclopedia of the History of Missouri," 1901, p. 557 a Creek named Tewanaye in 1802 had been found guilty of murder in New Orleans and in a return trip Tewanaye had tried to escape and crippled McCoy, https://books.google.com/books?id=3ZB5AAAAMAAJ&pg=PA143#v=onepage&q&f=false

3 Louisiana State Museum, *Louisiana History: The Louisiana Purchase* (Louisiana State Museum, n.d.), https://louisianastatemuseum.org/louisiana-history-louisiana-purchase

4 Louisiana State Museum, *Louisiana History: The Louisiana Purchase*.

5 "How the Louisiana Purchase Changed the World," *Smithsonian Magazine*, https://www.smithsonianmag.com/history/how-the-louisiana-purchase-changed-the-world-79715124/

6 Louisiana State Museum, *Louisiana history: The Louisiana Purchase*.

7 U.S. Census Bureau, *Historical Population Estimates: 1790 to 2020* (2023), https://www.census.gov/data/tables/time-series/demo/popest/2020s-counties-total.html

8 William C. C. Claiborne to James Madison, July 26, 1803, https://www.loc.gov/resource/mjm.07_0923_0924/?sp=1

9 Carr, *Cave-in-Rock Pirates and Outlaws*.

10 Ronald R. Morazán, "Records of the Cabildo: Miscellaneous Documents Relating to River Pirates," *Louisiana History: The Journal of the Louisiana Historical Association*

42, no. 2 (2001): 209–16, http://www.jstor.org/stable/4233736 It appears that Morazán credited Coates for this information.

11 Roxby, *Sam Mason: Wheeling's Deadliest Outlaw.*
12 Guild, "Old Times in Tennessee."
13 Rothert, *The Outlaws of Cave-In-Rock.*
14 Publications of the Mississippi Historical Society, Volume 11.
15 From personal communication, David R. Chittenden, September 19, 2019 and Chittenden's post on https://www.findagrave.com/memorial/192984249/samuel_ross-mason
16 Coates, *The Outlaw Years.*
17 Rothert, The Outlaws of Cave-In-Rock.
18 Coates, *The Outlaw Years.*
19 Claiborne, *Official Letter Books of W.C.C. Claiborne, 1801–1816*, p. 392.
20 To James Madison from William C. C. Claiborne, March 15, 1804, Founders Online, National Archives, https://founders.archives.gov/documents/Madison/02-06-02-0550
21 Rothert, *The Outlaws of Cave-In-Rock.*
22 Claiborne, *Official Letter Books of W.C.C. Claiborne, 1801–1816*, p. 91.
23 Claiborne, *Official Letter Books of W.C.C. Claiborne, 1801–1816*, p. 40.
24 Mason (Samuel) Trial Records.
25 Draper n.d:306.
26 Draper n.d.:312.
27 Draper n.d.:311.
28 Draper n.d:317.
29 Elizabeth Mason Briscoe. Findagrave, https://www.findagrave.com/memorial/203251121/elizabeth_briscoe
30 Dorsey Magnus Meason. Findagrave, https://www.findagrave.com/memorial/223809507/dorsey-magnus-meason

Chapter 11

1 Ward, *Between the Lines: Banditti of the American Revolution.*
2 There is no record of Mason or his brother having property on the Monongahela River, though there is a record of land in Kentucky, the ownership of which was contested because Mason's brother, Joseph Mason (Meason), died after giving a nuncupative (oral) will to two witnesses, one of whom was his sister, Rachael Thompson. In the oral will, Joseph left his land (in Kentucky) to his nephew, Joseph Worthington, Rachael Thompson's son from her first marriage.
3 Coates, *The Outlaw Years.*

4   J. Roxby, "Sam Mason: Wheeling's Deadliest Outlaw," 2015, https://weelunk.com/sam-mason-7032/

5   Roxby, "Sam Mason."

6   Roxby, "Sam Mason."

7   Roxby, "Sam Mason."

8   Smith, *Gangs and the Military.*

9   Questioning God or seeking understanding at life's end reflects a universal curiosity about our existence and purpose. The Bible acknowledges the human desire for wisdom, yet reminds us that some mysteries remain hidden until they are revealed by God (Deut. 29:29; 1 Cor. 13:12). These verses highlight that while we may "see in a mirror, dimly," we will one day "know just as [we are] known."

10 Throughout Scripture, the pursuit of understanding life's deeper questions is encouraged, though full understanding often comes only in God's presence. This mirrors the sentiment of seeing clearly in the life to come, as described in passages like 1 Cor. 13:12, where the partial nature of earthly knowledge gives way to complete clarity.

11 The decision to accept Jesus as one's Savior is depicted in Scripture as a choice that must be made during one's lifetime. The imagery of "after the bell rings, the whistle blows, or the trumpet sounds" conveys the finality of this choice upon death, aligning with biblical themes of urgency and preparedness (cf. Heb. 9:27; 2 Cor. 6:2). Once life has ended, the opportunity to make this decision passes, underscoring the significance of deciding before it is, as Scripture says, "too late."

Appendix A

1   Old Fort Niagara, https://www.oldfortniagara.org

2   See Ohio County Public Library, https://www.ohiocountylibrary.org/history/5541 and the *Wheeling Intelligencer*, July 15, 1908, http://ohiocountywv.advantage-preservation.com/viewer/?k=alley&i=f&d=852-12312020&e=zane%20cabin&m=between&ord=e1,k1&fn=wheeling_intelligencer_usa_west_virginia_wheeling_715_english_3&df=1&dt=5

3   Interestingly, she is sometimes referred to as the first female president, as it's pretty much known that Wilson suffered from severe ill health in the last year of his second term and wasn't really capable of any type of decision-making.

4   James White Fort, https://www.jameswhitesfort.org

5   Ramsey House, https://www.ramseyhouse.org/

6   Kentucky Historical Society, "Town House of Maj. Richard Bibb," https://history.ky.gov/markers/town-house-of-maj-richard-bibb

7   Farmer and Frenchman Winery, https://farmerandfrenchman.com/

8   J. Harris, "Exploring America's Rivers: From History to Habitat at Inland Waterways Museum in Paducah," October 26, 2020, https://www.paducah.travel/blog/stories/

NOTES

post/exploring-americas-rivers-from-history-habitat-at-inland-waterways-museum-in-paducah/

9. "Drought Status Update for the Midwest," US Drought.gov., https://www.drought.gov/drought-status-updates/drought-status-update-midwest-us-2023-06-23

10. Mason's sister Rachel was listed in their father's (Thomas Mason/Meason's) will in 1779 as Rachel Worthington, wife of Robert Worthington, Jr. Following Robert Worthington's death, she married Joseph Thompson. That's who she was married to when she was living at Cape Girardeau.

11. M. J. Wagner, *Archival and Historic Investigations for the Cherokee Trail of Tears in Union County* (National Park Service, 2003), https://www.nps.gov/trte/learn/historyculture/upload/Archival-and-Historical-Investigations-of-Union-County-508.pdf

12. Bumbu Rum Company – The Bottle, https://bumbu.sovereignbrands.com/the-bottle/

13. Colbert Ferry Natchez Trace.

14. Gordon House and Duck River Ferry Site Natchez Trace, https://www.natcheztracetravel.com/natchez-trace-tennessee/columbia-centerville-tn/83-gordon-house-and-duck-river-ferry-site.html

15. The Cabildo. Wikipedia, https://en.m.wikipedia.org/wiki/The_Cabildo

16. Lafitte's Blacksmith Shop. Wikipedia, https://en.m.wikipedia.org/wiki/Lafitte%27s_Blacksmith_Shop

17. Steven A. Grasse, "Wine." Essay, in *Colonial Spirits: a Toast to Our Drunken History; Being: a Revolutionary Drinking Guide to Brewing and Batching, Mixing and Serving, Imbibing and Jibing, Fighting and Freedom in the Ruins of the Ancient Civilization Known as America* (New York: Abrams Image, 2016), 69–86, https://www.amazon.com/Colonial-Spirits-Toast-Drunken-History/dp/1419722301; and David Hancock, "Commerce and Conversation in the Eighteenth-Century Atlantic: The Invention of Madeira Wine," *The Journal of Interdisciplinary History* 29, no. 2 (1998): 197–219, https://doi.org/10.1162/002219598551670

18. T. Jefferson, *The Garden Book*. [Digital Edition] (Monticello: Thomas Jefferson Foundation, 1959), https://www.monticello.org/research-education/thomas-jefferson-encyclopedia/garden-book/

19. General Orders, June 9, 1777, *Founders Online*, National Archives, https://founders.archives.gov/documents/Washington/03-09-02-0646. [Original source: *The Papers of George Washington*, Revolutionary War Series, vol. 9, *28 March 1777–10 June 1777*, ed. Philander D. Chase. Charlottesville, VA: University Press of Virginia, 1999, pp. 651–2.]

Appendix B

1. Compiled from references herein to supplement Bell's list, https://wvancestry.com/Files/Samuel_Mason_1739-1803.pdf

Appendix C

1. E. Nicodemus, "The Mostly True Story of Simon Girty: The Renegade of the Ohio Frontier," *Weelunk*, September 23, 2020, https://weelunk.com/mostly-true-story-simon-girty/
2. De Hass, *History of the Early Settlement and Indian Wars*.
3. E. Nicodemus, "The Mostly True Story of 'Betsy' Zane," February 7, 2016, https://weelunk.com/the-mostly-true-story-of-betsy-zane/
4. Nicodemus, "The Mostly True Story of 'Betsy' Zane."
5. Eric Sterner, "Betty Zane and the Siege of Fort Henry, September 1782," *Journal of the American Revolution* (2020), https://allthingsliberty.com/2020/01/betty-zane-and-the-siege-of-fort-henry-september-1782/
6. Sam Mason. Baseball Reference, https://www.baseball-reference.com/register/player.fcgi?id=mason-002sam

BIBLIOGRAPHY

Bell, Raymond M. "Samuel Mason 1739–1803: Captain in Virginia, Judge in Pennsylvania, River Pirate in Kentucky, Desperado in Mississippi. Washington, Pennsylvania." 1985. https://wvancestry.com/Files/Samuel_Mason_1739-1803.pdf.

Benedict Arnold Commits Treason. "This Day in History." *History.com,* September 21, 1780. https://www.history.com/this-day-in-history/benedict-arnold-commits-treason.

Brodhead, Col. *Daniel Sr.* The State Society of the Cincinnati of Pennsylvania, n.d. https://pasocietyofthecincinnati.org/gallery_post/col-daniel-brodhead-sr/.

Carr, Todd. *Cave-in-Rock Pirates and Outlaws.* Charleston, SC: The History Press, 2019.

Claiborne, W. C. C. *Official Letter Books of W.C.C. Claiborne, 1801-1816.* Jackson, MS: State Department of Archives and History, 1917. https://archive.org/details/officialletterb00rowlgoog/.

Claiborne, W. C. C. to James Madison, July 26, 1803. https://www.loc.gov/resource/mjm.07_0923_0924/?sp=1.

Coates, Robert M. *The Outlaw Years; the History of the Land Pirates of the Natchez Trace.* New York: Macaulay Company, 1930.

Daen, Laurel. "Revolutionary War Invalid Pensions and the Bureaucratic Language of Disability in the Early Republic." *Early American Literature* 52, no. 1 (2017): 141–167. https://www.jstor.org/stable/90009795.

Daniels, Jonathan. *The Devil's Backbone: The Story of the Natchez Trace,* 1962. New York, NY: McGraw-Hill.

De Hass, Wills. *History of the Early Settlement and Indian Wars of West Virginia: An Account of the Various Expeditions in the West, Previous to 1795.* Philadelphia, PA: King & Baird, 1851. https://archive.org/details/historyofearlyse00deha/page/n7/mode/2up.

Draper, Lyman C. *Manuscript Collections.* Wisconsin Historical Society, n.d. Various references.

"Drought Status Update for the Midwest U.S." Drought.gov. https://www.drought.gov/drought-status-updates/drought-status-update-midwest-us-2023-06-23.

Dunphy, Mike. "Tasting Table. Here's What Our Founding Fathers Drank at George Washington's Farewell Party." August 4, 2024. https://www.tastingtable.com/1632124/george-washington-bar-tab-party/.

Eckert, Allan W. *That Dark and Bloody River.* New York: Bantam Books, 1995.

Fenn, E. A. "Biological Warfare in Eighteenth-Century North America: Beyond Jeffery Amherst." *The Journal of American History* 86, no. 4 (2000): 1552–1580. https://doi.org/10.2307/2567577.

Finley, A. C. *The History of Russellville and Logan County, KY.* Russellville, KY: A. B. Willhite, 1876, Reprint c. 2000, p. 42 (page number from reprint).

Flores, Dan L. "Biography of Anthony Glass, (unknown–1819)." Texas State Historical Association, 1952. https://www.tshaonline.org/handbook/entries/glass-anthony.

"French and Indian War Militia and Provisioners to the (Frederick County, Virginia) Militia." 1758, March. http://files.usgwarchives.net/va/frederick/military/frenchindian/fiw_frederick.txt.

General Orders, *Founders Online,* National Archives. June 9, 1777. https://founders.archives.gov/documents/Washington/03-09-02-0646. [Original source: *The Papers of George Washington*, Revolutionary War Series, vol. 9, *28 March 1777–10 June 1777*, edited by Philander D. Chase. Charlottesville, VA: University Press of Virginia, 1999, pp. 651–652.]

Glass (Anthony) Papers unspecified — Box: 2E559 Dolph Briscoe Center for American History, Natchez Trace Small Manuscript Collections. https://collections.briscoecenter.org/repositories/2/archival_objects/42969.

Glasson, W. H., and D. Kinley. *Federal Military Pensions in the United States.* New York: Oxford University Press, 1918. https://archive.org/details/federalmilitaryp00glasuoft/page/n5/mode/2up?q=1778.

Guild, Josephus C. "Old Times in Tennessee, with Historical, Personal, and Political Scraps and Sketches." 1878. https://archive.org/details/oldtimesintennes00guil_0.

Harriss, Joseph A. "How the Louisiana Purchase Changed the World." *Smithsonian Magazine.* 2003. https://www.smithsonianmag.com/history/how-the-louisiana-purchase-changed-the-world-79715124/.

Head, D., and T. Hemmis. *A Republic of Scoundrels: The Schemers, Intriguers, and Adventurers Who Created a New American Nation.* New York: Simon & Schuster, 2024.

Heinz History Center. *Fort Pitt During the Revolutionary War: General Brodhead's Expedition,* 2017. https://www.heinzhistorycenter.org/blog/fort-pitt-museum-fort-pitt-during-the-revolutionary-war-general-brodheads-expedition/.

Jefferson, Thomas. *The Garden Book.* [Digital Edition] Monticello: Thomas Jefferson Foundation, 1959. https://www.monticello.org/research-education/thomas-jefferson-encyclopedia/garden-book/.

Kings Mountain Battle. *Encyclopedia of North Carolina,* edited by William S. Powell. University of North Carolina Press, 2006. https://www.ncpedia.org/kings-mountain-battle.

"Lach, Jr., Edward L. Mason, Samuel 1750–July 1803." 1999. https://doi.org/10.1093/anb/9780198606697.article.2000644.

"Little Prairie Pemiscot County, Missouri." Roots Web, 2018. https://sites.rootsweb.com/~mopemisc/pc-towns/LittlePrairie.htm.

Lochte and Markgraf. "Samuel Mason: The Cave-In-Rock Pirate Who Prowled the Region's Waterways." *WKMS,* June 18, 2015. https://www.wkms.org/arts-culture/2015-06-18/samuel-mason-the-cave-in-rock-pirate-who-prowled-the-regions-waterways/.

"Madison, James from William C. C. Claiborne, 15 March 1804, Founders Online, National Archives," https://founders.archives.gov/documents/Madison/02-06-02-0550.

BIBLIOGRAPHY

"Minute (or Order) Book for the Virginia Court Held for Ohio County Virginia." Annals of the Carnegie Museum. Historic Pittsburgh, 1904. https://historicpittsburgh.org/islandora/object/pitt%3A31735038275974/viewer#page/12/mode/2up.

Mississippi Department of Archives and History (MDAH). "Mason (Samuel) Trial Records. Call Number Z/0273.000, MDAH, Archival Reading Room, Manuscript Collection. Jackson, Mississippi." 1803. http://opac2.mdah.state.ms.us/phpmanuscripts/z0273.php.

Morazán, Ronald R. "Records of the Cabildo: Miscellaneous Documents Relating to River Pirates." *Louisiana History: The Journal of the Louisiana Historical Association* 42, no. 2 (2001): 209–16. http://www.jstor.org/stable/4233736.

Musgrave, Jon. "The Boat-Wreckers—Or Banditti of the West." *Jon's Southern Illinois History Page*, 1999. http://www.illinoishistory.com/plug.html.

Nicodemus, Earl. "Geo-history: The Gnadenhutten Massacre." *Weelunk*, May 6, 2020. https://weelunk.com/geo-history-gnadenhutten-massacre/.

Nicodemus, Earl. "The Mostly True Story of 'Betsy' Zane." February 7, 2016. https://weelunk.com/the-mostly-true-story-of-betsy-zane/.

Nicodemus, Earl. "The Mostly True Story of Simon Girty: The Renegade of the Ohio Frontier." *Weelunk*, September 23, 2020. https://weelunk.com/mostly-true-story-simon-girty/.

Nogay, Michael E. *Every Home a Fort, Every Man a Warrior: Stories of the Forts and Men in the Upper Ohio Valley During the American Revolutionary War*. Steubenville, OH: Tri-State Publishing Co., 2009.

Papers of Thomas Jefferson, vol. 2, 1777–18 June 1779, edited by Julian P. Boyd. Princeton, NJ: Princeton University Press. 1950.

Preston, David. "When Young George Washington Started a War." *Smithsonian Magazine*, 2019. https://www.smithsonianmag.com/history/when-young-george-washington-started-war-180973076/.

Rothert, Otto. *The Outlaws of Cave-in-Rock: Historical Accounts of the Famous Highwaymen and River Pirates Who Operated in Pioneer Days Upon the Ohio and Mississippi Rivers and Over the Old Natchez Trace*. Cleveland, OH: Arthur H. Clark, 1924. https://archive.org/details/outlawsofcaveinr00roth/page/n9/mode/2up.

Rowland, D. "Mississippi: Comprising Sketches of Counties, Towns, Events, Institutions, and Persons, Arranged in Cyclopedic Form." Atlanta, GA: Southern Historical Publishing Association, 1907.

Roxby, Joe. *Sam Mason: Wheeling's Deadliest Outlaw*, 2002/2015. https://weelunk.com/sam-mason-7032/.

Smith, Carter F. *Gangs and the Military: Gangsters, Bikers, and Terrorists with Military Training*. Lanham, MD: Rowman & Littlefield, 2017.

Smith, Ryan. "Cargo Theft on the Rise – Report." *Insurance Business*, January 16, 2023. https://www.insurancebusinessmag.com/us/news/marine/cargo-theft-on-the-rise--report-432971.aspx.

Sterner, Eric. "Betty Zane and the Siege of Fort Henry, September 1782." *Journal of the American Revolution*, 2020. https://allthingsliberty.com/2020/01/betty-zane-and-the-siege-of-fort-henry-september-1782/.

Strobel, Christoph. "Indigenous Peoples Day Offers a Reminder of Native American History – Including the Scalping They Endured at the Hands of Colonists," October 3, 2023. https://theconversation.com/indigenous-peoples-day-offers-a-reminder

-of-native-american-history-including-the-scalping-they-endured-at-the-hands-of-colonists-214433.

Swisher, James K. "Lord Dunmore's War: The Battle of Point Pleasant Shawnee Indians and Virginians Waged a Thunderous and Bloody Battle at Point Pleasant during the Conflict Now Known as Lord Dunmore's War," 2003. https://warfarehistorynetwork.com/article/lord-dunmores-war-the-battle-of-point-pleasant/.

"The Census of Henderson County, Kentucky (formerly known as Red Banks/Charleston)," 1792. https://occgs.com/projects/rescue/locations/kentucky/HENDERSON%20County-VITAL%20RECORDS.pdf.

Torrence, Robert H. Torrence and Allied Families. Philadelphia, PA: Wickersham Press, 1938. https://archive.org/details/torrencealliedfa00torr/page/n9/mode/2up.

Upstander Project. "Phips Bounty Proclamation." 2025. https://upstanderproject.org/learn/guides-and-resources/first-light/phips-bounty-proclamation#:~:text=In%201755%2C%20Spencer%20Phips%2C%20lieutenant,pursuing%2C%20captivating%2C%20killing%2C%20and.

"Virginia Magazine of History and Biography." Richmond, VA: Virginia Historical Society, 1893. https://archive.org/details/virginiamagazin02socigoog/.

"Virginia Northern Neck Land Grants, compiled by Gertrude F. Gray, Baltimore." Baltimore: Genealogical Publishing Co., 1983. https://www.familysearch.org/en/search/catalog/511490.

"Virginia Places – How Colonists Acquired Title to Land in Virginia." 1773, April 5. http://www.virginiaplaces.org/settleland/headright.html.

Wagner, Mark J. "Archival and Historic Investigations for the Cherokee Trail of Tears in Union County, Illinois." National Park Service, 2003. https://www.nps.gov/trte/learn/historyculture/upload/Archival-and-Historical-Investigations-of-Union-County-508.pdf

Walser, Lauren. "King's Tavern in Natchez, Mississippi More: Historic Bars." National Trust for Historic Preservation, 2017. https://savingplaces.org/stories/kings-tavern-in-natchez-mississippi.

Ward, Flora L., and Dorothy S. Lotito. "Officers and Men of the Frederick County Militia in the Year 1756. San Diego Chapter, D.A.R.," 1963. https://www.familysearch.org/library/books/viewer/221509/.

Winchester, Virginia. George Washington's Mount Vernon, n.d. https://www.mountvernon.org/library/digitalhistory/digital-encyclopedia/article/winchester-virginia.

Wiseman, Charles M. L. *Pioneer Period and Pioneer People of Fairfield County*. Columbus, OH: Ohio. F.J. Heer Printing Co., 1901. https://www.loc.gov/item/02012647/.

Wood, Colin J. "Bacheller vs. Wilkinson: The Quest to Understand Benedict Arnold at Saratoga." *Journal of the American Revolution*, 2024, September. https://allthingsliberty.com/2024/09/bacheller-vs-wilkinson-the-quest-to-understand-benedict-arnold-at-saratoga/.

INDEX

Abram's Delight
   museum in Winchester,
      Virginia   17, 182
Adams, John
   presidency and Quasi-War   87
   White House occupancy   80,
      101, 196
Al Capone
   comparison to Sam Mason   166–7
Algiers (New Orleans)
   The Little House   159, 195
Allegheny River
   formation of Ohio River   20, 29,
      54
Alston, Peter
   connected to May aliases   85,
      152, 216
Alston, Philip
   counterfeiting operations and
      associates   81, 85
Appalachian frontier
   settler life and conditions   5,
      11–14, 17, 19, 20, 22, 25,
      27–9, 31, 33
Army cantonments
   Cantonment Wilkinson   97,
      150
associate judges
   duties and authority   65
Audubon, John James
   observation of Mason in
      1815   165

Baker, Colonel Joshua
   robbery on Mississippi
      River   115, 117, 119, 162
   robbery on Natchez Trace   107,
      109, 132, 135, 137, 138,
      140, 141, 162
   pursuit of Mason gang   108,
      132
   letter to Governor Claiborne   115
banknotes
   counterfeit and genuine in Mason
      inventory   125–6, 128,
      130–1, 133–7, 139–40, 165
Battle of Brandywine
   Washington's defeat and
      retreat   36, 45–7, 60
Battle of Fort Necessity
   Washington's defeat and
      surrender   20–1, 23
Battle of Germantown
   fog and friendly fire   36, 45
Battle of Jumonville Glen
   precursor to French and Indian
      War   21
Battle of King's Mountain
   Patriot victory and Ferguson's
      death   60, 61

Battle of Lexington and Concord
  "shot heard 'round the world"   34
Battle of Paoli
  brutality and American
    losses   45, 46
Battle of Point Pleasant
  outcome of Dunmore's War   33,
    34, 47
Battle of Saratoga
  Arnold's charge and British
    surrender   46, 59, 97
Bayou Pierre, Mississippi
  Mason's residence   107, 126,
    130, 135–6, 139, 140, 157,
    163
Beaver Creek, Tennessee
  Harpe family residence   156
behavioral theories
  Cultural Deviance Theory   168
  Life Course Theory   168–9
  Social Disorganization
    Theory   168
Bill of Rights
  religious freedom protections   76
Black Bart (Bartholomew Roberts)
  pirate career and death   92
Blackbeard (Edward Teach)
  comparison to Mason   92
Blount, William   183
Bonnie Elizabeth Parker and Clyde
    Chestnut Barrow
  compared to Mason's mobility
    tactics   103–4
Bradford, David
  sent to arrest Mason   77
Brodhead, Daniel
  Thompson Island expedition   57–8
  command at Fort Pitt   61, 63, 65
Briscot (Philip)
  Mason's son-in-law   126, 134,
    138, 157–8, 163

British colonial forces
  strategy and presence in
    colonies   20–2
British counterfeiting strategy
  during Revolutionary War   82
Buffalo Creek, Pennsylvania
  Mason's farm location   53
Butler's Rangers
  in second siege of Fort Henry   67

Cabildo, The
  site of Louisiana Purchase
    transfer   150, 158, 194
Cairo, Illinois
  proximity to New Madrid   73,
    105, 107, 110, 189
Cantonment Wilkinson
  named after General
    Wilkinson   97, 150
Capone, Al, see Al Capone
Caruthersville, Missouri
  site of Little Prairie   118, 145
Cave-In-Rock, Illinois
  Mason's pirate headquarters   85,
    87, 90, 95, 98, 188
  strategic river location   89, 104
  tavern operation   88
Census of 1790
  national population and
    details   39, 79
Census of 1792 (Henderson
    County)
  listing of Masons and
    Kuykendalls   80, 83–4
Christian Lenape Indians
  massacred at Gnadenhutten   66,
    67
Claiborne, William C. C.
  Mississippi Territorial
    Governor   115–6, 147,
    149–52, 154

INDEX

reward for Mason capture 117–8
correspondence with President Madison 151, 154–5
Clemens, Jeremiah
 visit to Mason in Kentucky 77
Coast Guard (U.S.)
 early enforcement authority 96, 177
Colonel Fluger/Plug
 legendary river pirate 97–8
 methods and historical doubt 215
counterfeiting
 methods and materials 77, 80, 142
 postcolonial economic impact 81–2
 federal legislation against 82–3, 88
Crow's Island (Island 94)
 Natchez Trace gang headquarters 118
Cultural Deviance Theory, see behavioral theories

Dillinger, John
 comparison to Mason's methods 103–4
Diamond Island
 gang activity and hideout 83–5, 190, 216
Dorsey, Rosanna
 marriage to Sam Mason 27, 152
 children with Sam Mason 27–8
Duff, John McElduff
 counterfeiter and Mason's brother-in-law 81, 86, 137
Dunmore, Lord
 governor of Virginia 42
 military campaign planning 33–4

Dunmore's War
 causes and outcomes 32, 40, 56, 97
 Battle of Point Pleasant 33, 47
 Treaty of Camp Charlotte 33
Dunn, Captain John
 appointed constable of Red Banks 84
 murdered by Mason gang associate 84
 conflict with Mason family 84–5
Durbin, Thomas
 killed by Thomas Mason 84

Eliot, Charles William, see Harvard, Charles W.
escape from custody (Mason)
 Pointe Coupee incident 148
 newspaper reports 149
execution (Sutton and May)
 location and method 153
 public display of heads 153
 mistaken identity controversy 153–5

Flatboats
 construction and use 107, 115, 116, 122, 183
 targets for pirates 47, 88–9, 93, 94, 98, 127–8, 130, 132
Ford, James
 possible alias user at Cave-in-Rock 88, 114
 ferry operation 88
 rumored gang leader 88
Fort Duquesne
 predecessor to Fort Pitt 20, 29, 178
Fort Fincastle
 early name of Fort Henry 30, 34

Fort Henry
  construction and layout   30, 31
  Mason's involvement   33, 36, 39–40, 48–50, 61
  strategic location   32–3
  first and second sieges   40–3, 65–9
Fort Massac (Illinois)
  strategic post on Ohio River   96–8, 189
  rebuilt by Washington   97
Fort Mifflin
  bombardment and evacuation   47
Fort Niagara
  site of 1764 treaty   26
  current historical site   177
Fort Pitt
  strategic river location   29, 178
  support to Fort Henry   31, 40, 43, 61, 65, 67
  biological warfare incident   25
  Mason's shooting incident   29–30
Fort Pickering (Chickasaw Bluff)
  Sutton's enlistment   155
France
  colonial possessions in North America   34, 46, 87, 97, 102, 144, 149–50
  role in Louisiana transfer   118
frontier
  justice
    associate judges and justices of the peace   63–4
    role in remote settlements   64
  policing
    watch systems and militias   96, 103, 169
    vigilante Regulators   84–5, 87, 89, 96, 102

Gage, Thomas
  British general at start of Revolution   34
Gallows Field (Old Greenville)
  execution site of Sutton and May   153, 215–16
Gates, Horatio
  command at Saratoga   46
Genealogy, Mason family
  Francis Mason   4
  Lemuel Mason   4
  George Mason   4
  Thomas Mason (father)   5–7, 16, 212
  descendants   5, 6, 153, 155, 167
Geography, *see* Mississippi River; Ohio River
Girty, George
  led second Fort Henry siege   67–8, 95
Girty, Simon
  alleged leadership at Fort Henry siege   42–3, 95
  Loyalist activity   42, 67
  comparison to Harpes   95
Glass, Anthony
  Natchez merchant and Mason accomplice   122, 130, 135, 137
  served as fence for stolen goods   139
  staged robbery   131, 133, 142, 164
Gnadenhutten Massacre (1782)
  execution of Christian Indians   66–7
Gordon House and Duck River Ferry Site
  site along Natchez Trace Parkway   194
Greenville, Mississippi (Old Greenville)

INDEX

Sutton and May hanged
    there   152–3, 215–16
Green River (Kentucky)
    land between Green and
      Cumberland petitioned   79
Gum Springs (Tennessee)
    robbery site of Kentucky
      boatmen   121

Harpes, Micajah and Wiley
    background and post-war
      crimes   94–5, 120, 122
    brutality and conflict with
      Mason   155
Harpe, Wiley (a.k.a. Little Harpe)
    misidentification as Sutton   131,
      152–3, 155–7, 215
Harrison, General
    acquaintance of Mason   127,
      163–4
Heinz History Center, Pittsburgh
    Revolutionary War exhibit   178,
    217
Henderson, Kentucky (Red Banks)
    Mason's relocation and
      activity   80, 83–5, 89, 102,
      152, 186
    criminal hub   80
Hewitt
    accomplice of Mason gang   83–5
Holston River
    Mason squats near in
      Tennessee   69, 183
Horse theft
    Mason's arrest in Virginia   23, 50
    May's activity in Indiana   85

Illinois Campaign (1778)
    Clark's expansion into Northwest
      Territory   48, 168
Indian diplomacy

Treaty of Fort Niagara   26
Treaty of Camp Charlotte   33
Indian raids
    response by Mason's militia   40
    Pontiac's Rebellion   25
Indian relations, wartime
    Moravian Christian tensions   40,
      66–7
    raids and retaliation   67–9
Indian tribes
    in Fort Henry siege
      (Mingoes, Shawanese,
      Wyandotts)   42
industrial revolution
    influence on frontier   79
Irvine, William
    command at Fort Pitt during
      1782   67

Jackson, Andrew, see Jackson
    Square
Jackson Square, New Orleans
    location of Louisiana
      transfer   158, 194
Jamestown, Virginia
    Francis Mason arrival   4, 212
James White's Fort
    founding of Knoxville   70–1,
      184
    early frontier structure   70
Jefferson, Thomas
    presidency and ideals   55, 101,
      150, 196–7
    views on religion and liberty   10,
      15, 35, 76, 198
    on U.S. Mint and land
      bounties   83
John Jay, see Treaty of Paris (1783)
John Mason, see Mason, John (son)
Joseph Mason, see Mason,
    Joseph (son)

justice of the peace
- Mason elected in Washington County, Red Banks 63, 80
- role in frontier communities 128, 137

Keelboats
- size, use, and upstream travel 93–4, 218

Kimble, Martha Mae Latham
- DAR record reference 27

King's Tavern (Natchez)
- location and atmosphere 122–3, 145, 193
- connection to Mason 122

Knoxville, Tennessee
- founding and early years 184
- Mason's squat on Sevier's land 69–70

Kuykendall, Adam/Abner
- relationship with Mason family 83, 158

La Fête Wine Bar, Birmingham
- final stop and meal 196

land ownership
- Mason's property and taxes 69, 75, 163–4
- disputed claims and petitions 57, 79, 212–13

Lemuel Mason, *see* Genealogy, Mason family

life course theory, *see* behavioral theories

Little Prairie, Missouri
- Mason's arrest and trial site 123–6
- community characteristics 118–9

Logan County, Kentucky
- Revolutionary veteran settlement 77
- petition for creation 79

Louisiana Purchase
- territorial background and timeline 102, 118
- transfer ceremonies 150, 194

Louisiana Territory
- Spanish control pre-1803 102, 150, 216

McClure, David
- debt owed by Mason 49

McConnel, James
- road survey with Mason 39

McCoy, Captain Robert (Don Robert)
- coordinated arrest of Mason 123–6
- transport to Natchez 147–8
- rumored killed in escape 148

Mason, Dorsey (son)
- lived in Ohio, married Hannah Meason 27, 157–8

Mason, Elizabeth (daughter)
- lived in Bayou Pierre 27, 83, 157

Mason, Elizabeth or Mary
- marriage to Kuykendall 83

Mason, Isaac (brother)
- industrial success, ties to Ben Franklin 6–7

Mason, John (son)
- 1792 Census 63
- arrest and first trial with Sam 109, 130
- arrest and second trial with Sam 125
- testimony details 134
- married Margaret Douglas 157

Mason, Joseph (brother)
- joined Illinois Campaign 168, 212, 224

Mason, Magnus
- youngest Mason son, testimony 125, 135, 139–40, 158

INDEX

Mason, Marguerite (daughter-in-law)
   testimony summary   138
Mason, Mary (daughter)
   possibly married a Kuykendall   7
Mason, Samuel, Jr. (son)
   became Texas planter   158
   ancestor of Texas Governor Briscoe   158
   trial testimony   139
Mason, Samuel, Sr.
   militia captain and justice   39, 63
   river and land piracy   88–9, 92–3, 107, 118, 161
   headquarters at Cave-In-Rock, Wolf Island, other places   116, 118–19, 162
   arrest, escape, and execution   117, 123–5, 132, 138, 145, 148
   interview and trial testimony   131–4
Mason, Thomas (brother)
   joined Illinois Campaign   168, 212, 224
Mason, Thomas (son)
   threatened Dunn   84
   killed Durbin   85
   arrest, interview and trial testimony   125, 128, 130, 136–8, 141
   little known post-trial   157
McCulloch, John
   survived 1782 attack   43
McCulloch, Samuel
   heroic leap at Wheeling Hill   43
   life, death and legacy   40, 43
McElduff, John, see Duff, John McElduff
Merchants, see Glass, Anthony; Audubon, John James
military forts (1700s)
   design and purpose   28–32
   role in frontier communities   25, 28–9
military pensions
   early American policy and inconsistencies   56–7
Military Trained Gang Member (MTGM)
   Mason as earliest known   169
Mississippi River
   piracy along   90, 92
   geography and conditions   48, 79, 83, 93, 104
   commercial importance   102–3
modern piracy
   Falcon Lake and smuggling   91
Monongahela
   Mason's land claim and relatives   126, 163
Moravian Indians
   slaughter at Gnadenhutten   66–7
Mount Pleasant (Sevier estate)
   Sevier family residence   70, 76

Natchez, Mississippi
   center of investigation and reports   116
   historical atmosphere   80
Natchez Trace
   pirate ambush route   107–8, 117–18
   traveler dangers and landmarks   10
Native Americans, see Indians
New Madrid, Missouri
   trial site and administrative center   103, 105, 117, 123
   impact of earthquakes   105, 192
New Orleans, Louisiana
   arrival of Mason and trial documents   147, 148

city's colonial and early U.S. roles   90, 107, 121

Ohio County, Virginia
  Mason family relocation to   28, 39–40
  court records and civic roles   49, 58, 180
Ohio River
  strategic river base for Mason   28, 32, 53, 80, 85, 89
  flatboat traffic and piracy   8, 48, 80, 97
organized crime
  comparison of Mason to Capone   166–7
  structure and tactics   167–8

Patterson
  knowledge of gang activity   131, 142, 164
  family seen wearing stolen goods   131, 164
Peltier, Estache
  witness to threats against Derousse   80, 143–4
Pentecost, Dorsey
  commissary appointment   35
Peyroux de la Coundreniere, Don Henri
  issued Mason's passport   102–3
  Presided over Mason's trial   124–47
Philadelphia, see U.S. Mint; Washington, George
pillory punishment
  Mason's sentence   109
piracy, general
  definitions and legal distinctions   90–4
  comparison to privateering   91
Port Gibson, Mississippi

  location near Burnet's cabin   116, 152
Presbytère, The
  architectural significance and function   159, 195
privateering
  government-sanctioned piracy   3, 22, 35, 87, 91–2, 195
property inventory (Mason gang)
  items including cash, clothing, scalps   125–6, 133, 141
Proclamation of   1763
  land restriction west of Appalachians   25

Quasi War (U.S. and France)
  naval conflict   87, 96

Ramsey, Mr.
  associate of Mason in Cape Girardeau   127, 163
Ramsey House, Knoxville
  home of Francis A. Ramsey   184
Red Banks (Henderson), see Henderson, Kentucky
Red River (Kentucky/Tennessee)
  location tied to Mason's movement   76, 84, 121
Regulators (vigilantes), see frontier, policing
religion and government
  pre- and post-Revolutionary shifts   15, 172
  church-state separation   76
  Protestantism   15, 126, 134, 136, 139–40, 162, 195
religious reflections
  sin, self-sabotage, and legacy   170–2
  moral introspection and faith   5, 14–15, 172

INDEX

Rittenhouse, David
   appointed first Mint director   83
river piracy, see piracy; river
rivers, see Mississippi River; Native American river systems; Ohio River
Rogers (Natchez companion)
   with Baker during robberies   107–8, 138

St. Francois robbery
   Glass robbed by Sutton, Wigger, and others   128–31
Salcedo, Manuel de
   cooperation with Claiborne   47–8, 115
   Spanish governor of Louisiana   115, 147
Sam Mason, see Mason, Samuel, Sr.
scalping
   colonial practices and bounties   12, 54–5, 66
   items found in Mason gang inventory   42, 125
Scott, Molly
   alternate powder runner account   69, 214
Sevier, Colonel James
   denied Sutton was Harpe   215
Sevier, John
   first governor of Tennessee   60
   eviction of Mason from land   69–70, 75
Shepherd, David
   commanded Fort Henry   32, 35, 40
   orders from Brodhead   61
Shelby, Isaac
   leadership in Patriot forces   60
slaveholding
   Mason's ownership and Indian theft   69, 84, 89

economic context   14, 76, 78, 96, 118
smallpox
   biological warfare at Fort Pitt   26
Social Disorganization Theory, see behavioral theories
Spain
   controlled Louisiana Territory   34, 79, 97, 102, 105, 118, 147
   granted Mason passport   102–3
Spanish passport system
   Mason's exploitation of   103–4
Sutton, John (a.k.a. Taylor, Wells)
   trial testimony and contradictions   115, 122, 127–31, 141–2
   claimed reward for Mason's head   152–7
   identity dispute as Wiley Harpe   155–7, 215
Sycamore Shoals
   Overmountain Men and land purchase site   60, 182–3

taverns
   community importance in Revolutionary era   11, 16, 53–4
   used as pirate headquarters   83–4, 88–9
Taylor, see Sutton, John
Tennessee River
   geographic importance to Mason's route   121, 184, 187
Territorial governors, see Claiborne, William C. C.; Blount, William
Thompson, Mr.
   Mason's brother-in-law at Cape Girardeau   134, 163, 190
Thompson Island expedition
   Mason's participation   57

Trace robbery, see Natchez Trace
trial (1803)
  multi-day proceeding in New
    Madrid 124–45
  testimonies summarized 126–44
  trial (New Madrid), see trial (1803)

U.S. expansion
  population growth in frontier
    states 8, 19, 32, 39, 79,
    102, 118, 150
United States Mint
  foundation and early coin
    production 82–3
  Coinage Act of 1792 83

Valley Forge
  Continental Army
    encampment 47
Van Norstrand, Andrew
  folk song "Samuel Mason" 90
Van Norstrand, Noah
  folk song "Samuel Mason" 90
Vidal, Secretary of War (Spanish)
  transferred Mason case
    jurisdiction 147
Vigilantism, see frontier, policing

Washington, George
  early activity 5, 11
  Fort Necessity and
    Brandywine 20–2, 45
  presidency and river fort
    strategy 79–80, 83, 87,
    97
  ordered Fort Massac rebuilt 97
Water, Richard Jones, Dr
  vouched for Mason 102–3
West Point

  target of Benedict Arnold's
    treason 59
western frontier, see Appalachian
    frontier; Mississippi River;
    Ohio River
Whitney, Eli
  cotton gin and musket
    standardization 79
Wilkinson, General James
  military support in Louisiana 46,
    97, 150
Williamson, David
  led militia in Gnadenhutten
    Massacre 66–7
Wilson's Liquor Vault, see Cave-in-
    Rock
Winchester, Virginia
  home to Mason family 4–6
  strategic importance 23
Wolf Island
  pirate hideout location 104
  river geography and low water
    study 104
women in Mason's gang
  roles in deception and
    seduction 89

Zane, Ebenezer
  Fort Henry and road
    development 31, 39, 43
  property and block house 32,
    67–9
Zane's cabin
  source of gunpowder during
    siege 68
Zeisberger, David
  Moravian missionary
    intelligence 40

ABOUT THE AUTHOR

Dr. Carter F. Smith, a man of many hats (some worn while pursuing miscreants of all stripes), directs the Masters in Criminal Justice for Middle Tennessee State University's Department of Criminal Justice Administration. His credentials stack as high as a pirate's treasure chest: a Bachelor's in Public Management from Austin Peay State University, a Law Degree from Southern Illinois University, and a Doctorate from Northcentral University. Before turning to academia, Carter's career as a Special Agent in the US Army's Criminal Investigations Division (CID) took him on adventures worthy of any eighteenth-century novel. Over a remarkable twenty-two-year career, Carter roamed far and wide, from the hills of Kentucky to far-off posts in Germany and Korea, with short stints in Panama and Indonesia, investigating crimes that ranged from the dastardly to the bureaucratically bold. His roles were as varied as his titles—Special Agent In Charge, evidence custodian, team chief, and Chief of Investigative Support. Since trading the field for the classroom, Dr. Smith has imparted his wisdom to students across military and academic settings. He's also made memorable appearances as a guest expert for news outlets near and far, including the History Channel's Gangland series. With a scholarly record longer than a riverboat cargo list, his eclectic collection of books includes *Gangs and the Military: Gangsters, Bikers, and Terrorists with Military Training*; *Gangs and Organized Crime*; *Gangs*; *Private Security Today*, and *The Emergence of The Relationship Economy: The New Order of Things to Come*. In his free time, Dr. Smith enjoys growing vegetables and herbs, and learning about things that may or may not seem relevant to many other people, a pastime no doubt influenced by his finely tuned investigator's desire to learn everything. Learn more and connect at http://carterfsmith.com/.